BEST DAY HIKES
ON THE
ARIZONA
NATIONAL SCENIC
TRAIL

Best Day Hikes on the Arizona National Scenic Trail

Published by Wilderness Press
Distributed by Publishers Group West
First edition, second printing 2023

Editor: Kate Johnson
Cover design: Scott McGrew
Cartography: Scott McGrew and Steve Jones
Photos: Sirena Rana, except as noted on page
Interior design: Annie Long and Monica Ahlman
Proofreader: Emily C. Beaumont
Indexer: Joanne Sprott/Potomac Indexing

Library of Congress Cataloging-in-Publication Data

Names: Rana, Sirena, 1974– author.
Title: Best day hikes on the Arizona National Scenic Trail / Sirena Rana.
Description: First edition. | Birmingham, AL : Wilderness Press, [2020]
Summary: "The 800-mile Arizona National Scenic Trail (AZT) crosses the state, from Mexico to Utah. It
    travels up and down Sky Island mountain ranges, across the saguaro-studded Sonoran Desert, through
    the largest ponderosa pine forest in the world, past Arizona's highest peak, and from rim to rim of
    Grand Canyon. But you don't need to hike the entire route to experience its historical, geological,
    and botanical significance. Many scenic views and important sites are accessible within a few hours'
    journey. Trail expert Sirena Rana guides you along the most interesting and accessible portions of
    the trail in 30 carefully crafted routes. Each entry includes navigational information and interpretive
    facts about the trail's cultural history, natural history, and geography." —Provided by publisher.
Identifiers: LCCN 2020016154 (print) | LCCN 2020016155 (ebook) | ISBN 9781643590097 (pbk.)
    ISBN 164359009X (pbk.) | ISBN 9781643590103 (ebook)
Subjects: LCSH: Hiking—Arizona—Arizona Trail—Guidebooks.
Classification: LCC GV199.42.A72 D84 2020 (print) | LCC GV199.42.A72 (ebook)
    DDC 796.5109791—dc23
LC record available at loc.gov/2020016154
LC ebook record available at lccn.loc.gov/2020016155

♣ WILDERNESS PRESS

An imprint of AdventureKEEN
2204 First Ave. S., Ste. 102
Birmingham, AL 35233
800-678-7006, fax 877-374-9016

Visit wildernesspress.com for a complete listing of our books and for ordering information. Contact us at our website or at facebook.com/wildernesspress1967 with questions or comments. To find out more about who we are and what we're doing, visit adventurewithkeen.com/blog.

Cover photos: (Front) The author strides among wildflowers in the Gila River Canyons (Hike 11, page 108). (Back, top to bottom) AZT sign at the Picketpost Trailhead (see Hike 13, Picketpost, page 123); equestrians in Cienega Creek Natural Preserve (see Hike 6, Gabe Zimmerman Trailhead to Colossal Cave, page 71).

Safety Notice Though the author and publisher have made every effort to ensure that the information in this book is accurate at press time, they are not responsible for any loss, damage, injury, or inconvenience that may occur while using this book—you are responsible for your own safety and health on the trail. The fact that a hike is described in this book does not mean that it will be safe for you. Always check local conditions (which can change from day to day), know your own limitations, and consult a map.

BEST DAY HIKES
ON THE
ARIZONA
NATIONAL SCENIC
TRAIL

SIRENA RANA

 WILDERNESS PRESS . . . *on the trail since 1967*

Best Day Hikes on the Arizona National Scenic Trail

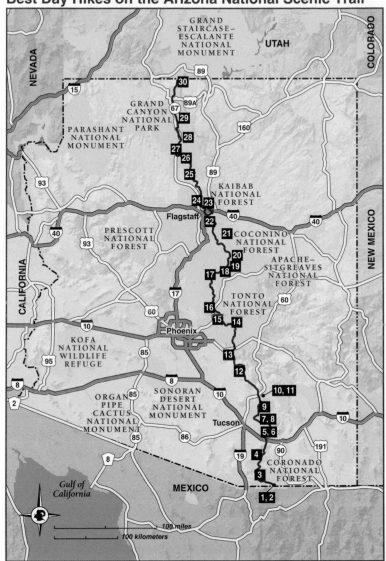

Table of Contents

Metal signs on the Arizona National Scenic Trail (AZT) list mileages to Utah and/or Mexico.

Map Legend

←→ → Directional arrows	Featured trail	Alternate trail
Freeway	Highway with bridge	Minor road
Boardwalk	Stairs	Unpaved road
Railroad	Power line	Ski lift/tram
Park/forest	Water body	River/creek/ intermittent stream

⌐ Bench	⋈ Footbridge	📷 Photo opportunity
⌒ Bridge	•—• Gate	🏕 Picnic shelter
▲ Campground	● General point of interest	🚽 Pit toilet
▲ Campground (hike-in)	♠ House/building	📡 Radio tower
‡ Cemetery	⑦ Information kiosk	♦♦ Restroom
✔ Dam	♠ Park office/ranger station	🔭 Scenic view
⛶ Drinking water	P Parking	♦ Trailhead
	▲ Peak/hill	⊙ Tunnel

Dedication

*To Brian Dufault for supporting my Arizona Trail dreams, and to my father,
Budh Prakash Rana, for instilling in me a love of the outdoors and photography.*

Acknowledgments

THIS BOOK TOOK OVER TWO YEARS OF WORK from proposal to completion, and I was fortunate to have the support of the following folks during the process:

Thanks to Brian for supporting my dreams and holding down the house while I was away on the Arizona Trail and the many scouting trips for this book.

I am forever grateful for my parents—Anna and Budh Prakash Rana, but especially my dad, for inspiring a love of the outdoors when I was growing up. He's also a great support crew and has come out to Arizona to join me for part of my 2008–09 section hike, most of my 2014 thru-hike, and even some of the research for this book. Despite being a native of India who lives in Chicago, he's seen more of Arizona than most Arizonans. Thanks also to my aunt Candida Kyle, who took me on my first camping trip with my uncle Patrick and taught me to appreciate nature as a child. Gratitude to Wilderness Press for publishing this book and to my editor, Kate Johnson.

The Arizona Office of Tourism supported my research for this book, and eight of my articles about the trail are published on its AZT landing page (arizona .com/uniquely-az/unique-communities/arizona-trail). Gossamer Gear (gossamergear.com) has sponsored me since my 2014 Arizona Trail Trek and supplied me with the equipment I needed for researching the book. Huppybar (huppybar.com), makers of Wild Mesquite, the official energy bar of the AZT, provided tasty snacks, and the skirt I wore for most hikes was supplied by Purple Rain Adventure Skirts (purplerainskirts.com). Summit Hut (summithut.com) has been a great supporter of my adventures and was my first sponsor back in 2008.

Many people hosted me during my research and writing, and I am especially thankful to Leigh Anne and Denny Thrasher, Anne and Greg McGuffey, Sarah Weichberger, Li Brannfors, Geneva Hickey, Niall Murphy and Kyle Meehan, and Bernie and Margie Stalmann. Thanks also to Eve Lindsey, Cate Bradley, Christy Snow, and Jeff Harris, Heather "Anish" Anderson, Liz "Snorkel" Thomas, Terri

Gay, India Hesse, Wendy Lotze, and Meredith Marder for their help. I appreciate the time that Madeline Shewalter took to speak to me about Dale and the early days of scouting and creating the trail. I enjoyed working with Lyle Balenquah, Hopi archaeologist and artist, on the information about ancestral lands in this book. Much gratitude to Roger Naylor for his thoughtful foreword (see page x).

Micro Chicken, Sirena's adventure companion since 2011

I am grateful for all the folks who supported me on the trail and during the planning process for my hikes in 2008–09 and 2014. The Arizona Trail and the Arizona Trail Association have been the catalyst for many dear friendships. A special shout-out goes to the volunteer crew I worked with to build the trail in southern Arizona, and to Mark Flint and Dave Hicks.

Though I spent a lot of time outdoors as a child with my best friend Kristin, I didn't grow up hiking and camping. I wrote this book so that even beginners can safely enjoy the AZT. I kept in mind while writing and researching what I would have wanted to know all those years ago when I moved to Arizona from the Chicago suburbs and started hiking.

Much of this book was written outdoors: on the AZT at High Jinks Ranch, in the Gateway Community of Summerhaven, near Saguaro National Park, or in a hammock hung along the trail. I find writing outside to be particularly productive, and I'm thankful to have been able to draw inspiration from nature while working on this book. Last but certainly not least, thanks to Dale Shewalter for his vision and hard work toward creating a trail for generations to enjoy.

Patreon Subscribers

Big thanks to my Patreon community for their support: Cate Bradley, Candida Kyle, Clara Hughes and Peter Guzman, John Officer, Gabbacia + Roberto, Mila Besich, Joe Mckenna, Steven Haubner, Jillian Glassett, Merina Karpen, Margo Stoney, Margie Roesch, Anne McGuffey, Alex Araiza, Greg Brush, and Rozanne Cazzone.

Join the Patreon community at patreon.com/desertsirena to receive newsletters, videos, behind-the-scenes looks at my creative process and trail design, and advance notice of events and new projects. You might even catch a glimpse of my adventure companion, Micro Chicken!

—*Sirena Rana*

Foreword

By Roger Naylor

ARIZONA IS A STATE LOADED WITH ICONS. The sculpted layers of Grand Canyon, the elegant saguaro cactus, Sedona's red rocks, and the monoliths of Monument Valley leap to mind.

Then there's one of Arizona's most unforgettable sights: Sirena Rana, rocking a colorful skirt and a big smile while hiking deep into the outback.

If you've spent any time at all on the Arizona National Scenic Trail—and thanks to this book, that just became much easier for everyone—there's a good chance you've encountered Sirena. If she's not hiking it, she's making repairs to the trail. She is a force of nature, a sweet and charming dynamo, and the very embodiment of inspiration. In many ways she's Arizona's own personal trainer. She coaxes us off the couch into the great outdoors where we can listen to what quiet sounds like, breathe clean air, and get moving again.

Her passion comes naturally. It was hiking that gave Sirena her life back while recovering from a devastating accident. It was the outdoors that saved her. It's no wonder she wants to return the favor. She works tirelessly to promote and protect our public lands. And there is no place she cares more about than the AZT—that long, lanky route snaking up the state from south to north, from Mexico to Utah.

Sirena is one of the leading experts on the AZT, having completed it twice. With this book she unravels the mystique of the 800-mile-long pathway and makes it accessible to just about anybody with a pair of hiking boots.

Each chapter takes a segment of the trail and whittles it down into an easily managed day hike. The information is comprehensive, providing directions, mileages, elevations, hiking times, scenic descriptions, and pertinent details. Sirena anticipates your questions and answers them. She also covers the Gateway Communities that hold the trail together, offering suggestions on what to see and do, and where to eat and stay in these small towns.

This is a book I've been eagerly awaiting ever since Sirena first told me about it. Like her, I'm an avid hiker. But I'm also a geezer who enjoys his comfort. I once wrote a book about my favorite Arizona hiking trails paired with nearby burger joints. That tells you plenty about my priorities.

It also explains why I need this book. My backpacking days are behind me, but I'm still out hoofing it on Arizona trails nearly every day. The astounding beauty of Arizona lurks just outside, and I want to experience it all. Thanks to Sirena, 800 miles of it just became more readily available. That means more lonely mountain ranges, rolling grasslands, sun-spanked desert, slashing canyons, and shady pine forests. Sirena serves them up in nice bite-size chunks, perfect for us day hikers.

So grab your water bottle and sunscreen. Lace up your hiking boots. Sirena Rana is showing us the way to some of Arizona's most scenic landscapes. Let's get out there and go see them.

Roger Naylor is one of Arizona's premier travel writers and a member of the Arizona Tourism Hall of Fame. He is the author of several books, including *Boots and Burgers: An Arizona Handbook for Hungry Hikers.*

Sunset near the South Kaibab Trailhead (see Hike 27, page 212)

Recommended Hikes

Note: An asterisk (*) next to a hike's name indicates that the short hike option in the description is recommended—for example, turning around at Forest Service Road 4110 instead of going all the way to Gardner Canyon in Hike 4 (page 59).

Hardest Hikes

Easy Hikes

Scenic Hikes

All are scenic, but the following are standouts:

Steep Hikes

Flat Hikes

Best Hikes for Solitude

Best Hikes for Kids

Best Wildflower Hikes

Best Geology Hikes

Best Desert Hikes

Best Forest Hikes

Best Grassland Hikes

Best High-Elevation Hikes (More Than 6,000')

Best Hikes for History

Best Hikes by Season
WINTER

SPRING

SUMMER

FALL

Introduction

The AZT at a Glance

The Arizona National Scenic Trail, also known as the Arizona Trail and the AZT for short . . .

- Stretches 800 miles, from Mexico to Utah.

- Connects deserts, mountains, forests, canyons, communities, and people.

- Is shared by day hikers, backpackers, mountain bikers, equestrians, runners, cross-country skiers, snowshoers, photographers, birders, goat and llama packers, and even the occasional unicyclist.

- Was designated a National Scenic Trail in 2009.

- Connected across the state on December 16, 2011.

- Traverses 3 national parks, 1 state park, 6 wilderness areas, 4 national forests, 33 Gateway Communities (see page 26), and 9 major mountain ranges.

- Is the only National Scenic Trail in the U.S. that crosses one of the Seven Natural Wonders of the World: Grand Canyon.

About the Arizona National Scenic Trail (AZT)
One Man's Vision: How the AZT Came to Be

DALE SHEWALTER GREW UP in Geneva, Illinois, and his love of the outdoors was inspired by his parents, who saved to send him and his brother to camp each year. After going to graduate school at the University of Arizona, he became a beloved math teacher in Flagstaff. He longed to hike the Appalachian Trail but couldn't manage the time off. One day, on a hike to Coronado Peak in Coronado National Memorial during the 1970s, he got the idea to create a long-distance trail running from north to south across Arizona.

In 1985 he hiked from the U.S.–Mexico border to the Arizona–Utah line, researching a route that would connect the state's many public lands, historical sites, diverse landscapes, and small towns. Dale was so inspired by that journey that he took a yearlong sabbatical from teaching to work for Kaibab National Forest, meeting with many land-management agencies to promote his idea for a trail that would run the length of the state. For many years, he traveled with his projector, screen, and slides to give presentations to hiking, biking, and equestrian groups; outdoors stores; and anyone else who might be interested.

1

The idea began to catch on, and Kaibab National Forest designated its Trail 101 as the first official segment of what was originally called simply the Arizona Trail. With his wife, Madeleine, and their son, Zane, Dale spent many weekends thereafter camping, scouting, and helping to sign the new trail. He teamed up with other hikers, bikers, and equestrians to scout and lay out the segments. Over the years the AZT gradually took shape, pieced together from both existing trails and newly created ones.

Dale Shewalter (1950–2010) is acknowledged as the "Father of the Arizona Trail." Photo: Bob Rink

On March 30, 2009, Dale saw his original concept designated as a National Scenic Trail—joining such hallowed hiking routes as the Appalachian, Pacific Crest, and Continental Divide Trails— thanks in part to the efforts of Gabe Zimmerman, an aide of U.S. Representative Gabrielle Giffords. Sadly, Dale passed away in 2010, just a year before the trail finally became contiguous across the state. Memorial benches honoring Dale and his parents are located along the AZT and in several Gateway Communities.

The Arizona Trail Association (ATA)

The ATA was established in 1994 as a 501(c)(3) nonprofit organization. Its mission: to protect, maintain, enhance, promote, and sustain the Arizona Trail as a unique encounter with the land. The ATA spearheaded one of the largest volunteer projects in the state's history in constructing and connecting the trail from Mexico to Utah.

The association's programs and activities are funded by individual members and donors, along with the ATA's official Business Partners and Legacy Partners. Federal grants, special fundraising events, and retail sales also help support the organization. The ATA is a member of the nonprofit **Partnership for the National Trails System** (pnts.org), which advocates for land preservation and stewardship resources for the 11 National Scenic Trails and 19 National Historic Trails.

The ATA's website, **aztrail.org**, contains a wealth of information about trail conditions, events, and planning resources. ATA members get access to exclusive online content, as well as discounts on official merchandise and purchases from ATA Business Partners such as REI, That Brewery, and Summit Hut. Membership fees start at $35 per year ($25 per year for middle school, high school, and college students); see aztrail.org/get-involved/join for details.

The ATA is always looking for volunteers to help with trail maintenance and rerouting (see below). Volunteers are also needed for the following tasks: running events, mailings and office work, fundraising, outreach booths at community events, and speaking engagements. Visit aztrail.org/get-involved/volunteer for more information.

TRAIL BUILDING AND MAINTENANCE

The construction of the AZT was the largest volunteer project in the state's history. The trail was connected from Mexico to Utah near the Gila River in 2011, and you can visit this spot on Hike 12, Gila River Canyons (page 116).

Though the AZT is now completely contiguous across the state, the ATA continues to improve upon its work through reroutes that make the trail more sustainable, as well as new construction to move sections that previously utilized dirt roads onto singletrack trail.

The AZT is maintained largely by volunteer Trail Stewards—groups or individuals who adopt segments of the trail. In remote areas or areas where extensive work may be needed, members of the Conservation Corps often pitch in to help.

You can help keep the trail clear by reporting downed trees, overgrown or washed-out trail sections, or damaged tread by filling out a Trail Conditions Form on the ATA website: aztrail.org/the-trail/trail-conditions-form.

GATEWAY COMMUNITIES

When Dale Shewalter first conceived a trail across Arizona, an important part of his vision was connecting people to the small towns along the way. The Gateway Community Program was developed to foster relationships between the AZT and the people, businesses, and organizations in these towns. It also promotes economic development in these communities through ecotourism. This program is near and dear to my heart: I served as the ATA's Gateway Community Liaison from 2011 to 2016.

Each hike in this book is connected to one of the Gateway Communities, with recommendations for the all-important posthike meals, lodging, services, and nearby attractions. Note that not every Gateway Community is represented; for a full list, see aztrail.org/explore/gateway-communities.

YOUTH PROGRAMS

The ATA's **Seeds of Stewardship** and **Gear Girls** youth programs (aztrail.org/youth) aim to pass on a love and appreciation of the outdoors to the next generation.

Seeds of Stewardship works with middle and high school students in AZT Gateway Communities. Using a three-pronged approach of experience, education, and service learning, they strive to engage, inspire, and empower youth, helping encourage stewardship of the outdoors.

Working with grades 4–8, Gear Girls uses mountain biking, trail work, cross-country skiing, and snowshoeing to build confidence, outdoor competence, community, and character. The participants learn practical skills in these areas while also developing character skills such as mindfulness, teamwork, and determination, all of which will prepare them for life's challenges.

My AZT Story

My very first hike on the AZT (though I didn't know it was part of the AZT at the time) was in 1994, on the South Kaibab Trail to Cedar Ridge. I was moving from the Chicago suburbs to Tucson, without ever having visited the state before, to study archaeology at the University of Arizona.

In 1997, during my last semester at UA, I was hit by a truck while I was walking across the street, and it changed my life forever. I developed a chronic pain condition called fibromyalgia that left me very ill for many years. I lost my job, and for a while I was also bedridden, depressed, and uncertain of what the future held.

Eventually I started to take small walks with my boyfriend Brian and my dog, Zeus, a big German Shepherd mix. Even though I would be tired and sore afterward, being outside lifted my spirits and temporarily distracted me from the pain. Small hikes turned into longer ones as I slowly built up my stamina and strength. Brian lost interest as my hikes became all-day affairs and it was just Zeus and me out in nature.

In the early 2000s I often hiked the Bellota Trail in the Catalina Mountains. I saw the AZT signs, but I was still a novice hiker and thoughts of long-distance journeys were still far off.

In 2001 I went on my first backpacking trip on the AZT, down the South Kaibab Trail to the Bright Angel Campground at Grand Canyon for two nights and back up the Bright Angel Trail. It was the hardest thing I'd ever done, but I was enchanted by the Grand Canyon and backpacking.

In May 2007 I went to the town of Oracle, north of Tucson, to go for a hike. I stopped in at a business in town to ask for suggestions, and they directed me to the AZT at the American Flag Ranch Trailhead (see Hike 10, page 99). I made it a little past the Oracle Ridge Trail junction before I had to turn around for the day. When I arrived at the trailhead, I noticed a big ARIZONA TRAIL sign with a map on it. As I considered the north–south span of the trail, I wondered, "How on Earth does someone hike across Arizona? There's no water!"

That question led me to start researching the AZT and long-distance hiking in general. Here's a quote from a journal entry I wrote around that time: "As I look at a map of AZ, I realize many of the places I want to explore are on the AZT. San Francisco Peaks, Superstitions, Mogollon Rim, Grand Canyon, Huachucas, Arizona Strip, Patagonia, Rincons, and 4 Peaks."

I began planning a thru-hike for the following year. I had a lot to learn, and there weren't very many resources for the AZT at the time. I spent a lot of time calling Trail Stewards and seeking advice from other hikers and the trail-building crew I had been volunteering with.

My thru-hike became a section hike when the Great Recession happened and I could no longer afford to take the necessary time off work all at once. I decided to dedicate my hike to fibromyalgia awareness and serving as a positive role model for people struggling with this condition. I also raised money for the National Fibromyalgia Association.

On February 25, 2008, I began hiking with friends on AZT Passage 1, from the U.S.–Mexico border to Parker Canyon Lake. For the next 15 months, I section-hiked the trail, learning many things about backpacking, long-distance hiking, and myself. The AZT was about 60 miles from being completed at the time, and from time to time I joined other hikers in working on those sections. Mostly, though, I was on my own—and when I say "on my own," I mean I hardly ever saw another person on the trail. I completed my first AZT long-distance hike at the American Flag Ranch Trailhead—the same place where I had first gotten the idea to hike the trail—on May 12, 2009, Fibromyalgia Awareness Day.

Completing the hike was bittersweet; I'd had a grand adventure, but now it was over. I decided to give presentations about my hike and promote the

The author finishes her 2009 AZT section hike. Photo: Terri Gay

AZT—I would talk about it to anyone who would listen. The trail had given me so much: confidence in myself, appreciation for Arizona's incredibly diverse environments, and new friends I'd made along the way. I always say that the Sirena who started the trail was a completely different person from the Sirena who completed the trail.

I continued to help build the trail, and I was one of the people on the crew that connected the final piece of the AZT at a ceremony along the Gila River on December 16, 2011. To this day I'm involved with trail maintenance as one of the Trail Stewards for Passage 12c: Cody Trail (see Hike 10, page 99).

From 2011 to 2016 I served as the Gateway Community Liaison for the ATA. I was asked to take the job by former Executive Director Dave Hicks as the trail was coming close to completion. He said, "We need someone enthusiastic out there on the ground and shaking hands."

When I first started the job, hardly anyone knew about the AZT. I would go into businesses, chambers of commerce, and visitor centers, and I'd get blank stares when I asked if they knew that Arizona had a National Scenic Trail spanning the length of the state. Through many years of traveling to these towns and educating folks about the trail, the Gateway Communities learned about the AZT. In turn, they saw the increased economic benefits of trail users coming in and spending money on food, lodging, and other items in town.

In 2014 I completed the AZT a second time on what I called the Arizona Trail Trek. This was a thru-hike to promote the AZT, the guidebook *Your Complete Guide to the Arizona National Scenic Trail,* and the AZT's Gateway Communities. From mid-March to the end of May, I not only walked the entire 800 miles but also held 12 fundraisers in the Gateway Communities (all with music, food, and Arizona Trail Ale); did countless newspaper, TV, and radio interviews; took more than 100 people with me on the trail on five public backpacking trips and seven day hikes; and raised almost $18,000 for the ATA. You can read journals from my thru-hike on my website, sirenarana.com.

The Gateway Community Program flourished during the five years I worked for the ATA. Not only are trail users now welcomed with open arms, but the Gateway Communities' economic landscape has also changed as a result of embracing the AZT, and the communities are proud to be a part of the trail's culture.

After working for the ATA, I founded a consulting company, Trails Inspire, which promotes the outdoors through writing, photography, public speaking, and trail design. (See trailsinspire.com and page 255 for more information.) The AZT will always be close to my heart, though, and from that comes this book.

So often when I talk to people about the AZT, they shut down, thinking that hiking an 800-mile trail couldn't possibly be something they could do. But the great thing about the AZT is that you can choose your own adventure: there are many ways you can experience it without having to complete the whole thing. No matter how long or how short the hike, as long as you're on the AZT, you're part of its magic. I am excited to provide a resource that makes the AZT more accessible to hikers of a wide range of abilities and experience. The book you're reading is the culmination of 13 years of hiking, building, working, and playing on this trail I love so much. I invite you to share your own adventures on social media with the hashtag #DayHikesAZT.

Hiking the AZT
Hike Your Own Hike (HYOH)

THIS TERM IS USED in the long-distance-hiking community, but it's relevant for day hikers as well. What it means is that your hiking experience is unique to you and you alone, and you shouldn't compare it with the experiences of others. Like to take long breaks and stare at clouds while another hiker might do their whole hike without stopping? HYOH. Do you take everything but the kitchen sink with you while others have tiny packs? HYOH. Is your idea of a good day one where you hike 3 miles while for another person it might be 20? HYOH.

The 10 Essentials

This list of hiking gear was originally developed by The Mountaineers, a non-profit outdoors organization, in the 1930s and first appeared in print in the guidebook *Mountaineering: The Freedom of the Hills* (1974). The 10 Essentials work together to help keep you safe on the trail.

1. *Navigation:* maps, altimeter, compass, GPS device, personal locator beacon or satellite communicator, extra batteries or battery pack

2. *Headlamp or flashlight,* plus extra bulb and batteries

3. *Sun protection:* sunglasses, sun-protective clothes, hat, sunscreen, and lip balm

4. *First aid:* including foot care, insect repellent, and tweezers for areas with cactus

5. *Knife,* plus a repair kit for gear

6. *Fire:* matches, lighter, and tinder

7. *Shelter:* carried at all times; for day hikes, can be a light emergency bivy sack

8. *Extra food:* trail mix, granola bars, or other high-energy snacks

9. *Extra water:* more than you think you'll need (a good general rule is 0.5 liter an hour, twice that in hot weather), or the means to purify water you find along the trail. (*Note:* Many of these hikes have no water available.) Water report for the Arizona Trail can be found at aztwaterreport.org.

10. *Extra clothes:* raingear; a change of socks and shirt; and, depending on the season, a warm hat and gloves

Some of my favorite gear for day-hiking the AZT

Hiking poles are not included in the official 10 Essentials list, but they can be very helpful on the uneven, rocky trails of Arizona. I also carry a **hiking umbrella** made by Gossamer Gear (gossamergear.com) that is very light but sturdy, as well as a **whistle,** for signaling for help.

An organization called The 11th Essential (11thessential.org) suggests adding a **stuff sack** to your pack for collecting trash that you may find along the trail. Organizations in Arizona such as Keep Nature Wild (keepnaturewild.com) and Natural Restorations (naturalrestorations.org) do cleanup events both on and off the AZT; check their websites for details. **Note:** When picking up trash, take care to not collect anything that may have cultural value (such as Indigenous artifacts) or historical value (items more than 50 years old).

Leave No Trace

The Leave No Trace Center for Outdoor Ethics was founded on seven conservation principles, summarized below and at the National Park Service website: nps.gov/articles/leave-no-trace-seven-principles.htm. For further discussion, see lnt.org/why/7-principles.

1. PLAN AHEAD AND PREPARE

- Be aware of any regulations and special concerns regarding the area in which you plan to hike.
- Prepare for extreme weather, hazards, and emergencies.
- Schedule your trip to avoid times of high use.
- Visit in small groups when possible. Consider splitting larger groups into smaller ones.
- Repackage food to cut down on waste.
- Use a map and compass or GPS unit instead of marking paint, rock cairns, or flagging.

2. TRAVEL AND CAMP ON DURABLE SURFACES

- Durable surfaces include maintained hiking trails and designated campsites; rock, gravel, or sand; dry grasses; or snow.
- Camp at least 200 feet from lakes and streams.
- Don't create new campsites or alter existing ones.
  #### In popular areas
  - Use existing trails and campsites.
  - Walk single file in the middle of the trail, even when it's wet or muddy.
  - Keep campsites small. Focus activity in areas where vegetation is absent.

In pristine areas
- Disperse use to prevent the creation of new campsites and trails.
- Avoid places where impacts are just beginning.

3. DISPOSE OF WASTE PROPERLY

- Pack it in, pack it out. Carefully check your campsite, food-preparation areas, and rest areas for trash or spilled food. Pack out all garbage and leftovers.
- Use existing toilet facilities whenever possible. Otherwise, deposit solid human waste in catholes dug 6–8 inches deep and at least 200 feet from water, camp, and trails. Cover and disguise the cathole when finished.
- Pack out toilet paper and other hygiene products.
- When bathing or washing dishes, carry the water 200 feet away from streams or lakes, and use small amounts of biodegradable soap. Scatter strained dishwater.

4. LEAVE WHAT YOU FIND

- Preserve the past: feel free to examine and photograph cultural or historical structures and artifacts, but do not touch them.
- Don't disturb rocks, plants, or other natural objects.
- Avoid introducing or transporting nonnative plant species.
- Do not build structures or furniture, and do not dig trenches.

5. MINIMIZE CAMPFIRE IMPACTS

- Use a lightweight stove for cooking and a candle lantern for light.
- Where fires are permitted, use established fire rings, fire pans, or mound fires.
- Keep fires small. Use only down and dead wood from the ground that can be broken by hand.
- Burn wood and coals to ash, put out fires completely, and scatter the cooled ashes.

6. RESPECT WILDLIFE

- Observe wildlife from a distance. Do not follow or approach them.
- Don't feed animals. This damages their health, alters their natural behaviors, habituates them to humans, and exposes them to predators and other dangers.
- Protect wildlife and your food by storing rations and trash securely.
- Keep pets under control at all times, or leave them at home.

7. BE CONSIDERATE OF OTHER VISITORS

- Respect other visitors and protect the quality of their experience.
- Yield to other users on the trail.
- Step to the downhill side of the trail when you encounter horses and their riders.

- Camp and take breaks away from trails and other visitors.
- Let nature's sounds prevail.

© 1999 Leave No Trace Center for Outdoor Ethics (lnt.org). Reprinted with permission.

Solo Hiking

Conventional wisdom holds that hiking by yourself is a bad idea, but it's one of my greatest joys. That said, it does takes extra planning and care—especially in unfamiliar areas without cellular coverage. Here's how to stay safe on the trail. (See next page for solo hiking tips for women.)

- **Always leave an itinerary** with someone. Include details about your route, what time you expect to be back, and instructions on what to do if you don't come back when expected.

- **Do your research!** Being well prepared is important when there's no one else around to ask for help. Study the conditions, weather, terrain, and navigation. I also research potential bailout points in case the hike doesn't go as planned.

- **Hike a trail you know well and that has cell reception** for your first solo trip.

- **The 10 Essentials** (see page 7) are even more important when you don't have hiking partners to help carry your gear or administer first aid in an emergency.

- If you plan to hike in an area without cellular reception, I highly recommend a satellite communicator (such as Garmin's inReach) that has tracking, weather forecasts, and two-way texting capabilities. Most importantly, it has an SOS function that can be used in case of an emergency to contact a search-and-rescue dispatcher. (See "Communication," page 14, for additional options.)

- Check before each hike to make sure that your first aid kit is well stocked and that any items used on the last hike have been replenished or replaced.

- Consider taking a wilderness first aid course, which will teach you how to handle basic backcountry emergencies as well as make evacuation decisions.

- Know what to do in case of an animal encounter (see page 31).

Maps, Apps, and More
NAVIGATION

When I section-hiked the AZT in 2008–09, navigation was one of my biggest challenges: much of the trail saw few visitors and signage was sparse, not to mention that parts of the trail had yet to be built. Having rehiked these sections while researching this book, however, I've found that trail conditions have improved greatly over the past decade. And when it comes to navigation, you have plenty of tools—this book being one of them—that can help you stay on the right track.

Solo Hiking Tips for Women

Hiking takes on yet another dimension for women who are going it alone on the trail. I often get surprised looks and a lot of questions when I mention that I prefer to hike by myself. There's really nothing quite like it. Having time in the outdoors completely to yourself is an incredible experience. Without someone else to talk to, I find myself truly immersed in the journey. My time is mine alone, and I can go at my own pace and stop for photography, reflection, cloud watching, a trailside dance party, or snacks anytime I want. Here are a few tips that I've picked up over the years.

- Be prepared to hear criticism or concern from people who think women shouldn't hike alone. *Ignore it.*

- If you're trying to overcome your fears of hiking alone, I've found that it helps to make a list of those fears, along with solutions for managing them. When I was first going solo, for example, I was very nervous about getting lost, so I jotted down the different resources I would take along with me to keep myself on track and the steps I would take in case I got lost.

- Don't give out your location on social media in real time. Either hold off on posting until you get home or describe where you are only in very general terms.

- Never volunteer to people you meet on the trail that you're hiking by yourself. Say "we" instead of "I."

- Trust your intuition. If you run across someone who makes you feel unsafe, go with that feeling and have a few scenarios ready just in case—you could claim, for instance, that the rest of your group is right behind you, or that your hiking partner stopped for just a second back on the trail.

- Finally, remember that bear spray also works on humans.

MAP AND COMPASS Using these tools is a skill that takes a bit of practice but is well worth it—smartphones and GPS units, after all, can run out of power, get lost, or just stop working. The maps in this book are schematic rather than topographic; the appropriate U.S. Geological Survey (USGS) 7.5-minute topographic map is listed for each hike. Free printable topo maps are available at usgs.gov and websites such as topoquest.com. **REI** has a good online guide to navigation (rei.com/learn/expert-advice/navigation-basics); plus, there are classes you can take and orienteering groups you can join.

GUTHOOK GUIDES ARIZONA TRAIL APP (ATLAS GUIDES) Based in the Gateway Community of Flagstaff, Atlas Guides has revolutionized mobile navigation for long-distance trails and trail systems worldwide, including the AZT. Available for iOS and Android, the software is part of a library of digital maps for specific trails. In addition to the AZT, trails represented include the Appalachian Trail (AT) and the Pacific Crest Trail (PCT), among others. (Ryan Linn, Atlas Guides' cofounder and software developer, has hiked the AT and PCT under the trail name Guthook.) The AZT app costs $9.99 at the time of this writing.

Developed in cooperation with the ATA, the AZT software includes waypoints for trailheads, junctions, and water sources, along with information about Gateway Communities. You can plan your hike ahead of time as well as see crowdsourced information and comments about the latest trail conditions.

The app works in airplane mode—after you've downloaded it and set it up, it doesn't require a data/Wi-Fi connection to function; that said, you shouldn't rely on it as your only navigational tool on the trail. To be safe, carry an external battery pack, plus nondigital backup tools such as paper maps and a compass.

GPS Today's mapping apps can perform many of the same functions as dedicated GPS units. I use **Gaia**, which has both free and pay versions. A GPS watch or smartwatch can perform some of the same functions as a handheld unit or a mobile app.

AZT SIGNAGE The AZT passes through many different land-management agencies, each with its own signage. In addition, the ATA has put up many signs and other methods of marking the trail.

Wooden Signs These are often used in national forests and state and national parks.

Metal AZT Mileage Signs These list the distance south to Mexico and north to Utah.

Small Metal AZT Signs These are posted at critical junctions for wayfinding.

Carsonite Posts These thin brown posts usually have a directional arrow and an AZT sticker.

Cairns Stacks of rocks marking the trail; these can range from small piles to towers that are waist-high or taller. The problem with cairns is that they can occasionally lead you astray onto a route that deviates from the AZT.

Signs on Trees In areas that receive heavy snow, such as the Mogollon Rim and the Kaibab Plateau, AZT signs may be placed high up on tree trunks.

AZT Stickers These may be found on gates, signs, or other places to aid navigation.

GATES No discussion of the AZT is complete without a mention of gates. Arizona is ranch country, and the rule for gates is to read the signs and "leave it how you found it." If a sign says to keep a gate closed or if you find it closed, please shut it behind you. If you find a gate open, leave it open—a rancher could be moving stock around, and closing it could cut off the animals' water source. This rule also applies to gates that you might find while driving.

AZT Super Gate These attractive metal gates with AZT emblems are designed and fabricated by Tucson artist Rob Bauer (see page 113). They're easy to use, and quite a few have very scenic views.

Metal Gate These come in many sizes with a variety of closures.

Cowboy Gate This type of gate is strung with barbwire and has a post-and-loop closure— look to the side for a loop of wire, lift it off the post so the gate goes slack, and then step through. Replace the post and pull it upright to get the loop back over it. Tightly strung gates can require a bit of force to open and close, especially if you're hiking solo.

ROUTE-FINDING TIPS

For me, doing volunteer trail work has been invaluable in helping me develop my orientation skills—by learning what goes into building and maintaining a trail, you also learn clues to finding it if you get off-course.

KEEP YOURSELF FOUND Familiarize yourself with the trail description before your hike, and consult the description and your navigational tools during the hike. Does the description say the trail climbs but you're going downhill? Find yourself on the map or the app.

LOOK BACK While you're hiking, take a moment to look back at where you came from, especially at trail junctions. This will help with navigation on your return trip.

LOOK AROUND Clues that you're on the trail include footprints, cut branches and vegetation from trail maintenance, and rockwork on the tread. Check for cairns or signage.

STOP If you think you might have gotten off the trail, take a moment to assess the situation before moving forward. Continuing to hike and hoping that you'll find the trail again can get you even more off-track—and in the desert, that can be quite the spiny situation.

REVERSE COURSE If you just can't figure out the way forward, go back the way you came until you're certain that you're back on the trail.

COMMUNICATION

At press time, parts of the AZT remain out of cellular range or have spotty coverage at best; reception can also vary depending on your wireless carrier. When you leave details about your itinerary with someone (see page 11), also let that person know if you expect to be hard to reach due to poor cell coverage.

I recommend taking along a **backup power source** for your smartphone: a battery case, a portable charger, or (for older phones) spare removable batteries, especially if you're using your phone to navigate and take photos. (I use an Anker portable charger, but there are many other brands to choose from.) To help prolong battery life, put your phone in airplane mode—which disables voice, text, Bluetooth, data, and Wi-Fi—unless you absolutely need access to those features. The Guthook Guides Arizona Trail App (see page 12) works in airplane mode, as do some other navigation apps.

If you'll be hiking often in an area without cell service, I also recommend buying or renting a **satellite communicator,** a GPS device that can be used for messaging in addition to navigating and tracking your route. I own a Garmin inReach, which comes with two-way texting, preset messages, and weather forecasts, along with an SOS button that you can use to contact a search-and-rescue service in case of an emergency. The SPOT satellite messenger is another option with several models available. I've used both and prefer the Garmin inReach.

Prices for satellite communicators start at around $350 for the device itself, plus the cost of a satellite subscription, which varies according to levels of service similar to a cellular plan. (At the time of this writing, Garmin's satellite plans start at $11.95 per month for a yearly plan or $14.95 per month for a plan without an annual contract.)

Personal locator beacons (PLBs), such as the ACR ResQLink, transmit your location to a search-and-rescue service; they lack messaging capabilities, but they don't require a satellite subscription to work. Prices are comparable to those of satellite communicators. If you have only an occasional need for one of these devices, do an online search for "satellite communicator rentals."

Trail Conditions

Conditions on trails and roads can change due to factors including weather, fire, construction, and reroutes. Before you head out, check the "Passage" listing in each hike description for a page at the ATA website that contains detailed information about a particular AZT passage, or trail section.

Each passage is subdivided into segments that are maintained by **Trail Stewards.** These volunteers cut back brush, repair tread, and are available to answer questions about their segment. For example, I share Trail Steward duties for the

Cody Trail segment of Passage 12, Oracle Ridge, with Arizona Zipline Adventures. Steward and public-land contacts for each passage are listed at aztrail.org /explore/trail-stewards.

If you find a tree down or a stretch of trail that's overgrown or washed out, the ATA has a feedback form online at aztrail.org/the-trail/trail-conditions -form. The passage pages on the website also list updates about road conditions and closures; in addition, you can contact the land-management agencies listed in the hike descriptions.

Sharing the Trail

Observing proper etiquette helps everyone get along when sharing a multiuse, nonmotorized trail such as the AZT. Here are some general guidelines.

- Hikers going downhill should yield to those heading uphill.

- Horses are allowed along the length of the AZT; in the Gateway Community of Flagstaff, the trail's Equestrian Bypass diverts around the city's east side. If you encounter a horse and rider while hiking, step off the trail and greet the rider so that the horse hears your voice and isn't startled.

- Mountain bikers yield to hikers and horseback riders. Mountain bikes are allowed on the AZT *except* where it passes through wilderness areas and national parks. AZT Passage 11b, the Pusch Ridge Wilderness Bypass, was developed for mountain bikers; the Guthook Guides Arizona Trail App (see page 12) also shows alternative routes. ATA members (see page 3) have access to exclusive web content, including maps and GPS data created specifically for mountain bikers; see aztrail.org/explore/mountain-bikers for more information. In Grand Canyon National Park, cyclists who are riding the trail must either dismantle their bikes at the trailhead, strap them to their backs, and carry them from rim to rim across the canyon or have them shuttled around and cross on foot. *Note:* Electric bikes (e-bikes) are prohibited on the AZT, which is for nonmotorized vehicles only.

When and Where to Go
Elevation Is Everything

Many people mistakenly think of Arizona as one big desert, when in fact it contains a staggering amount of geological and biological diversity. From the Sky Islands of southern Arizona, which rise more than 9,000 feet, to the rocky peaks in the central part of the state, to the forested Colorado Plateau (7,000') and

Ancient Trails Through Ancestral Lands By Lyle Balenquah, Hopi

I know for certain that my Hopi ancestors were long-distance travelers. During one of my own wanderings in desert canyons of the Southwest, I gazed upon a 1,000-year-old rock art panel that clearly depicted a line of four individuals, stick figures, loaded with packs. Each figure was shown leaning slightly forward under the weight of a heavy load. They were placed on the cliff face traversing a long, thin fracture in the canyon wall that led my gaze around the corner, as if indicating they still had some miles to go.

Since time immemorial, foot trails in the American Southwest have served as important travel corridors for Indigenous peoples. These trail systems, some of which cover hundreds of miles, connected people from distant regions and different cultural backgrounds. Some trails served as routes to hunting and gathering areas, or to locations where natural materials could be obtained such as salt and turquoise. Other routes led to sacred places where prayers and offerings were deposited. Whatever the purpose, trails enabled the ancient people of the Southwest to travel extensively across the landscape.

Many of the trails we use today were first established by Indigenous peoples. The landscapes these routes travel through are richly detailed in their respective cultural histories. Specific landmarks along these trails have unique Indigenous place-names and recall significant historical people or events.

These landscapes are not unknown or forgotten. Yet this Indigenous presence is often overlooked as various Western designations of land ownership have been enacted on ancestral lands. This has resulted in the removal of Indigenous peoples, their place-names and histories, from many of the areas we currently experience as hikers and backpackers. Modern Indigenous communities maintain their connections to these lands through traditional use, ceremony, and preservation of cultural history. Learning these histories as part of our pretrip research, then acknowledging these Indigenous connections along the trail, is one way that we can show respect for those who have journeyed these landscapes before us.

Today, many Indigenous people continue to use trails as part of their traditional obligations. They come as hikers and backpackers, too, recreating as well as remembering their cultural histories. By following these ages-old trails, Indigenous people continue to honor the traditions and values passed on to them by their ancestors.

Lyle Balenquah, Hopi, is an archaeologist, ethnographer, educator, and outdoor guide. For more than 15 years, he has worked throughout the American Southwest documenting ancestral Hopi settlements and their lifeways. Currently an independent consultant, he previously held positions with the National Park Service, the Hopi Tribe, and the Museum of Northern Arizona. Lyle holds bachelor's and master's degrees in archaeology from Northern Arizona University.

For more information, see the "Ancestral Lands" section of each hike profile, along with Appendix 1 (page 239).

the Kaibab Plateau (9,000') north of Grand Canyon, Arizona contains all of the natural diversity of a drive from Mexico to Canada.

The term *life zones* was coined by C. Hart Merriam (1855–1942), a naturalist and cofounder of the National Geographic Society, during an 1889 expedition to northern Arizona, during which he studied the plant and animal life of the San Francisco Peaks, Painted Desert, and Grand Canyon. Merriam observed that in general, as you gain elevation, temperatures gradually decrease as precipitation gradually increases, approximately 3°F per 1,000 feet.

The concept of life zones, or biotic communities, has been refined over time, and the diagram on the next page notes the plants that are contained in each life zone. The diagram also illustrates differences in vegetation on south-facing versus north-facing slopes.

The table below explains these life zones in greater detail.

LIFE ZONE	ELEVATION	DESCRIPTION	AVERAGE TEMPERATURE	AVERAGE ANNUAL RAIN/SNOW	COMMON PLANTS
Lower Sonoran	100' to 3,500'	low, hot desert	low: 47°F high: 93°F	3"–12"	creosote bush, Joshua tree, saguaro
Upper Sonoran	3,500' to 6,500'	desert steppe, chaparral	low: 43°F high: 78°F	10"–20"	sagebrush, scrub oak, Colorado pinyon, Utah juniper
Transition	6,000' to 8,500'	open woodland	low: 25°F high: 64°F	18"–26"	ponderosa pine
Canadian	8,000' to 9,500'	mixed-conifer forest	low: 25°F high: 61°F	25"–30"	Rocky Mountain Douglas-fir, quaking aspen
Hudsonian	9,500' to 11,500'	spruce forest	low: 21°F high: 43°F	30"–40"	Engelmann spruce, Rocky Mountain bristlecone pine
Arctic–Alpine	11,500' to 12,700'	alpine meadows, tundra	low: 16°F high: 48°F	35"–40"	lichen, grass

The point of all this scientific stuff, in a nutshell: it's important to research the elevation of the hike you're planning to do. You may assume, for instance, that any hike in southern Arizona will be hot and dry, but that's not the case. Hike 2, Miller Peak (page 46), reaches an elevation of more than 9,000 feet—and snow often remains on the mountain well into spring. See pages xv–xvi of "Recommended Hikes" for a list of this book's best hikes by season.

Wheelchair Accessibility

Five hikes in this book include very short sections of the AZT that meet the accessibility criteria of the Americans with Disabilities Act (ADA): Hike 5, Gabe Zimmerman Trailhead to Rattlesnake Mural (page 65, 300 feet); Hike 6, Gabe

Arizona's Life Zones

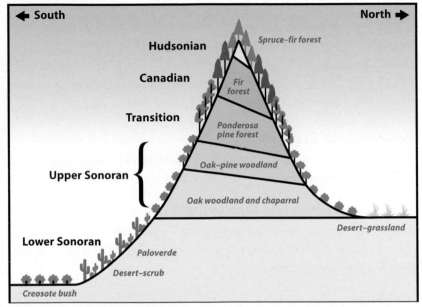

Illustration: Steve Jones (adapted from *Biotic Communities of the American Southwest: United States and Mexico*, edited by D. E. Brown) (University of Utah Press, 1994)

Zimmerman Trailhead to Colossal Cave (page 71, 300 feet); Hike 24, Buffalo Park (page 196, 0.4 mile); Hike 29, East Rim Viewpoint to Tater Canyon (page 229, 0.2 mile); and Hike 30, Stateline Trailhead to Coyote Valley Overlook (page 235, 0.1 mile). For other hikes, I've included detailed information about the trail surface and grade in the descriptions, as well as information about what accessible facilities, if any, are available at the trailheads.

Hiking with Dogs

With the exception of service animals as defined by the ADA (see ada.gov /regs2010/service_animal_qa.html), dogs are prohibited in **Coronado National Memorial** (see Hikes 1 and 2, pages 40 and 46); **Saguaro National Park** (between Hike 6, page 71, and Hike 7, page 79); **Pusch Ridge Wilderness** (see Hike 8, page 87); and **Grand Canyon National Park** below the rim (see Hikes 27 and 28, pages 212 and 223). These restrictions also apply to emotional-support animals.

When it comes to the rest of the AZT, however, just because dogs are allowed on the trail doesn't always mean it's a good idea to bring them along.

The hot, dry southern and central deserts of Arizona can be extremely tough on dogs, especially if they're not used to the environment; carrying enough water for both you and your pet is a must. The terrain can be tough on tender paws; bring along a dog first aid kit that includes tweezers for cactus spines. Plus, there are poisonous critters and prickly plants to be aware of.

If you do bring your dog, please keep it on a leash to avoid potential run-ins with other hikers, pets, and wildlife, and please clean up after it.

How to Use This Book

The section on the following pages walks you through this book's organization, making it easy and convenient to plan great hikes on the AZT.

The Overview Map and Map Legend

The overview map, on page iv, opposite the Table of Contents, displays the primary trailheads for all 30 hikes. A legend explaining the map symbols used throughout the book appears on page vii.

Trail Maps

In addition to the overview map on the inside cover, a detailed map of each hike's route appears with its profile. On each of these maps, symbols indicate the trail-head, the complete route, significant features, facilities, and topographic landmarks such as creeks, overlooks, and peaks.

To produce the highly accurate maps in this book, I used a handheld GPS unit to gather data while hiking each route, then sent that data to Wilderness Press's expert cartographers. Be aware, though, that GPS readings can vary from unit to unit, and your device is no substitute for sound, sensible navigation that takes into account the conditions that you observe while hiking.

Elevation Profile

Each hike also includes this diagram in addition to a trail map. The at-a-glance information preceding each hike description also lists the hike's accumulated elevation gain (see page 24).

The elevation profile represents the rises and falls of the trail as viewed from the side, over the complete distance (in miles) of that trail. On the diagram's vertical axis, or height scale, the number of feet indicated between each tick mark lets you visualize the climb. To avoid making flat hikes look steep and

How Do You Say That?

You'll see these words occasionally throughout this book, but if you're not from Arizona, you may not know how to pronounce them:

AGAVE (ah-GAH-vay)	**MESQUITE** (mes-KEET)
CHOLLA (CHOY-ah)	**MOGOLLON** (MO-go-yawn)
KAIBAB (KYE-bab)	**OCOTILLO** (oh-co-TEE-yoh)
MAZATZAL (MAH-zat-zal or Madda-ZELL)	**SAGUARO** (sah-WA-roh)

Trail-Terms Glossary

BENCHED TRAIL A trail that is cut into the side of a slope or cliff.

BUTTE An isolated hill with steep sides and a flat top.

CAIRN A stack of rocks used to aid navigation. Be careful about trusting cairns—they may be for a trail other than the AZT, or they may have been placed there by someone who was off-route themselves.

CANYON A large, deep, steep-sided gorge that often has a river or creek running through it. In Arizona, these waterways may run only seasonally.

CARSONITE POST A 3- to 5-foot-tall, thin, brown post with AZT stickers, used to aid navigation.

CONTOUR A trail that stays level while traversing a slope. A *rolling contour* has up-and-down variations.

DOUBLETRACK A trail or roadbed that is two parallel tracks.

DRAINAGE A land area where precipitation collects and drains off into a common body of water, such as a river or lake. Also called a *drainage basin* or *watershed*.

MESA An isolated, flat-topped hill with steep sides. (*Mesa* means "table" in Spanish.)

PLATEAU An extensive land area with a relatively level surface that is considerably higher than adjoining land on at least one side. Plateaus are often divided by deep canyons; for example, Grand Canyon cuts through the Kaibab Plateau.

RAVINE A small, narrow, steep-sided valley that is smaller than a canyon and is usually worn by running water.

SADDLE A low point between two hills.

SINGLETRACK A trail that is wide enough for one person at a time.

SWITCHBACK A section of trail or road that zigzags back and forth to aid in negotiating steep ascents or descents.

TRAVERSE A lateral movement across a landform.

WASH A permanently or seasonally dry creekbed.

steep hikes appear flat, varying height scales provide an accurate image of each hike's climbing challenge.

The Hike Profile

Each profile opens with the hike's star ratings, followed by a list of key at-a-glance information. Each profile also includes a map (see "Trail Maps," above) and an elevation profile (also see above). The main text for each profile consists of four sections: **Overview, On the Trail, Gateway Community,** and **Getting There.**

STAR RATINGS

Each hike was assigned a one- to five-star rating in each of the following categories: scenery, trail condition, suitability for children, level of difficulty, and degree of solitude. The star ratings break down as follows:

SCENERY One of my aims in writing this book was to cherry-pick the absolute best scenery of the AZT accessible by passenger vehicle; as a result, you'll find no hikes rated below four stars in this category.

TRAIL CONDITION There's no denying that Arizona is a very rocky and rugged state—if you're used to smooth hiking trails, it can be a bit of an adjustment. The Trail Condition rating incorporates my evaluation of the tread, routing, and grade of the trail. I've also included notes about the types of tread you'll encounter on each hike in the description.

What this rating *doesn't* take into account is whether the trail is overgrown or not; this varies throughout the year, as Trail Stewards maintain the AZT. To get more information about trail conditions before your hike, you can contact the Trail Steward for the hike's AZT passage at aztrail.org/the-trail/trail-stewards. Fires and subsequent flooding can also affect trail conditions. You can also report overgrown trail conditions, damaged tread, or downed trees at the AZT website: aztrail.org/the-trail/trail-conditions-form.

DIFFICULTY This rating considers the length of the hike, the terrain and trail tread, the accumulated elevation gain, and the trailhead elevation.

CHILDREN A number of the short hike options are suitable for kids (see "Recommended Hikes," page xiii, but you can always improvise and turn around at any point. The ATA has a **Junior Explorer Handbook** available for download at aztrail .org/youth/junior-explorers. Tip: Bring along a small toy to take photos of on your journey as a fun activity.

SOLITUDE On a number of these hikes, you'll feel like you have Arizona all to yourself. On others, you'll be sharing the trail with other hikers, mountain bikers, equestrians, and trail runners. See "Sharing the Trail," page 16, for etiquette tips to ensure that everyone has a great time on the AZT.

The AZT is gaining in popularity every year, so some of these ratings may change as the years pass. For example, when I section-hiked the AZT in 2008–09, I rarely saw anyone else, but during my

Family time in the snow Photo: India Hesse

research for this book, I regularly ran into other trail users. If you're on the trail during thru-hiker season, you might encounter many of them in one day.

AT-A-GLANCE INFORMATION

DISTANCE Hiking distances were calculated based on GPS tracks that I recorded during my research; these tracks were then used to generate the maps for each hike.

Note that the distances in this book may vary somewhat from those posted on trail signs. Possible reasons could include recent reroutes that have changed the distance of the trail, a different starting point in the GPS track, or the inclusion of side trips in the total hike distance.

CONFIGURATION The hikes in this book are generally classified as **(1) out-and-backs, (2) point-to-points,** and **(3) loops.** Some hikes combine these elements.

Out-and-Back This type of hike starts and ends at the same trailhead, taking you out in one direction and then back the way you came; the scenery is generally different on the return trip, however. Most of the hikes in this book are out-and-backs— the routes are straightforward, and only one vehicle is necessary to get to them.

Point-to-Point (One-Way) This hike configuration starts in one place and ends in another, requiring a two-vehicle shuttle: you drive to the end trailhead, place one car there, and then drive to the beginning trailhead to start the hike. Hikes in this book with shuttle options are Hike 6, Gabe Zimmerman Trailhead to Colossal

Cave (page 71); Hike 14, Vineyard Trailhead to Mills Ridge (page 130); and Hike 21, Mormon Lake (page 177). If you don't have two vehicles, you could simply double the mileage by doing an out-and-back—but be sure to take that extra mileage into account when planning your hike.

Loop Like an out-and-back, a loop starts and ends at the same trailhead, but whereas an out-and-back is linear, a loop is more circular (though not perfectly so). The loop hikes in this book incorporate trails that aren't part of the AZT. They are, as follows, Hike 9, Marshall Gulch–Aspen Loop (page 93); the Pine Loop in Hike 17, Highline: Pine Trailhead to Red Rock Spring (page 157); Hike 24, Buffalo Park (page 196); and the Aspen Nature Loop in Hike 25, Aspen Nature Loop to Bismarck Lake (page 205).

Short Hike Option Most of the descriptions also list an alternative turnaround point for shortening the hike. If you're a novice hiker, you don't have a lot of time, or you have kids with you, consider one of these shorter options.

HIKING TIME I estimated hiking times using the calculator at TrailsNH.com: see trailsnh.com/tools/hiking-time-calculator.php. For each hike, I entered the distance and elevation gain in the fields provided, along with estimates for pace (given as a range of Slow–Run), trail surface (Easy–Tough), and pack weight (Light–Very Heavy).

I provide a range of hiking times, as the difficulty of a trail is somewhat subjective and depends on how much time you take for snack and lunch breaks, photography, birding, or any other activity that requires stopping. This book is written with beginners in mind, and the ranges in the hiking times reflect that as well.

ELEVATION GAIN The hike's accumulated elevation gain (AEG) takes into account all ascents along the route. For example, Hike 3, Canelo Pass to Meadow Valley (page 52), has 375 feet of elevation gain and 400 feet of elevation loss on the way out, along with 400 feet of elevation gain and 375 feet of elevation loss on the way back; thus, the total out-and-back AEG equals 775 feet.

OUTSTANDING FEATURES This entry lists the highlights of the hike, including scenic views, historical sites, water features, and seasonal displays such as wildflowers and fall color.

LAND-MANAGEMENT AGENCY The AZT passes through numerous types of public lands—national forests, national and state parks, U.S. Bureau of Land

Management sites, and county and city property—as well as privately owned lands. This entry provides the contact information for the relevant agency that administers the land traversed by a particular hike.

MAPS In addition to the maps included in the book, this entry lists the appropriate USGS 7.5-minute topographic quadrangle (1:24,000-scale) for the area in which the hike is located. Topo maps are available at usgs.gov, sciencebase.gov, topoquest.com, and many other websites, often at no cost.

AZT PASSAGE The AZT consists of 43 *passages*, or sections, which vary in length from 8 to 35 miles. This entry tells you which passage a particular hike travels along. Note that none of the hikes in this book cover a full passage—rather, they make use of the best and most accessible parts of the AZT.

ANCESTRAL LANDS Although the AZT does not directly pass through lands that belong to sovereign tribal nations, it's important to remember that all of Arizona originally belonged to the Indigenous peoples who lived here long before European and American colonization changed their ways of life forever. This entry names the tribe that inhabited the land prior to colonization, as well as current tribes that are connected to the region. See page 17 for a discussion of Indigenous perspectives on the AZT, and see Appendix 1 (page 241) for contact information for tribal nations located near the trail.

SEASON This entry lists the best times of year to hike in terms of accessibility, weather, and seasons for wildflowers and fall color. See "Elevation Is Everything" (page 16) for a discussion of how elevation affects temperatures throughout Arizona, and see "Recommended Hikes" (pages xv and xvi) for a list of hikes by season.

ACCESS Lists applicable entrance fees, permits, trail-access hours, seasonal closures, and restrictions (such as prohibitions on dogs).

THE HEART OF THE HIKE

OVERVIEW This paragraph provides a concise summary of what to expect on the trail.

ON THE TRAIL (DESCRIPTION) This section guides you on the hike route from start to finish, noting important turns and junctions, special sights along the way, and alternative routes.

GATEWAY COMMUNITY Gateway Communities are an essential part of the AZT. When Dale Shewalter established the trail, he considered these communities vital to the user experience. These hiker-friendly cities and towns provide lodging, supplies, attractions, and places to savor the all-important posthike meal and beverage. Gateway Community signs welcome you on the roads into town.

Following "On the Trail," each hike includes a Gateway Community write-up, consisting of basic statistics about the town (its distance from the hike, population, and elevation); a short summary of the community's offerings; and listings for specific points of interest.

As the former Gateway Community Liaison for the ATA, I've spent lots of time in these unique places, and I have lots of recommendations for things to see and do. If you'd like to expand your hike to an overnight or weekend adventure, I've also included suggestions on where to camp in the area, both in developed campgrounds and dispersed backcountry areas nearby.

Finally, please keep in mind that phone numbers, websites, operating hours, and prices that were accurate at the time of publication can change. In light of the ongoing public health emergency, it's especially important to call or check online for the very latest information well in advance of your hike.

GETTING THERE Driving to trailheads on the AZT can be an adventure in and of itself. The good news: none of the hikes in this book require a four-wheel-drive vehicle to reach them—most access roads, in fact, are asphalt- or gravel-paved. All of the roads in this book are suitable for passenger vehicles. (Only three hikes in this book should not be accessed in low-clearance vehicles: Hike 4, page 59; Hike 15, page 139, and Hike 20, page 172.)

Trailhead Here you'll find the trailhead's GPS coordinates and elevation in feet. For point-to-point hikes, information for both the starting and ending trailheads is listed.

Road Conditions Where access roads are dirt instead of paved, I indicate whether they can be accessed by all vehicle types.

Facilities Conveniences are often few and far between on the AZT. Many trailheads have no restrooms, water, or picnic tables—just a dirt parking pullout. Make sure to bring all the water you need, and then some (see page 29). Keep a couple of gallons of water in the car in case of emergency.

Directions I've included detailed turn-by-turn driving directions as well as information about grades and road conditions for dirt roads. It's best to follow the directions as written, as online mapping services will sometimes take you on a different route.

Note: As a transplant from the flat, paved suburban Midwest, I found that driving up mountains and on dirt roads took some getting used to. Some of these drives are guaranteed to dirty up your vehicle, and a couple may even make your heart race, but in return you'll be rewarded with superb scenery and access to wonderfully remote places. Where the drives involve roads with steep drop-offs and no railings, I've made sure to note it in the directions.

Hiking the Entire AZT

If you're interested in hiking all of the AZT, there are two ways to do it: thru-hiking and section hiking. See Appendix 2 (page 243) for a list of Arizona Trail resources to help plan your hike.

Thru-Hiking

On your AZT hikes, you may encounter people who are doing the whole 800 miles. You'll probably be able to tell who they are by their well-worn gear and insatiable hiker hunger. They may introduce themselves by an unusual trail name, like "Snorkel," "Hiker Box," or "Wonder Woman." These are thru-hikers, and there are two thru-hiking seasons on the AZT. **Northbounders (NOBOs)** start at the Mexican border in the spring, usually in March or April, and hike toward Utah. **Southbounders (SOBOs)** set out in the opposite direction, usually in September or October. Thru-hikers use the Gateway Communities to resupply and rest along their journey.

Hiking during these two times of year avoids the cold of the northern passages of the trail and the heat of its southern passages; indeed, thru-hikers are often said to be following the wildflower blooms north and the fall colors south. Completion times vary, but most hikers take anywhere from 45 days to three months from start to finish. When I thru-hiked the AZT in 2014, it took me two and a half months, from mid-March to the end of May.

At the time of this writing, the fastest known time (FKT) for thru-hiking the AZT is 14 days, 12 hours, and 21 minutes, set by Josh Perry in October 2019. That's more than 50 miles a day, and he was self-supported, meaning that he carried all of his own gear and had to stop in towns to resupply. The self-supported FKT for women is 19 days, 17 hours, and 9 minutes, set by Heather "Anish" Anderson in October 2016.

If you cross paths with thru-hikers, offer them some food—chances are they're hungry from burning up to 5,000 calories a day. Thru-hikers call these acts of kindness *trail magic*.

Section Hiking

Are you interested in taking on the entire AZT but you don't have the time, resources, or desire to hike for months on end? Then section hiking is for you. This has many advantages: you can choose to hike the sections during the best seasons, it's easier to fit in hiking while working a full-time job, you can change your plans if the weather turns bad, and it's gentler on your body than the day-after-day beating you take on a thru-hike.

Section hiking is how I first completed the AZT: I hiked on my days off from work, and occasionally for a week at a time, for 15 months. Some folks take a year, others take a decade. Section hiking lets you go at whatever pace is right for you.

Available through the ATA, *The Arizona Trail Day Hiker's Guide* ($33) is geared to section hikers. This three-ring-bound book breaks up the 800 miles into 89 day hikes ranging from 3.8 miles to 13.8 miles long, with an average distance of about 9 miles per hike. You can order it online at aztrail.org/product-category/books.

If you complete the whole AZT, you can submit your information and complete a survey to get a finisher's copper belt buckle. You can see a list of finishers on the ATA website: aztrail.org/the-trail/trail-finishers.

Desert Hiking Tips and Tricks

Four Rules to Live by in the Desert

1. Don't touch spiny plants or critters.

2. Don't put your hands or feet where you can't see them.

3. Kick rocks over before putting your hands on them.

4. Bring more water than you think you'll need.

The desert is a very different environment from what most people are used to. Coming to Arizona from the Chicago suburbs, I found it intimidating at first, but the more I learn about this state, the more I appreciate the hardy plants and creatures that call the desert home. I've learned quite a few tips and tricks in my quarter century of living here that go a long way toward staying comfortable on the trail.

Hydrate and Refuel

A good general guideline is to carry 0.5 liter (16 ounces) of water per person, per hour, in cool weather and 1 liter (32 ounces) per person, per hour in warmer weather. If you've already gone through more than half of your water halfway through the hike, consider turning around early. Another good reason to carry plenty of water: high elevations are dehydrating.

It's not enough to just chug water nonstop while you hike—in fact, that can lead to a dangerous condition called hyponatremia. Your body loses salts and minerals when you sweat, though you might not realize how much you're sweating because it evaporates quickly in the desert. You need to replace them while you rehydrate, either by eating salty snacks or by consuming electrolyte-replacement drinks, tablets, chews, or gels.

One of the first signs of dehydration is irritability. Are you in a lousy mood? Are you starting to think your hiking partners are a bunch of jerks? If you take a moment to drink and eat, you'll be surprised at how much better you feel. You can even prehydrate by making sure to drink plenty of water the night before.

It's always a good idea to carry snacks in your pack even on short hikes. For longer hikes, pack a lunch to eat on the trail. In hot weather, salty snacks like pretzels or trail mix will help to replace salts lost by sweating (see above).

Spines and Prickles and Barbs, Oh My!

As the first rule in the box opposite indicates, the vegetation of Arizona, especially that in the southern part of the state, is best admired from a distance. Sometimes, however, accidents happen despite your best efforts to avoid them, so it's wise to carry a pair of tweezers in your first aid kit to remove spines. And it's not just the large spines you need to worry about—the small, hairlike glochids (bristles) of prickly pear are just as uncomfortable but harder to find.

Remove as many spines as you can in the field before they have a chance to break off or scrape against your clothing. Back at home, use this trick to

Prickly pear (foreground) and cholla cacti and acacia and mesquite trees are prevalent in the southern part of the state, and all have spines to be avoided.

remove any remaining spines: apply a thin layer of white school glue to affected skin, cover it with gauze, let it dry, and then peel it off.

Sometimes spines get embedded underneath the skin, in which case you should remove them as you would splinters, using one of these techniques: pluck out the spine with tweezers (disinfect it first with rubbing alcohol); cover it with duct tape and then pull it off (and hopefully the spine with it); expose the spine with a needle (again, disinfect it first), then pull it out with tweezers; or try drawing it out with hydrogen peroxide or a mixture of water and baking soda or Epsom salts. When spines can't be removed, the body often encapsulates them in scar tissue, and they may emerge months later.

Some people may experience dermatitis, a rash or bumps on the skin. Spines that get embedded near joints can cause inflammation—in this case, you might need to seek medical treatment instead of trying to remove them yourself.

Cholla cactus (aka jumping cholla) is segmented, with loosely attached spines. These can come off the plant when you brush by, or segments that have fallen on the ground can get kicked up and embed themselves in your skin. The spines are barbed and difficult to remove. The best implement for cholla removal is a comb—place it behind the cholla segment, and pull away from the skin. If you don't have a comb, use sticks to dislodge the segment, but be careful of flying segments when they come loose.

Wildlife

You could very well complete all of the hikes in this book and never encounter any of the creatures described below. Nevertheless, it's good to know what to do in case of an encounter.

MAMMALS

BLACK BEARS AND MOUNTAIN LIONS Should you have a run-in with a cougar or a bear, face the animal, make yourself seem as large as possible—raise your hands and put up your hiking poles—and either stand your ground or move sideways slowly. Make noise: yell, clack your hiking poles together, or bang a piece of metal with a rock. **Do not run or turn your back**—that triggers the animal's prey response. If you're attacked, fight back with everything at your disposal: sticks, rocks, backpack, or bare hands. Jaguars have also been recorded in the grasslands of southern Arizona but are so elusive that even researchers hardly ever see them.

JAVELINAS Javelinas (hah-va-LEE-nas) have sharp tusks and may rush toward you if threatened. Though they look like pigs, they are part of the peccary family. They have poor eyesight and generally aren't aggressive toward humans unless you get between them and their babies. Javelinas can be aggressive toward dogs, though, so leash your pets.

Javelina
Photo: Dennis W. Donohue/Shutterstock

Diamondback rattlesnake

SNAKES, SCORPIONS, BUGS, AND STINGING INSECTS

SNAKES Arizona has 13 species of rattlesnakes along with numerous nonvenomous species. Observe the second and third rules in the box on page 28, and be aware of your surroundings, as many snakes have incredibly effective camouflage. If you get bitten, call 911 immediately. If you're in an area without cell reception, walk slowly back to your vehicle, and drive to an area with cell service and or a hospital as soon as possible. **Do not tie a tourniquet around the bite or try to slice the wound and suck the poison out.**

Tip: If you like to listen to music while you hike, put in just one earbud so you can hear the rattlesnake's signature warning sound. Be aware, however, that rattlers don't always warn before they strike.

The small, light-brown Arizona bark scorpion packs a potent poison.

SCORPIONS At 1–3 inches long, the **Arizona bark scorpion** is the smallest and most venomous of the species found in the state. Follow the second and third rules on page 28 to minimize contact with them. Scorpions are most active during warmer months and at night. They may sting if disturbed while hiding under rocks or branches. Most stings in healthy adults can be managed with first aid at home. Children under age 9, people with high blood pressure, and anyone who is allergic to scorpions should seek immediate medical treatment.

SPIDERS There are several types of spiders to be aware of in Arizona. **Tarantulas** are found across the state and are more prevalent in the summer and fall seasons. Though they look like something out of a horror movie, they're generally docile, although they do have two methods of defense if provoked: (1) the spider waves its legs to release irritating hairs, called urticating hairs, from its abdomen, or (2) in rare cases it will bite, which causes localized pain at the site.

Female **black widow spiders** are identified by a red hourglass shape on the abdomen. Black widows are not aggressive, but their venom is extremely potent. People who are bitten should seek medical attention; be especially aware that black widow bites can be life-threatening in young children.

TARANTULA HAWKS These large (2-inch-long) wasps with black bodies and bright copper- or orange-colored wings don't sting humans very often, but rest assured it's not an experience you want to have. Though their sting is said to be the second most painful in the insect kingdom, the pain is short-lived, and stings don't require medical attention unless you're allergic to wasps and bees. On the other hand, the pain *can* be distracting enough to make you injure yourself in some other way as you flail around in agony. If you do get stung, immediately drop to the ground and try to tough it out for 5–10 minutes.

Tarantula hawks are named for the prey they seek: they sting a tarantula, paralyzing it without killing it; drag it to their burrow; and lay an egg inside. The larva feeds on the tarantula, grows into an adult, and emerges from it as a wasp. The desert is a tough place indeed.

Unlike its prey, the tarantula hawk has a sting that lives up to its fearsome appearance.   Photo: @N8TRGRL

BEES While the larger and venomous animals in the desert get a lot of attention, bees can be one of the most dangerous encounters, especially if one is allergic to them. Of the many types found in the desert, the Africanized honey bee (AHB), an invasive hybrid species, is especially aggressive. When disturbed, patrolling bees will "bump," or run into, the target. If this occurs, protect your face and run away until you are outside of the defensive area, which can be up to a half mile away from the hive. Do not swat at or try to kill the bees as that will attract more; they tend to sting in greater numbers.

Seek medical attention immediately if you have been stung many times, have a reaction that makes you feel ill, or are short of breath. If you are allergic to bees, carry a kit with Benadryl and an epinephrine auto-injector (such as EpiPen).

BIRDING ON THE AZT

The AZT passes through many birding hot spots and migration corridors. Visit the **Arizona Important Bird Areas Program** website (aziba.org) for more information, including a downloadable map (click "Resources," then "Map Resources").

Desert Environment Tips and Tricks

Sun and Shade

The sun in Arizona is very intense, even when the weather isn't particularly hot. Here's some advice.

It might seem counterintuitive to wear long sleeves and pants on a hike in the desert, but they provide shade, UV protection, and evaporative cooling as you sweat.

Protect the back of your neck and ears from sunburn with a wide-brimmed hat, a neck flap, or a lightweight hoodie paired with a baseball cap or visor. Shirts with thumb holes protect the backs of your hands; you can also wear lightweight UV gloves. Choose sunglasses with UV protection.

When it comes to sunscreen, use a product with an SPF of at least 30 (check the expiration date), and apply it every 2 hours (don't forget your ears) or after you get wet.

One of my favorite pieces of gear is **Gossamer Gear's trekking umbrella** (gossamergear.com)—shade is at a premium in the heat, after all, so why not carry your own? A regular umbrella will do in a pinch, but most aren't made to withstand high winds without turning inside out. Look for a model with a silver reflective surface made from carbon fiber; light and sturdy, it can be carried in your hand or attached to your pack. You can also set it up to shade you while you take a break, and if you carry a trekking umbrella, you don't need to wear a sun hat. Put a wet bandanna on your head and you've got a great way to provide evaporative cooling.

COOLING METHODS

Here's an easy one: wear a wet bandanna on your neck for even more cooling. Make sure to pack extra water for this purpose. This fools your body into thinking it's cooler than it is, because it gets temperature cues from the blood flowing through the carotid artery in your neck. You could buy special cooling towels, but an old-fashioned cotton bandanna works just as well.

A trick for especially hot hikes: wet a long-sleeved cotton T-shirt and put it in a waterproof bag. When you're at your hottest, put on the wet shirt and enjoy the evaporative cooling. (On the other hand, if it's hot enough to use this trick, you might just consider hiking in a cooler, higher elevation instead.) Hiking past water in hot weather? Wet your head and sleeves.

Cold Weather

The desert is a place of extremes—sometimes you can be sweltering in the heat and then shivering from the cold within the space of a couple of hours. Prepare for these temperature swings by packing layers. A lightweight jacket is handy to have in your pack; for colder weather, pack a down jacket, hat, scarf, and gloves. Don't wear cotton when it's cold or temperatures fluctuate—that fabric stays wet for a long time and can cause hypothermia. Instead, opt for synthetics or fleeces that wick away moisture.

To avoid sweating in cold weather, remove a layer when you warm up—when you're climbing a hill, for instance—and then put it back on later when you've cooled down.

Wind

Arizona can be a windy place, especially in the spring, so check the forecast and pack a wind-blocking layer like a rain jacket or wind shirt. When you take a break, make sure that your stuff is weighted down and garbage is packed away so the wind doesn't scatter it and create a mess. A hat with a chin strap helps you hang on to it in high winds.

Monsoon

This weather phenomenon brings heavy rain and lightning storms to Arizona, generally from July to mid-September. The monsoon has a pattern of building during the heat of the day, with storms occurring in the afternoon. Make sure to check the weather before you hit the trail—it's generally best to be done with your hike by the afternoon during monsoon. See the next two sections for more information about monsoon conditions.

Flash Floods

When it rains heavily in the desert, the ground can't soak it all in, and the rainwater forms runoff streams, which combine in larger drainages to form flash floods. These can be extremely dangerous and can occur even when there is no storm directly overhead.

Avoid crossing flooded waterways—the water is likely thick with sticks, logs, rocks, and other debris that can injure you. Also take flash floods into consideration when driving: **do not attempt to drive your vehicle through swift-moving water.** As little as 6 inches of water can damage a passenger vehicle.

Lightning

Here are some tips from the National Lightning Safety Institute (see lightning safety.com/nlsi_pls/ploutdoor.htm).

AVOID metallic objects; high ground; solitary tall trees; close contact with others (spread out 15–20 feet apart); contact with dissimilar objects (such as water and land, boat and land, rock and ground, tree and ground); and open spaces.

SEEK clumps of shrubs or trees of uniform height; ditches, trenches, or the low ground; and a low, crouching position, with feet together and hands on ears, to minimize acoustic shock from thunder.

KEEP a high level of safety awareness for 30 minutes after the last observed lightning or thunder.

Other Concerns

Cryptobiotic Soil

Don't bust the crust! Cryptobiotic soil is composed of living organisms (such as algae and fungi) that form a crust on the dirt that resembles a black, bumpy mat. This crust, which can take hundreds of years to develop, plays a vital role in managing storm runoff and maintaining the structural integrity of the soil underneath. Stay on established trails, and take a look around you before wandering off the trail to take a break, snap photos, or use the restroom.

Avoid disturbing cryptobiotic soil, which is very fragile and important to desert environments.

Mine Shafts

Arizona has a long history of mining, and some of the AZT passes abandoned mine shafts. **Do not disturb them**—not only do mine shafts pose risks of rockfall and collapse, but many also serve as ecologically sensitive spaces for Arizona's diverse bat population.

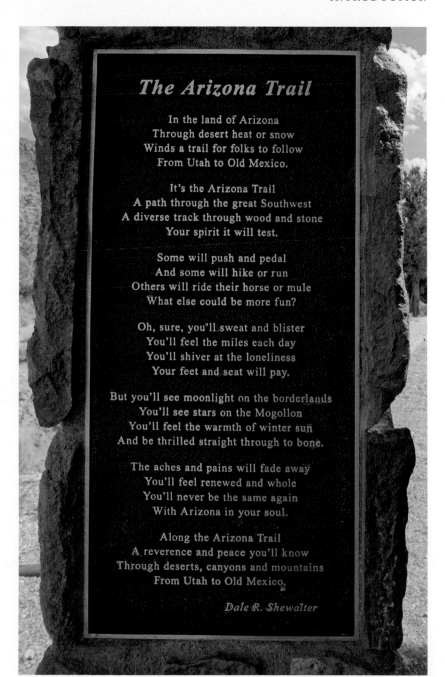

The Arizona Trail

In the land of Arizona
Through desert heat or snow
Winds a trail for folks to follow
From Utah to Old Mexico.

It's the Arizona Trail
A path through the great Southwest
A diverse track through wood and stone
Your spirit it will test.

Some will push and pedal
And some will hike or run
Others will ride their horse or mule
What else could be more fun?

Oh, sure, you'll sweat and blister
You'll feel the miles each day
You'll shiver at the loneliness
Your feet and seat will pay.

But you'll see moonlight on the borderlands
You'll see stars on the Mogollon
You'll feel the warmth of winter sun
And be thrilled straight through to bone.

The aches and pains will fade away
You'll feel renewed and whole
You'll never be the same again
With Arizona in your soul.

Along the Arizona Trail
A reverence and peace you'll know
Through deserts, canyons and mountains
From Utah to Old Mexico.

Dale R. Shewalter

Dale Shewalter, who conceived the AZT, wrote the poem on this obelisk at the trail's northern terminus.

South (Hikes 1–11)

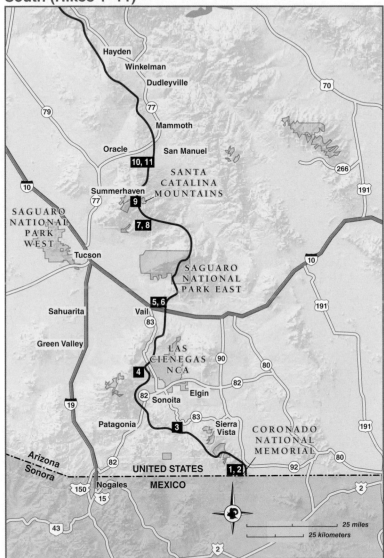

Hayden

Winkelman

Dudleyville

70

79

77

Mammoth

Oracle   San Manuel

266

10, 11

SANTA
CATALINA
MOUNTAINS

10

191

Summerhaven

77

9

SAGUARO
NATIONAL
PARK
WEST

7, 8

Tucson

SAGUARO
NATIONAL
PARK EAST

10

191

Sahuarita   Vail

5, 6

83

Green Valley

LAS
CIENEGAS
NCA

90

80

4

82

82   Sonoita   Elgin

19

83   Sierra
Vista

Patagonia

3

CORONADO
NATIONAL
MEMORIAL

Arizona
Sonora

82

UNITED STATES

1, 2

92

80

150   Nogales   MEXICO

2

15

N

43

25 miles

25 kilometers

2

Gateway Communities are highlighted in yellow.

Sunrise on the AZT at High Jinks Ranch (see Hike 10, page 99)

Montezuma Pass to Mexico
Journey to the Mexico border

> SCENERY: ★ ★ ★ ★
> TRAIL CONDITION: ★ ★ ★ ★
> CHILDREN: ★ ★ ★
> DIFFICULTY: ★ ★ ★
> SOLITUDE: ★ ★ ★

A view into Mexico from Border Monument 102

DISTANCE & CONFIGURATION: 3.8-mile out-and-back

HIKING TIME: 2–3 hours

ACCUMULATED ELEVATION GAIN: 900'

SHORT HIKE OPTION: You kind of miss the point of this hike if you shorten it. That said, you can always turn around sooner at any point as your schedule and circumstances dictate.

OUTSTANDING FEATURES: Southern terminus of the AZT at Border Monument 102; views into Mexico

LAND-MANAGEMENT AGENCY: Coronado National Memorial, 520-366-5515, nps.gov/coro

MAPS: USGS 7.5' *Montezuma Pass, AZ*

AZT PASSAGE: 1/Huachuca Mountains, aztrail.org/explore/passages/passage-1 -huachuca-mountains

ANCESTRAL LANDS: Tohono O'odham, Pascua Yaqui, Sobaipuri, Chiricahua Apache

SEASONS: Spring, fall, winter

ACCESS: Dogs prohibited in Coronado National Memorial; no fees or permits; open daily, sunrise–sunset; visitor center open daily, 8 a.m.–4 p.m. except December 25

Advisory

In July 2020 U.S. Customs and Border Protection began work on a road and 30-foot-tall wall through Coronado National Memorial, and the Arizona National Scenic Trail (AZT) is closed at the time of this writing inside the park. The road and wall are expected to block the view south from the southern terminus of the AZT and will travel through a protected habitat for endangered jaguars and ocelots. Projected completion date is June 2021; check the passage page (aztrail.org /explore/passages/passage-1-huachuca-mountains) or Coronado National Memorial (nps.gov/coro) for updates.

Overview

This day hike takes you through grasslands and oaks in Coronado National Memorial to the southern terminus of the AZT at the Mexico border. The AZT at the border has no vehicle access—you can get there only by hiking the 1.9 miles down and back from Montezuma Pass.

On the Trail

From the south end of the trailhead parking area, with the picnic ramada on your left and trail register on your right, follow the Yaqui Ridge Trail/AZT south as it switchbacks up the hill and comes to a junction with the Coronado Peak Trail in 500 feet. Dale Shewalter, "Father of the Arizona Trail," was hiking the Coronado Peak Trail when he got the idea for a trail across Arizona, from Mexico to Utah (see page 1); for this hike, though, take the left (southeast) fork at the junction to stay on the AZT. If you have energy to burn, the route to Coronado Peak is an 0.8-mile, 330-foot ascent with 360-degree views, along with interpretive signs about the Indigenous people of the area and Coronado's expedition.

Francisco Vázquez de Coronado was sent by Antonio de Mendoza, viceroy of New Spain, to find Cíbola, or the Seven Cities of Gold, in 1540. (A Franciscan priest, Fray Marcos de Niza, had returned from New Mexico saying he had seen these cities.) The entrada (expedition) party consisted of priests, 300 Spanish soldiers, several hundred Mexican allies, servants and slaves, and 1,500 stock animals.

The National Park Service website states: "While there is no physical evidence of the expedition in the present memorial, the park offers a sweeping view of the San Pedro River which is widely regarded as the corridor that the expedition used on their way north to the mythical Cíbola." The expedition traveled all the way to Kansas in 1542 before they realized the tales of cities

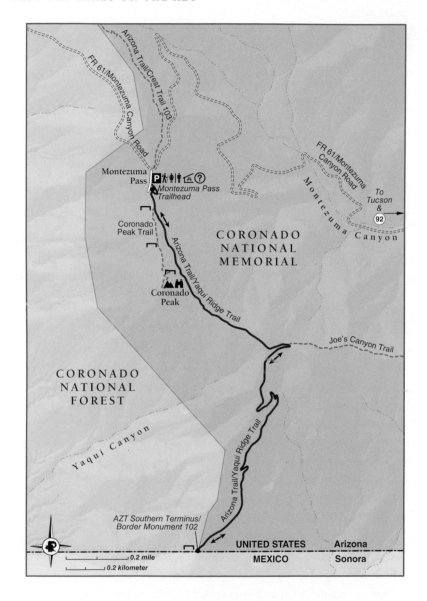

of gold were fantasy. The entrada resulted in the slaughter of many Indigenous people and forced them to abandon their pueblos—the beginning of a pattern that would continue as Europeans and then Americans continued to colonize the Southwest.

There is a brief climb for 0.3 mile; then the trail descends through grass-lands and Gambel oak. The mountain that dominates the view is San Jose Peak, in Mexico (8,858'). In 0.4 mile, reach a junction with Joe's Canyon Trail, which goes left (east) down to the visitor center you passed on your drive up—the AZT heads right (west), then curves south.

The trail begins descending on a series of switchbacks in 0.3 mile and then another switchback in 0.4 mile. It continues descending past rocky outcrops that are part of the Glance Conglomerate, a prehistoric sedimentary layer created from the erosion of small mountains, which filled the valley with rocks of varying types and sizes. Over time, the sediment and inclusions were compacted into what you are seeing today. Keep your eyes open for coatimundi, a raccoonlike creature with a long tail. Bands of coatimundi can consist of up to 30 individuals, and I've seen them on the hillside in this area.

In 0.1 mile the trail trends southwest toward Mexico. The obelisk of Border Monument 102 isn't visible until just before you reach the border. Reach the southern terminus of the AZT at 1.9 miles (5,903'). At the time of this writing, the border is marked by a three-strand barbwire fence; however there is now a border wall under construction. There is a bench nearby to take in the view. Border Monument 102 is one of 258 that mark Mexico's border with the US.

If you're here in March or April, you might see AZT thru-hikers beginning their journey northbound, and in November or December you may see them completing their journey southbound. The seasons for thru-hiking are determined by weather conditions: they follow spring northbound from Mexico and fall southbound from Utah (see "Thru-Hiking," page 27, for more information).

Return the way you came, making a left (west) turn at the Joe's Canyon Trail junction.

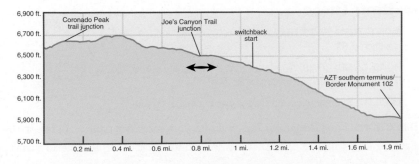

Gateway Community: SIERRA VISTA

DISTANCE FROM TRAILHEAD: 24.0 miles **POPULATION:** 43,888 **ELEVATION:** 4,633'

Site of the Fort Huachuca Army base, Sierra Vista is also a hot spot for birding that attracts avian enthusiasts from all over the world. The Nature Conservancy's **Ramsey Canyon Preserve** is home to more than 170 varieties of birds, including 14 species of hummingbirds. The 40.0-mile-long **San Pedro Riparian National Conservation Area** preserves the rich biodiversity along the San Pedro River, is home to historic and prehistoric sites up to 12,000 years old, and serves as an important habitat for 250 bird species that pass through during migration.

There are plenty of places to eat in Sierra Vista, but one of my favorites is **Bamboo Garden.** Sierra Vista also has German cuisine at **The German Café, Angelika's German Imports,** and **Bobke's for Lunch.** A full range of lodging options are available.

RAMSEY CANYON PRESERVE: 27 E. Ramsey Canyon Rd., 520-335-8740, tinyurl.com /ramseycanyonpreserve. Admission: $8/person, $5 for Nature Conservancy members. Open Thursday–Sunday, 8 a.m.–5 p.m. March 1–October 31, 9 a.m.–4 p.m. November 1– February 28.

SAN PEDRO RIPARIAN NATIONAL CONSERVATION AREA: 9800 E. AZ 90, 520-508-4445, sanpedroriver.org/wpfspr. Free entry, visitor center open daily, 9:30 a.m.–4:30 p.m.

BAMBOO GARDEN: 1481 E. Fry Blvd., Ste. 3, 520-459-1800, facebook.com/bamboo gardenssv. Open Tuesday–Saturday, 11 a.m.–9 p.m., Sunday, noon–9 p.m.

THE GERMAN CAFÉ: 1232 E. Fry Blvd., 520-456-1705, tinyurl.com/germancafesv. Open Monday–Saturday, 11 a.m.–9 p.m.

ANGELIKA'S GERMAN IMPORTS: 1630 E. Fry Blvd., 520-458-5150, tinyurl.com /angelikassierravista. Open Tuesday–Thursday, 10 a.m.–5 p.m., Friday, 10 a.m.–6 p.m., Saturday, 10 a.m.–3 p.m.

BOBKE'S FOR LUNCH: 355 W. Wilcox Dr., 520-458-8580, tinyurl.com/bobkesforlunch. Open Monday–Friday, 7:30 a.m.–2:30 p.m.

Getting There

MONTEZUMA PASS TRAILHEAD: N31° 21.022' W110° 17.126', elevation 6,575'

ROAD CONDITIONS: All vehicles; last 3.3 miles are graded dirt, suitable for passenger vehicles and trailers under 24'

FACILITIES: Restrooms and shaded picnic ramada; no water

DIRECTIONS *From Downtown Tucson:* From Congress Street and I-10, take I-10 East for 44.0 miles to Exit 302 for AZ 90 South (Fort Huachuca/Sierra Vista).

A different view into Mexico, this one from Montezuma Pass

In 32.0 miles keep right (south) to merge onto AZ 92 East; then continue south 14.0 miles to South Coronado Memorial Road. Turn right (south) and follow the road as it curves right (west) and becomes Montezuma Canyon Road; then, in 5.0 miles, reach the Coronado National Memorial Visitor Center, on the right. Stop in here to see the interpretive exhibits, including information about the Indigenous people and natural history of the region, as well as period chain mail and helmets. From the visitor center, continue west and then south 3.3 miles on Montezuma Canyon Road; this final, twisting stretch up to the Montezuma Pass Trailhead is graded dirt road. Look for the parking area on your left just before the road curves sharply right (northwest).

Scenic Route: From I-10 East, take Exit 281 for AZ 83 South, and drive 26.0 miles to Sonoita. Turn left onto AZ 82 East and, in 19.0 miles, turn right (south) onto AZ 90. In 14.6 miles keep right (south) to merge onto AZ 92 East; then continue south 14.0 miles to South Coronado Memorial Road, and proceed as above.

Note: On your return north, there are internal border-patrol checkpoints on AZ 90 at milepost 304 and on AZ 83 at milepost 40.8.

2

Miller Peak

High-elevation haven

SCENERY: ★ ★ ★ ★ ★
TRAIL CONDITION: ★ ★ ★
CHILDREN: ★
DIFFICULTY: ★ ★ ★ ★ ★
SOLITUDE: ★ ★ ★

The views into Mexico are fantastic as the Crest Trail climbs.

DISTANCE & CONFIGURATION: 10.4-mile out-and-back

HIKING TIME: 6–10 hours

ACCUMULATED ELEVATION GAIN: 3,290'

SHORT HIKE OPTION: 4.2-mile out-and-back to wilderness boundary (1,380' elevation gain)

OUTSTANDING FEATURES: Spectacular 360-degree views, diverse Sky Island environments

LAND-MANAGEMENT AGENCIES: Coronado National Memorial, 520-366-5515, nps.gov/coro; Coronado National Forest, Sierra Vista Ranger District, 520-378-0311, fs.usda.gov/coronado

MAPS: USGS 7.5' *Montezuma Pass, AZ* and *Miller Peak, AZ*

AZT PASSAGE: 1/Huachuca Mountains, aztrail.org/explore/passages/passage-1 -huachuca-mountains

ANCESTRAL LANDS: Tohono O'odham, Pascua Yaqui, Sobaipuri, and Chiricahua Apache

SEASONS: Spring, fall, winter (snow possible well into spring)

ACCESS: Dogs prohibited in Coronado National Memorial; no fees or permits; open daily, sunrise–sunset; visitor center open daily, 8 a.m.–4 p.m. except December 25

Overview

This hike on the AZT is one of the toughest in the book: it's long, steep, remote, and high-elevation. Make sure to check trail conditions before you go, as snow can linger past winter along the shaded parts of the trail. You'll be rewarded for your efforts with incredible views from the Crest Trail and Miller Peak (9,466').

Note: The lower the elevation where you live, the more this hike will affect your breathing. When hiking to a peak, you should set a strict turnaround time for the summit that allows for enough time to return safely before sunset. Watch your water intake as well; you'll want to turn around once you've finished half of your water supply. Temperatures vary widely on this hike due to the change in elevation—layers are key to staying comfortable (see page 33 for a discussion).

On the Trail

From the parking area (6,548'), cross the road and head right about 30 yards. Just before the cattle guard, the signed Crest Trail 103—which is contiguous with the AZT inside Coronado National Memorial—starts to your left (west). Another sign says FOREST BOUNDARY 2 MILES, MILLER PEAK 5.3 MILES. Miller Peak, which you'll visit shortly, isn't on the AZT, requiring a 1.0-mile round-trip from the junction with the Crest Trail, but the views from the top are worth it.

The trail immediately starts to climb north above the road. At 0.2 mile make two short switchbacks, and the trail continues north. In 0.3 mile make four more short switchbacks, and continue climbing to the crest of the ridge at a small saddle in 0.1 mile, and then another saddle in 0.1 mile. You have views of the San Rafael Valley to the left (southwest) and into Mexico to the south.

At mile 1.0, the trail curves left (northwest), and you can see Montezuma Pass and the Coronado Peak Trail to your right (south). In 0.25 mile the AZT curves right (northeast) and starts a series of switchbacks. You're heading for the saddle, or low point between two hills, that you see ahead. The vegetation is more open and exposed here. The trail passes through oak grasslands dotted with agave and beargrass.

Switchback and climb to reach the first of three mine shafts in 0.4 mile to your left (northwest). The shaft is gated to prevent people from going in but lets bats out. In 0.1 mile pass the second mine shaft on the right (northwest). Continue switchbacking uphill and, in 0.3 mile, pass mine shaft number three, which also has a metal tank, to the left (northwest).

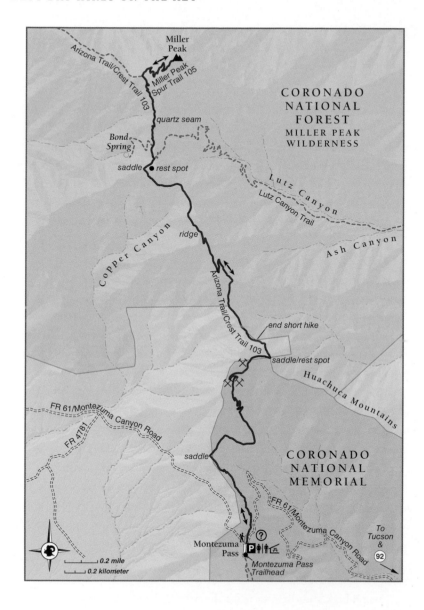

Finally, that saddle you've been eyeing is getting closer; keep climbing east toward the ridgetop. At 2.0 miles reach the saddle and a well-deserved break, just before the AZT heads left (northwest). A windswept alligator juniper to your right (south) makes a good rest spot.

The views from the saddle are fantastic. You can see into Montezuma Canyon and Mexico beyond to the southeast. Also to the east are the Mule Mountains near Bisbee, and beyond those the Chiricahua Mountains.

From the saddle climb a couple of switchbacks to reach the Miller Peak Wilderness boundary (7,794'). **This is the turnaround point for the short hike, at 2.1 miles and 1,380 feet of elevation gain.** You can see the other side of the ridge and Miller Peak ahead (northwest), along with Sierra Vista in the valley to the right.

The trail is cut across a steep slope but climbs gently. You may feel somewhat exposed as you continue through a burn area. In 0.3 mile the climb gets steeper and curves left (north) in 0.3 mile. Miller Peak comes into view again as the trail switchbacks to gain the crest of the ridge in 0.2 mile. It follows the ridgetop, then goes to the right (east) to travel below the ridge.

Reach the ridgetop again in 0.4 mile and cross over to the southwest side. This part of the trail has no shade, just small bushes. The Santa Rita Mountains and Mount Wrightson are visible to the west; in the distance to the left of that range, is Baboquivari Peak, the center of the Indigenous Tohono O'odham universe.

In 0.1 mile the trail curves right (northeast) and flattens as it descends for 0.2 mile; then it curves west (left). Switchback right (northeast) to go through another saddle in 0.3 mile. This makes a great spot to take another break before the next part of the journey and take stock of your water supply and energy before continuing. You'll find large ponderosa pines for shade and rocks to sit on just past the saddle on the right (southeast).

At mile 4.0, the AZT curves left northwest and passes through another small saddle at a junction with the Lutz Canyon Trail, which makes a hard right, heading east. (At the time of this writing, the sign at the junction was down on the ground. It reads LUTZ CANYON TRAIL #104–ASH CANYON ROAD

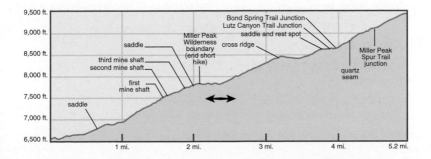

3.5 MILES.) In 0.1 mile you pass another junction with Bond Spring Trail 113 to the left (northwest).

The trail begins a series of short, steep switchbacks for 0.5 mile to reach the junction with Miller Peak Spur Trail 105, your route to the summit. The good news is that you have plenty of nice scenery to look at while you're catching your breath. In 0.2 mile walk over a giant seam of white quartz that cuts through the granite. The trail briefly levels just before you reach the aforementioned junction at 4.75 miles. The AZT continues on the Crest Trail, but you turn right (northeast) at the junction to head for the Miller Peak summit.

The trail switchbacks up the hill for 0.4 mile and reaches the ridge of the peak to follow it north to the summit. Pass a concrete foundation to your right (northwest) and then the summit cairn to your right at 5.2 miles (9,466').

The 360-degree views of southern Arizona and Mexico are incredible. Below, to the west, you can see the continuation of the Huachuca Crest. Tiny Parker Canyon Lake and the Canelo Hills (see next hike) are in the San Rafael Valley beyond the crest. Carr Peak is the next tallest in the range to the northwest and there is visibility all the way to the Santa Catalina and Rincon Mountains near Tucson. The Whetstone Mountains are to the north, the Dragoon Mountains to the northeast, and the Mule and Chiricahua Mountains to the east; to the south you see Montezuma Pass, Coronado Peak, and, beyond into Mexico, San Jose Peak. You can also see the ridge that you worked so hard to traverse on the Crest Trail.

The peak itself and the concrete foundation afford slightly different views—make sure to check out both. You've earned it!

Go back the way you came, making sure to turn left (southeast) back at the Crest Trail junction to follow it back to Montezuma Pass.

Gateway Community: SIERRA VISTA *(see page 43)*

DISTANCE FROM TRAILHEAD: 24.0 miles **POPULATION:** 43,888 **ELEVATION:** 4,633'

Getting There

MONTEZUMA PASS TRAILHEAD: N31° 21.022' W110° 17.126', elevation 6,575'

ROAD CONDITIONS: All vehicles; last 3.3 miles are graded dirt, suitable for passenger vehicles and trailers under 24'

FACILITIES: Restrooms and shaded picnic ramada; no water

DIRECTIONS *From Downtown Tucson:* From Congress Street and I-10, take I-10 East for 44.0 miles to Exit 302 for AZ 90 South (Fort Huachuca/Sierra Vista). In 32.0 miles keep right (south) to merge onto AZ 92 East; then continue south 14.0 miles to South Coronado Memorial Road. Turn right (south) and follow the road as it curves right (west) and becomes Montezuma Canyon Road; then, in 5.0 miles, reach the Coronado National Memorial Visitor Center, on the right. Stop in here to see the interpretive exhibits, including information about the Indigenous people and natural history of the region, as well as period chain mail and helmets. From the visitor center, continue west and then south for 3.3 miles on Montezuma Canyon Road; this final, twisting stretch up to the Montezuma Pass Trailhead is graded dirt road. Look for the parking area on your left just before the road curves sharply right (northwest).

Scenic Route: From I-10 East, take Exit 281 for AZ 83 South, and drive 26.0 miles to Sonoita. Turn left onto AZ 82 East and, in 19.0 miles, turn right (south) onto AZ 90. In 14.6 miles keep right (south) to merge onto AZ 92 East; then continue south 14.0 miles to South Coronado Memorial Road, and proceed as above.

Note: On your return north, there are internal border-patrol checkpoints on AZ 90 at milepost 304 and on AZ 83 at milepost 40.8.

The 360-degree views from Miller Peak are spectacular.

Canelo Pass to Meadow Valley

Solitude in the grasslands

> SCENERY: ★ ★ ★ ★
> TRAIL CONDITION: ★ ★ ★
> CHILDREN: ★
> DIFFICULTY: ★ ★ ★
> SOLITUDE: ★ ★ ★ ★ ★

3

Jasmine the Mini Donkey and Leigh Anne in Meadow Valley

DISTANCE & CONFIGURATION: 5.4-mile out-and-back

HIKING TIME: 3–4 hours

ACCUMULATED ELEVATION GAIN: 775'

SHORT HIKE OPTION: 2.6-mile out-and-back to saddle gate (400' elevation gain)

OUTSTANDING FEATURES: Grasslands of Meadow Valley, views of the San Rafael Valley and Santa Rita and Huachuca Mountains

LAND-MANAGEMENT AGENCY: Coronado National Forest, Sierra Vista Ranger District, 520-378-0311, fs.usda.gov/coronado

MAPS: USGS 7.5' *O'Donnell Canyon, AZ*

AZT PASSAGE: 3/Canelo Hills West, aztrail.org/explore/passages/passage-3-canelo-hills-west

ANCESTRAL LANDS: Tohono O'odham, Sobaipuri, and Pascua Yaqui

SEASONS: Winter, spring, fall

ACCESS: No fees or permits; open 24-7 year-round

Overview

This hike on the Arizona National Scenic Trail (AZT) takes you through the grasslands, oaks, and junipers of the Canelo Hills to beautiful Meadow Valley.

(*Canelo* means "cinnamon" in Spanish, a likely reference to the hills' reddish color.) The San Rafael Valley is a migration corridor for many species of birds; it was also used as a filming location for many Western movies.

This part of the AZT is very remote and takes a while to travel to. You probably won't see very many other people on the trail unless it's thru-hiker season.

On the Trail

An information kiosk at the trailhead (5,333') discusses the Canelo Hills East and West passages of the AZT, as well as safety in bear country and Leave No Trace principles. To your left (south), the AZT heads to Canelo Hills East and Parker Canyon Lake—for this hike, however, take the right (west) fork to Canelo Hills West. Reach a sign in 50 feet that says CANELO HILLS WEST #131, and lists distances to Meadow Valley, Red Bank Well, and Harshaw Road. Though the sign says Meadow Valley is 2.75 miles away, our destination is 2.2 miles away.

The AZT goes southwest through juniper, oak, and manzanita. The trail curves right (northwest) and climbs on rocky tread, then levels and curves southwest at 0.2 mile. In 0.1 mile you can see the path of the AZT as it curves right (west) up to the saddle. The path is flat and the views are open for 0.2 mile; then the trail climbs again. In 0.25 mile descend to a small drainage crossing and climb through a series of switchbacks. Take in views of the Huachuca Mountains to your right (east) and the Dragoon Mountains straight ahead (northeast) as you climb. The trail is steep and rocky in the final approach to the saddle. Reach a gate at the saddle, and the hike's high point, at mile 1.3 (5,581'). **This is also the turnaround for the short hike, at 1.3 miles and 400 feet of elevation gain.**

From the saddle there are views of Red Mountain near Patagonia and Saddle Mountain on the AZT to your right (northwest). Go through the gate, making sure to close it behind you, and descend on rocky tread to the right (northwest), with views of the San Rafael Valley to the left (southwest). Many scenes in the 1955 classic movie musical *Oklahoma!* were filmed in the San Rafael Valley and in Sonoita, Elgin, and Canelo. This side of the saddle has lots of varieties of agave: smooth-leaved beargrass, spiky Spanish bayonet, and serrated-leafed sotol.

In 0.25 mile the AZT crosses a small drainage and climbs; then the trail levels to contour on the side of the hill for 0.2 mile before resuming its descent. Contour across two small drainages, and descend to cross a third at mile 2.0. The trail curves right (west) and gently climbs northwest, then west to a junction in

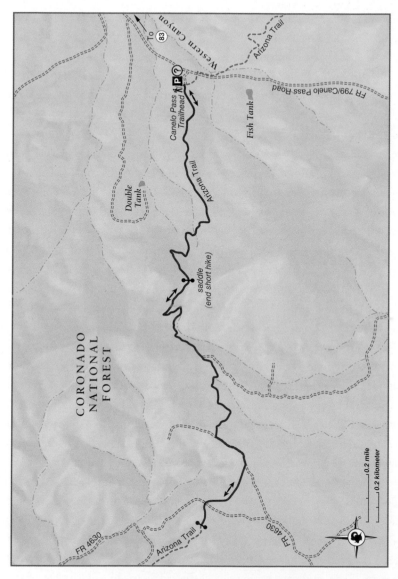

0.2 mile. Turn left (south) as directed by a wooden sign; you join a dirt double-track road coming in from the right (north). **Heads-Up:** Make a note of this junction so you don't miss it on your way back to the trailhead.

The Santa Rita Mountains and Mount Wrightson, the next Sky Island on the AZT, are visible to the right (northwest), and to the left (east) are beautiful rolling hills. Even though you're walking on a dirt road, the views in every direction are a delight.

The road curves right (west) and descends to a faint junction at the low point of the hike (5,299') in 0.2 mile. A wooden sign guides you to the right (west), and the trail climbs to the northwest. In 0.2 mile the road curves right (north). In 0.1 mile you reach a junction with a north–south dirt road—continue straight ahead (northwest) across this road on the singletrack trail. Reach the end of the hike 0.1 mile ahead at an AZT Super Gate with a great view of 9,456-foot Mount Wrightson and the Santa Rita Mountains beyond it (5,297').

Go back the way you came, making sure to go straight (south) at the first road junction and making sure to leave the road walk at the last junction, turning right (east) where the singletrack starts the climb to the saddle.

Gateway Community: PATAGONIA

DISTANCE FROM TRAILHEAD: 20.0 miles via FR 799 (graded dirt), 31.7 miles via AZ 83/AZ 82 (paved) **POPULATION:** 919 **ELEVATION:** 4,058'

The Gateway Community of Patagonia is a hub for recreation as well as a world-famous birding destination, thanks to places such as **Patagonia–Sonoita Creek Preserve, Tucson Audubon's Paton Center for Hummingbirds,** and **Patagonia Lake State Park.** The compact town center has everything a traveler needs within walking distance. Many artists make Patagonia their home, and this is reflected in its colorful atmosphere.

Lodging is available at the **Stage Stop Inn** and at many Airbnb properties. Patagonia Lake State Park has a developed campground, and primitive camping is allowed throughout Coronado National Forest free of charge.

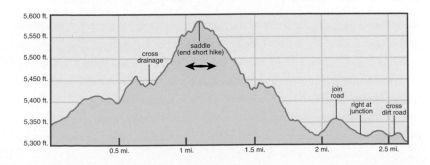

55

Dining options include **Velvet Elvis** for pizza; home-style cooking at the **Wild Horse Restaurant,** inside the Stage Stop Inn; bar fare at the **Wagon Wheel Saloon;** and pastries, sandwiches, and more at **Ovens of Patagonia.**

PATAGONIA–SONOITA CREEK PRESERVE: 150 Blue Heaven Rd., 520-394-2400, tinyurl .com/pscpreserve. Admission: $8/person, children under age 13 free. *April–September:* Open Wednesday–Sunday, 6:30 a.m.–4 p.m. *October–March:* Open Wednesday–Sunday, 7:30 a.m.–4 p.m.

TUCSON AUDUBON'S PATON CENTER FOR HUMMINGBIRDS: 477 Pennsylvania Ave., 520-415-6447, tinyurl.com/patoncenter. Free admission (donations welcome); gates open daily, sunrise–sunset.

PATAGONIA LAKE STATE PARK: 400 Patagonia Lake Rd., 520-287-6965, azstateparks .com/patagonia-lake. Admission: $15–$20/vehicle, $3/walk-in or cyclist; see website for camping reservations and fees (click "Reserve Campsites" at the top of the homepage). Open daily year-round; see website for park hours by season.

STAGE STOP INN: 303 McKeown Ave., 520-394-2211, stagestoppatagonia.com

VELVET ELVIS: 292 Naugle Ave., 520-394-0069, facebook.com/velvetelvispizza. Open Thursday–Sunday, 11 a.m.–8 p.m.

WILD HORSE RESTAURANT: Stage Stop Inn, 309 McKeown Ave., 520-394-2344, stage stoppatagonia.com/wild-horse-restaurant-saloon. Open Monday–Friday, 11 a.m.–9 p.m.; Saturday, 6 a.m.–9 p.m.; Sunday, 6 a.m.–8 p.m.

WAGON WHEEL SALOON: 400 Naugle Ave., 520-394-2433, facebook.com/wagonwheel saloon. Food served daily, 6:30 a.m.–8 p.m. Bar hours vary (up to 2 a.m.); call to confirm.

OVENS OF PATAGONIA: 277 W. McKeown Ave., 520-394-2330, ovensofpatagonia.com. Open Monday–Saturday, 8 a.m.–6 p.m., Sunday, 9 a.m.–5 p.m.

Gateway Community: SONOITA

DISTANCE FROM TRAILHEAD: 19.0 miles **POPULATION:** 818 **ELEVATION:** 4,987'

Gateway Community: ELGIN

DISTANCE FROM TRAILHEAD: 14.0 miles **POPULATION:** 161 **ELEVATION:** 4,728'

Sonoita and Elgin are the heart of southern Arizona's wine country. A **self-guided tasting tour** visits 13 wineries (see the first website below for a map); you can also hire a guide from **Arizona Winery Tours. Arizona Hops and Vines** is a standout vineyard in the region, with fun festivals and events. If beer is more your style, **Copper Brothel Brewery** has you covered and also serves bar fare.

About 10 miles north of Sonoita, the historic **Empire Ranch** was established in 1876. The ranch complex, anchored by a 22-room adobe house, was privately owned until the U.S. Bureau of Land Management bought it in 1988. It has also served as a filming location for numerous movie Westerns, along with the TV series *Bonanza* and *Gunsmoke*.

Numerous hotels and guest ranches offer overnight stays, among them the **Sonoita Inn** and **Rancho Milagro Bed & Breakfast;** Airbnb rentals are available as well. Most restaurants and services are located near the intersection of AZ 82 and AZ 83. **The Steak Out** is Western-themed with live music; **The Cafe** serves Italian-inspired dishes along with steaks, burgers, and sandwiches and has patio seating. For breakfast and lunch in a no-frills setting, try the **Sky Island Diner.** Despite its Mexican-sounding name, **Tia 'Nita's Cantina** serves Italian favorites and pizza.

SONOITA & ELGIN TASTING ROOMS (SELF-GUIDED TOUR): sonoitaelginchamber.org /winetasting.html

ARIZONA WINERY TOURS: 520-338-9302, azwinerytours.com

ARIZONA HOPS AND VINES: 3450 AZ 82, 301-237-6556, azhopsandvines.com. Open Thursday and Sunday, 10 a.m.–4 p.m., Friday and Saturday, 10 a.m.–6 p.m.

COPPER BROTHEL BREWERY: 1/3 AZ 83, 520-405-6721, copperbrothelbrewery.com. Open daily, 11 a.m.–9 p.m.

EMPIRE RANCH: Empire Ranch Road, between mileposts 39 and 40 on AZ 83, about a mile south of the border-patrol checkpoint; 888-364-2829, empireranchfoundation.org. Free admission; open daily, sunrise–sunset.

SONOITA INN: 3243 AZ 82, 520-455-5935, sonoitainn.com

RANCHO MILAGRO BED & BREAKFAST: 140 Camino Agave, 520-269-1462 or 520-604-7534, ranchomilagrobnb.com

THE STEAK OUT: 3243 AZ 83, 520-455-5205, azsteakout.com. Open Monday–Thursday, 5 p.m.–9 p.m.; Friday, 5 p.m.–10 p.m., Saturday, 11 a.m.–10 p.m.; Sunday, 11 a.m.–9 p.m.

THE CAFE: 3280 AZ 82, 520-455-5044, cafesonoita.com. Open Sunday–Wednesday, 11 a.m.–3 p.m.; Thursday–Saturday, 11 a.m.–8 p.m.

SKY ISLAND DINER: 3270 AZ 82, 520-455-3787, facebook.com/skyislanddiner. Open Tuesday–Sunday, 8 a.m.–4 p.m.

TIA 'NITA'S CANTINA: 3119 AZ 83, 520-455-0500. Open Thursday, 3–9 p.m.; Friday, 3–10 p.m.; Saturday, 11 a.m.–10 p.m., Sunday, 11 a.m.–7 p.m.

Getting There

CANELO PASS TRAILHEAD: N31° 30.773' W110° 33.494', elevation 5,343'

ROAD CONDITIONS: All vehicles; graded dirt road for 2.9 miles

FACILITIES: None

DIRECTIONS From downtown Tucson (Congress and I-10), take I-10 East for 23.0 miles to Exit 281 for AZ 83 South; then drive 33.0 miles to the Gateway Community of Sonoita. (**Note:** You will pass an internal border-patrol checkpoint at milepost 40.8 that will require a stop on your way back north.) At the stop sign at the junction with AZ 82, continue straight (south). In 0.3 mile AZ 83 curves to the left (east); then, in 3.1 miles, stay right at the junction to continue south on AZ 83. In 1 mile, reach a junction with a road to the Gateway Community of Elgin to your left (east). In another 3.9 miles, pass a winery and a yellow sign on your right that says ROUGH ROAD NEXT 4 MILES; then, 0.1 mile farther, the road curves left (east) at a sign for Parker Canyon Lake.

In 0.6 mile AZ 83 makes a sharp turn to the right (south) and then turns left (east) 0.4 mile later. In 1.2 miles curve right (southwest); then, another 1.2 miles ahead, curve left (southeast). In 1.4 miles enter Coronado National Forest. Drive 2.7 miles, and then turn right to continue south on AZ 83. In 0.9 mile, where AZ 83 curves left (east) at another sign for Parker Canyon Lake, keep straight to continue south on Canelo Pass Road, a graded dirt road suitable for passenger vehicles. *Zero your odometer here.*

A sign for Forest Service Road 799 lists mileages to the San Rafael Valley, Lochiel, the Gateway Community of Patagonia, and the border town of Nogales. At mile 0.6 pass a sign that says CANELO PASS ROAD STRAIGHT, UMPIRE RANCH LEFT. Then make a slight turn right (southwest) to stay on Canelo Pass Road.

At mile 2.8 pass a small sign on your right (west) indicating that the trail is ahead, then a sign that says HORSE AND PEDESTRIAN CROSSING. The right (west) turn for the Canelo Pass Trailhead is just past the horse-crossing sign at mile 2.9. Look for a circular driveway at the trailhead—keep right here. Reach a sign for HORSE TRAILER PARKING on the right; cars should pull around to the left. Parking, an information kiosk, and the Canelo Pass Trailhead are 0.1 mile ahead in the west part of the circle. Four parking spots are directly across from the trailhead; more are available if you continue around the circle. *Please don't block the turnaround for horse trailers.*

4

Kentucky Camp to Gardner Canyon

Gold mines and scenic beauty

SCENERY: ★ ★ ★ ★
TRAIL CONDITION: ★ ★ ★
CHILDREN: ★ ★ ★
(short option)
DIFFICULTY: ★ ★ ★
SOLITUDE: ★ ★ ★

ARIZONA
TRAIL

unnel Spring	6.6 ↑
ear Spring	10.1 ↑
alker Basin Tr.	13.2 ↑
lexico	79.1 ↑

Kentucky Camp Trailhead sign with Mount Wrightson (9,456') and the Santa Rita Mountains in the distance

DISTANCE & CONFIGURATION: 7.8-mile out-and-back

HIKING TIME: 4–6 hours

ACCUMULATED ELEVATION GAIN: 920'

SHORT HIKE OPTION: 4.0-mile out-and-back to FR 4110 (250' elevation gain)

OUTSTANDING FEATURES: Mining history of Kentucky Camp, interpretive signs, scenic grasslands, mountain views

LAND-MANAGEMENT AGENCY: Coronado National Forest, Nogales Ranger District, 520-281-2296, fs.usda.gov/coronado

MAPS: USGS 7.5' *Sonoita, AZ*

AZT PASSAGE: 5/Santa Rita Mountains, aztrail.org/explore/passages/passage-5 -santa-rita-mountains

ANCESTRAL LANDS: Tohono O'odham, Sobaipuri, and Pascua Yaqui

SEASON: Winter, spring, fall

ACCESS: No fees or permits; open 24-7 year-round

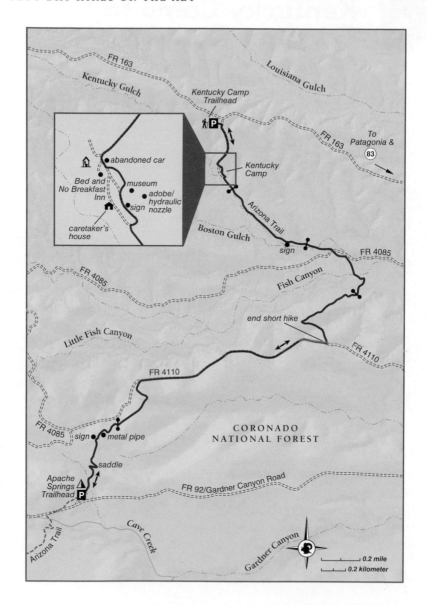

Overview

The Kentucky Camp area is steeped in history and preserves a series of buildings, tunnels, and trails connected to gold-mining operations from the early 1900s. Interpretive signs and a museum along the way help tell the story.

On the Trail

From the parking area (5,225'), go right (south) in 30 feet to descend onto Forest Service Road 4045 toward Kentucky Camp, and then pass through an AZT Super Gate in 100 feet. A sign listing mileages lets you know that you're 79.1 miles from Mexico. To the left (east) are the Whetstone and Mustang Mountains, and to the southeast are the Huachuca Mountains and the southern terminus of the AZT (see Hike 1, page 40). To the right (west) are the Santa Rita Mountains, with Mount Wrightson the high point at 9,456 feet, and Josephine Peak is to the left (south). In 0.25 mile the road curves left (southeast) and comes to Kentucky Camp proper after a descent of 100 feet.

An old adobe structure and car parts are on your left (north), a rental cabin signed BED AND NO BREAKFAST INN is on the right (south), and the toilet is straight ahead (west) in 50 feet. Curve left (southeast) to reach an AZT kiosk with information and maps and a box for donations. The caretaker of Kentucky Camp lives down the road about 0.1 mile south of the Bed and No Breakfast Inn.

At 0.3 mile reach the museum to your left (east). It has tables and Adirondack chairs on the porch, features exhibits about gold-mining days, and provides information about hiking in the area. A small adobe building to the south of the museum has a hydraulic nozzle in front of it that used pressurized water to blast gold from the earth.

The trail curves left (southeast) past the museum building and down the hill past the caretaker's cabin. In 0.1 mile pass a wooden AZT sign and an interpretive sign about Kentucky Camp. The AZT makes a turn to the right (west) and then immediately leaves the road to the left (south) on a singletrack tread. In 0.1 mile you pass through an AZT Super Gate and sign in at the trail register. The trail trends southeast, winding among grasses, oaks, junipers, and mesquite

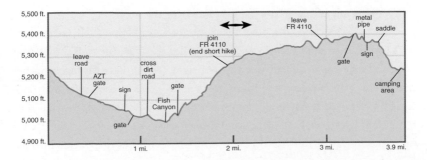

trees. In 0.4 mile, you reach a second interpretive sign; past it, the trail curves slightly left (east), joins a fence line 0.1 mile ahead, and then turns right (south) to pass through a small metal gate.

At 1.0 mile from the trailhead, the trail crosses a drainage and, in 0.1 mile, bends right across FR 4085, heading southeast. In 0.1 mile, the AZT curves left (east) and then right (southeast) to cross Fish Canyon another 0.1 mile farther. After a switchback left (east), then right (south) to climb out of Fish Canyon, the trail levels at the bottom of the canyon and passes through a small metal gate at 1.4 mile; then, over the next 0.1 mile, it curves right (west) and then left (southwest) before it starts to ascend.

In 0.3 mile you switchback left (southeast) and continue climbing toward a road junction. Views of the Rincon Mountains open to the north; Spanish bayonet, a variety of agave, grows near the trail. In 0.2 mile reach the aforementioned junction, with FR 4110. **This is the turnaround for the short hike, at 2.0 miles and 250 feet of elevation gain.**

Now continue right (west) and join the rocky doubletrack road heading uphill. Mount Wrightson dominates the skyline on the climb to the ridge. In 0.1 mile the AZT curves left (southwest), and views open in every direction. To the northwest are buttes of the Santa Rita foothills, and you can even see to the north a small part of the Santa Catalina Mountains near Tucson. In 0.2 mile the trail curves right (west) and then joins a fence line 0.1 mile after that.

The AZT curves left (southwest) in another 0.1 mile and proceeds west toward an intersection 0.2 mile farther; at this point, the road also starts a rocky ascent. Just before you reach the top of the climb, look to your left for a brown carsonite AZT sign. After 3.0 miles of hiking, you reach a junction and leave FR 4110 to the left (south) to continue on the AZT. **Heads-Up:** If you're not careful, this is the perfect setup for the classic AZT blunder: not paying attention, walking merrily down the road, and missing the turn.

Past the junction, the now-flat singletrack trail curves left (southeast) for 0.1 mile, then right (southwest). In another 0.2 mile, the trail climbs past a carsonite sign that directs you to turn right (west). Pass through another small metal gate and descend; then, in 0.1 mile, cross a metal pipe that once carried water used for hydraulic mining. Continue descending to reach a turn to the right (west), marked by another interpretive sign, which explains that it was easier to elevate the pipe on a masonry platform than to excavate into the bedrock. Masonry held the pipe in place, while short wooden trestles carried it across small drainages.

After the sign, the trail switchbacks south to cross the drainage, then climbs out the other side and runs parallel to the pipe among giant agave stalks. In 0.1 mile cross the pipe again at a rock wall with the pipe on the left (east). Then, in another 0.1 mile, reach a saddle where you can see Gardner Canyon and the Apache Springs Trailhead in the valley below.

The trail descends on a series of switchbacks and crosses the canyon bottom in 0.2 mile (5,220'). Reach a junction with a dirt parking area and a camping loop at the Apache Springs Trailhead; then curve right (southwest) and continue on the road, ignoring the trail that continues to the west in 100 feet. Reach the trailhead parking and information kiosk at 3.9 miles. (One of the signs at the trailhead says KENTUCKY CAMP 5.2 MILES—that's wrong, so ignore it.) You don't have a lot of options for seating—just a couple of rocks—but there is some shade under the trees.

When you're ready, go back the way you came. Remember that you'll rejoin FR 4110 by turning right (east) and then leave it again 1.1 miles farther to the left (north). You can tell that the latter turn back onto the AZT is coming when you begin to descend from the ridge; you'll leave the road again 0.2 mile ahead. This second turn, which takes you back up Fish Canyon and through Kentucky Camp, may be partially obscured by a small mesquite tree—if you reach a small brown road sign for FR 4110 to your left, you've missed the turn.

Gateway Community: PATAGONIA *(see page 55)*

DISTANCE FROM TRAILHEAD: 22.0 miles **POPULATION:** 919 **ELEVATION:** 4,058'

Gateway Community: SONOITA *(see page 56)*

DISTANCE FROM TRAILHEAD: 4.0 miles **POPULATION:** 818 **ELEVATION:** 4,987'

Gateway Community: ELGIN *(see page 56)*

DISTANCE FROM TRAILHEAD: 13.0 miles **POPULATION:** 161 **ELEVATION:** 4,728'

Getting There

KENTUCKY CAMP TRAILHEAD: N31° 44.875' W110° 44.512', elevation 5,225'

ROAD CONDITIONS: No low-clearance vehicles; graded dirt for 5.1 miles

FACILITIES: None at parking area; restrooms, water, and picnic tables at Kentucky Camp in 0.3 mile

DIRECTIONS *From downtown Tucson:* From Congress Street and I-10, take I-10 East for 23.0 miles to Exit 281 for AZ 83 South (Sonoita/Patagonia). In 3.1 miles pass the Sahuarita Road Trailhead to your right (west), and pass a roadside table on your right (west) 8.7 miles after that. In 6.0 miles the speed limit decreases as drivers pass an internal border-patrol checkpoint at milepost 40.8. **Note:** This will require a stop on your way back north. Then, in 3.5 miles (21.3 miles from the I-10 exit), turn right (west) onto FR 92 (Gardner Canyon Road). *Zero your odometer here.*

At mile 0.7 turn right (northwest) onto FR 163 toward Kentucky Camp and a sign reading ROADS WITH VERTICAL ROUTE MARKER NOT MAIN-TAINED FOR PASSENGER USE. At mile 1.7 stay right (northwest) at a junction with a road to Santa Rita Abbey, and at mile 1.8 cross a cattle guard and a sign that says ENTERING PRIVATE PROPERTY—if you're doing an overnight trip, please be considerate and don't camp in this area. Then, in 0.4 mile, pass a sign on the right (north) that says ARIZONA TRAIL, KENTUCKY CAMP 3 MILES.

At mile 2.8 reach a junction with FR 4060 and stay left (south), following the signs for Kentucky Camp. Leave private property at mile 3.0 and enter Coronado National Forest; there is a sign for OHV information to the left (east) in 0.1 mile. Pass a junction with FR 162 on your right (west) at mile 3.9, and then the road climbs to a junction at mile 4.2 with FR 4085 to your left (east). Continue straight at the junction, and reach the Kentucky Camp Trailhead on your left (south) at mile 5.3. There is parking for about seven cars.

From Patagonia: Take AZ 82 northeast for 12.5 miles to the intersection with AZ 83, turn left (north), and drive 4.1 miles to FR 92 (Gardner Canyon Road). Then turn left (west), zero your odometer, and proceed as above.

White-tailed deer roam the grasslands.

5

Gabe Zimmerman Trail-head to Rattlesnake Mural

Desert vistas and a distinctive work of art

SCENERY: ★★★★
TRAIL CONDITION: ★★★★
CHILDREN: ★★★★★
DIFFICULTY: ★
SOLITUDE: ★★

Tucson artist Ed Muren III created this distinctive piece of public art to decorate the I-10 underpass in 2017.

DISTANCE & CONFIGURATION: 3.2-mile out-and-back

HIKING TIME: 1.5–2 hours

ACCUMULATED ELEVATION GAIN: 270'

SHORT HIKE OPTION: None (the hike is already short)

OUTSTANDING FEATURES: Rattlesnake mural, views of the surrounding mountains

LAND-MANAGEMENT AGENCIES: Pima County Natural Resources, Parks and Recreation, 520-724-5000, webcms.pima.gov/recreation

AZT PASSAGE: 7/Las Cienegas, aztrail.org/explore/passages/passage-7-las-cienegas

MAPS: USGS 7.5' *Vail, AZ*

ANCESTRAL LANDS: Tohono O'odham, Sobaipuri, and Pascua Yaqui

SEASON: Winter, spring, fall

ACCESS: No fees or permits; open 24-7 year-round

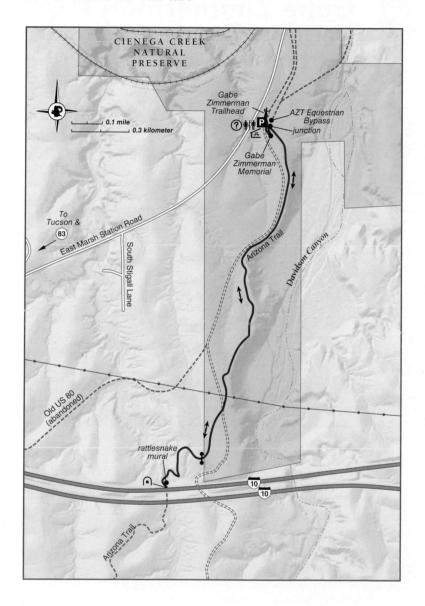

Overview

This short hike on the Arizona National Scenic Trail (AZT) passes through a beautiful stretch of desert on the way to a unique work of art on the I-10 underpass. It also visits a memorial to Gabriel "Gabe" Zimmerman. Spectacular views of the Santa Catalina Mountains and Rincon Mountains await you on your return to the trailhead.

On the Trail

This trailhead memorializes Gabriel "Gabe" Zimmerman (1980–2011), director of community outreach for U.S. Representative Gabrielle Giffords and lover of the outdoors. He organized many public events where voters could meet the congresswoman and talk to her about local issues; he was also instrumental in getting the AZT designated as a National Scenic Trail in 2009. Sadly, Zimmerman was one of six people killed in a shooting outside a Tucson supermarket during one of Giffords's "Congress on Your Corner" events on January 8, 2011. (Giffords, who suffered debilitating injuries and resigned from the House of Representatives to work on her recovery, is now an advocate for gun control.)

From the parking lot, go southeast through the gate and pass a map describing AZT Passages 7 and 8. (For more about the AZT leading northeast from the parking lot, see the next hike, Gabe Zimmerman Trailhead to Colossal Cave.) In 100 feet, reach a four-way junction and turn right (south) to visit the Gabe Zimmerman Memorial. The gravel path leads 200 feet to a seating area with art commemorating Zimmerman's life. Take some time to appreciate the scenery and perhaps leave a note in the register; then return the way you came. This is the end of the wheelchair-accessible portion of the hike. Back at the four-way junction, turn right to continue southeast.

Past the four-way junction on the left (north) side of the trail, a sign points out the different mountain ranges visible in this area and Cienega Creek, which is the tree-lined riparian area below the trail to the north. At 0.1 mile the trail splits, and a sign notes that horse riders keep to the left and hikers and bikers to

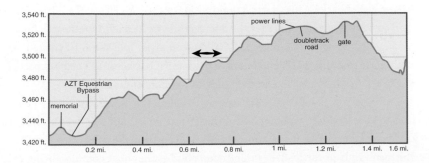

the right. The left fork is an equestrian bypass through Davidson Canyon that lets horses and their riders sidestep the concrete culvert that passes under I-10; since you're hiking, however, you take the right fork (southeast). Note that this AZT passage is popular with mountain bikers as well as hikers and equestrians, and you'll share the trail with cyclists to the underpass.

The clusters of tall, spiky, thorny things you see reaching toward the sky along the trail are ocotillos, which are among the fastest-growing plants on the planet. Just after it rains, the ocotillo grows small green leaves between its spines and uses them for photosynthesis, fueling the plant's growth until the leaves dry up and fall off. They also have beautiful orange-red blooms in spring that are very attractive to hummingbirds. Ocotillos' companion on the trail is creosote bush, a short, squatty shrub with an earthy scent that botanists call petrichor; locals know it simply as the smell of desert rain. Creosote bush has yellow blooms in spring and possesses many medicinal properties.

The trail hugs the rim of Davidson Canyon on your right (east) and gradually gains elevation. At 0.25 mile, I-10 comes into view. The mountain to the south is Mount Fagan, one of the Santa Rita Mountains; the range to the left (southeast) is the Empiritas.

At 1.0 mile the AZT turns southeast, crosses underneath a set of power lines just 0.1 mile farther, and then crosses a dirt doubletrack road right after that. Take the singletrack trail to the right (southwest). The trail descends as it nears the underpass. In 0.2 mile pass through a gate that also has a rollover ramp for bikes off to the side. Make sure to close the gate behind you.

After the gate, the trail briefly heads northwest and then switchbacks down the hill. As you hike, you can see a rattlesnake below you with its mouth wide open—actually a mural painted around the previously mentioned culvert that passes underneath the I-10 bridge. The trail curves southeast and descends toward I-10 on switchbacks. Cross a small drainage in 0.2 mile. You'll see the I-10 bridge, then curve away from it to enter the drainage and make a left (southeast), finally reaching the bridge at 1.6 miles (3,460'). Tucson artist Ed Muren III created the rattlesnake mural in 2017, and in only a few years it has become a beloved part of the AZT. (Visit his website, edmuren.com, to see more of his artwork.)

To keep yourself safe from real rattlesnakes, it's important to pay attention to where you're walking and to never put your hands or feet anywhere that you can't see (for more information about rattlesnake safety, see page 31). Thirteen kinds of rattlesnakes call Arizona home, the most common being the western diamondback. Their rattles are made from interlocking bands of keratin, similar to the material that makes up your fingernails.

After enjoying a break and some photos with the rattlesnake, return the way you came. On your return you'll have a short climb to the gate with views of the Santa Catalina Mountains in the distance to the northwest and Rincon Mountains to the north. To your right (northeast) is Rincon Peak, in the center (north) is Mica Mountain, and the mountain to the left (northwest) is Tanque Verde Peak.

The AZT continues northbound through Colossal Cave Mountain Park (see the next hike) and Saguaro National Park, up and over Mica Mountain, and then up and over the Catalinas through the Gateway Community of Summerhaven (see Hikes 7–9, starting on page 79).

As you get closer to the trailhead, the Tucson Mountains are visible in the distance to the left (west). Wildflowers and cacti bloom in the spring. The trail merges with the equestrian bypass coming in from the right (east) and passes the interpretive sign with the mountains. You'll pass the junction for the northbound AZT continuing into Cienega Creek Natural Preserve on your right, and you'll see the gate you came through and the trailhead straight ahead (northwest).

This hike can be combined with the short version of Hike 6 into Cienega Creek (page 71), which adds 1.4 miles out-and-back.

Gateway Community: VAIL

DISTANCE FROM TRAILHEAD: 6 mi **POPULATION:** 10,208 **ELEVATION:** 3,235'

Vail is nicknamed "The Town Between the Tracks." Though the AZT doesn't go directly to the cave at **Colossal Cave Mountain Park**, it's definitely worth the detour for a cave tour. The cave headquarters also has a café called The Terrace. The park's La Posta Quemada Ranch offers horseback riding, a petting zoo, a museum, a deli, and snacks.

Vail's dining options are concentrated around the area south of the railroad tracks. **Montgomery's Grill and Saloon** has a full bar and an outdoor patio. You can also head to **Arizona Pizza Company** for pies, salads, and wings; **Dairy Queen** for ice cream after your hike; or **Fito's Taco Shop** for Mexican favorites.

At the time of this writing, there are no hotels in Vail, but there are a number of Airbnb rentals available. Camping is available at Colossal Cave's **La Selvilla** and **El Bosquecito Campgrounds**.

COLOSSAL CAVE MOUNTAIN PARK: 16721 E. Old Spanish Trail, 520-647-7275, colossal cave.com. Click "Rates" at the website for information about the cave tours, horseback riding, camping, and the petting zoo. Open daily, 10 a.m.–5 p.m., except Thanksgiving and December 25.

MONTGOMERY'S GRILL AND SALOON: 13190 E. Colossal Cave Rd., Ste. 190; 520-762-0081, montgomerysvail.com. Open daily, 11 a.m.–9, 10, or 11 p.m. Hours are subject to change; call ahead to confirm.

ARIZONA PIZZA COMPANY: 13190 E. Colossal Cave Rd., 520-762-5500, azpizzacompany .com. Open daily, 11 a.m.–9 p.m.

DAIRY QUEEN: 13160 E. Colossal Cave Rd., 520-762-0343. Open Monday–Thursday, 10 a.m.–9 p.m.; Friday and Saturday, 10 a.m.–10 p.m.; Sunday, 11 a.m.–9 p.m.

FITO'S TACO SHOP: 13303 E. Colossal Cave Rd., 520-762-8888, tinyurl.com/fitos tacosvail. Open Monday–Saturday, 6 a.m.–10 p.m.; Sunday, 7 a.m.–10 p.m.

LA SELVILLA AND EL BOSQUECITO CAMPGROUNDS: Colossal Cave Mountain Park, 16721 E. Old Spanish Trail, 520-647-7275, colossalcave.com. Tent, RV, and horse trailer camping with picnic tables, grills, restrooms, and water (no hookups); $7.50–$12.50/night.

Getting There

GABE ZIMMERMAN MEMORIAL TRAILHEAD: N32° 00.832' W110° 38.848', elevation 3,446'

ROAD CONDITIONS: All vehicles; paved

FACILITIES: Shaded picnic bench at trailhead, a bike rack in the form of a snake, and (as of this writing) a portable toilet

DIRECTIONS From downtown Tucson (Congress Street and I-10), take I-10 East for 23.0 miles to Exit 281 for AZ 83 South (Sonoita/Patagonia). In 0.4 mile turn left (north) at the stop sign. Cross back over the freeway and, in 0.2 mile, turn right (northeast) at the sign that says FRONTAGE ROAD TO MARSH STATION ROAD; then, in 0.1 mile, turn right (southeast) onto Marsh Station Road. In 3.3 miles turn right (east) into the Gabe Zimmerman Memorial Trailhead. Please leave the gravel side of the parking lot open for horse trailers.

6

Gabe Zimmerman Trailhead to Colossal Cave

Creek-to-park adventure with saguaros along the way

SCENERY: ★ ★ ★ ★
TRAIL CONDITION: ★ ★ ★ ★
CHILDREN: ★ ★ ★ ★ ★
(short hike)
DIFFICULTY: ★ ★ /★ ★ ★
(point-to-point/out-and-back)
SOLITUDE: ★ ★

The Rincon Mountains with Cienega Creek fall colors below

DISTANCE & CONFIGURATION: 5.1-mile point-to-point or 10.2-mile out-and-back

HIKING TIME: 2–3 hours point-to-point, 4–5 hours out-and-back

ACCUMULATED ELEVATION GAIN: 567' point-to-point, 1,160' out-and-back

SHORT HIKE OPTION: 1.4-mile out-and-back to Cienega Creek Natural Preserve
(150' elevation gain)

OUTSTANDING FEATURES: Cienega Creek, Three Bridges, views of the Rincon Mountains

LAND-MANAGEMENT AGENCIES: Pima County Natural Resources, Parks and Recreation, 520-724-5000, webcms.pima.gov/recreation; Colossal Cave Mountain Park, 520-647-7275, colossalcave.com

MAPS: USGS 7.5' *Vail, AZ*

AZT PASSAGE: 8/Rincon Valley, aztrail.org/explore/passages/passage-8-rincon-valley

ANCESTRAL LANDS: Tohono O'odham, Sobaipuri, and Pascua Yaqui

SEASON: Winter, spring, fall

ACCESS: A free permit is necessary to visit Cienega Creek Natural Preserve unless you're staying on the AZT. For more information, see tinyurl.com/cienegacreekpermit. The preserve is open daily, sunrise–sunset.

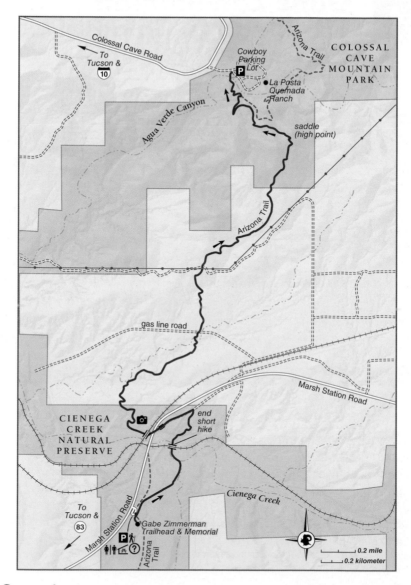

Overview

This section of the Arizona National Scenic Trail (AZT) passes through a beautiful riparian area in Cienega Creek Preserve and through the southernmost extent of the saguaro cactus on the AZT through Colossal Cave Mountain Park. You'll get spectacular views of the Rincon Mountains and even see a castle in the distance. It also visits a memorial to Gabriel "Gabe" Zimmerman.

To do this hike as a point-to-point (one-way), drop off one car at the end at the Cowboy Parking Lot at La Posta Quemada Ranch inside Colossal Cave Mountain Park, then drive to the Gabe Zimmerman Memorial Trailhead to start the hike. Be aware that the gates at Colossal Cave close at 5 p.m.

Note: This AZT passage is very popular with hikers, mountain bikers, and equestrians. Please observe proper trail etiquette: if you see horses on the trail, pull off to the side and greet the rider so that the horse hears that you are a human and not a predator. Mountain bikers yield to both hikers and horses. For more information, see "Sharing the Trail," page 16.

On the Trail

This trailhead memorializes Gabriel "Gabe" Zimmerman (1980–2011), director of community outreach for U.S. Representative Gabrielle Giffords and a lover of the outdoors. He organized many public events where voters could meet the congresswoman and talk to her about local issues; he was also instrumental in getting the AZT designated as a National Scenic Trail in 2009. Sadly, Zimmerman was one of six people killed in a shooting outside a Tucson supermarket during one of Giffords's "Congress on Your Corner" events on January 8, 2011. (Giffords, who suffered debilitating injuries and resigned from the House of Representatives to work on her recovery, is now an advocate for gun control.)

From the parking lot, go southeast through the gate and pass a map describing AZT Passages 7 and 8. In 100 feet, reach a four-way junction and turn right (south) to visit the Gabe Zimmerman Memorial. The gravel path leads 200 feet to a seating area with art commemorating Zimmerman's life. Take some time to appreciate the scenery and perhaps leave a note in the register; then return the way you came. This is the end of the wheelchair-accessible portion of the hike. Back at the four-way junction, continue straight (north) down the hill. (For more about the AZT leading southeast from this junction, see the previous hike.)

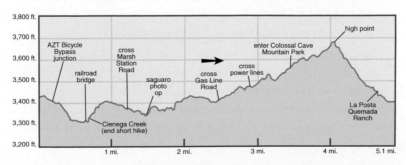

In 0.1 mile reach a junction with the AZT bicycle bypass. Take the trail on the right (northeast) and pass an interpretive sign talking about wildlife in the riparian habitat. Cottonwood, ash, and willow trees line the streamside habitat, providing a space for rich biodiversity of mammals, reptiles, birds, and insects. Because Cienega Creek has areas of perennial flow, it has been inhabited by humans for more than 12,000 years; there are numerous archaeological sites in the area. La Posta Quemada Ranch, inside Colossal Cave Mountain Park, which you'll visit farther ahead, has a small museum on-site that tells the story of the Indigenous people of the region and houses a collection of artifacts.

The trail descends, and Rincon Peak is straight ahead with Mica Mountain to the left (west). The northbound AZT goes up and over Mica Mountain near its 8,668-foot summit. This is the southernmost passage on the AZT that has saguaro cactus. You can see a couple of these cacti to your right (south) before you descend to the creek.

In 0.4 mile reach the bottom of a side canyon of Cienega Creek, and turn left (north) to take this sandy creekbed 0.1 mile into the creek's main stem. Cienega Creek changes course from time to time, so you may have to look for the best place to cross on rocks to keep your feet dry. Turn left (west) to follow the creek downstream as it curves to the right (north), and a railroad bridge comes into view. This area is called Three Bridges. Cross underneath the bridge, making sure there are no trains coming.

Stay to the right (east) side of the creekbed. In 0.2 mile, just before the creek curves to the left, look to your right for a small metal AZT sign pointing out of the creek. This is the low point of the hike, at 3,310 feet. **It's also the turn-around for the short hike, at 0.7 mile and 150 feet of elevation gain.**

Take a right (east) to follow the trail into a small side canyon and begin climbing out of Cienega Creek. Follow the trail in the side canyon, and in 0.1 mile the trail makes a switchback. The trail contours and climbs along the sides of small hills and then reaches a ridge. At mile 1.0, the trail meets a utility road at a T-intersection and makes a sharp turn to the left (west).

Reach a sign in 0.25 mile that says, "You are about to enter Union Pacific Railroad property. For your protection, please stay on the trail, and travel under the canopy as you pass beneath the overhead railroad tracks." The road crossing is directly ahead—turn on the crossing warning lights by pushing the button, and take care in crossing Marsh Station Road. On the other side, the trail curves left (south) briefly to follow the road before turning right (west) to cross under a second set of railroad tracks. Make sure that no trains are coming before you cross beneath the canopy.

Go through a fence line and the trail curves, then resumes a westward course. The clusters of tall, spiky, thorny things you see reaching toward the sky along the trail are ocotillos, which are among the fastest-growing plants on the planet. Just after it rains, the ocotillo grows small green leaves between its spines and uses them for photosynthesis, fueling the plant's growth until the leaves dry up and fall off. They also have beautiful orange-red blooms in spring that are very attractive to hummingbirds. Ocotillos' companion on the trail is creosote bush, a short, squatty shrub with an earthy scent that botanists call petrichor; locals know it simply as the smell of desert rain. Creosote bush has yellow blooms in spring and possesses many medicinal properties. You'll also encounter compass barrel cacti, so named because they lean to the south. The trail switchbacks, descends into the canyon, and crosses it past some stately saguaros that make a perfect backdrop for a photo in 0.3 mile.

Colossal Cave Mountain Park holds an annual celebration at the end of June, the Ha:san Bak festival, for the saguaro fruit harvest (see sidebar on the next page). The saguaro and its fruit are an important part of Indigenous Tohono O'odham culture. During the festival there are presentations, food, storytelling, and hands-on activities, as well as a workshop that teaches about the cultural significance and proper techniques for harvest and processing the fruit (or *bahidaj* in the Tohono O'odham language) from the saguaro (*Ha:sañ*).

Ascend out of the canyon, and reach the northern boundary of Cienega Creek Preserve at a fence line in 0.2 mile. The trail curves to the left (northwest) on a big slab of rock, crosses the canyon, and exits on the other side. The trail now trends to the northeast, staying to the east side of the canyon, which is to your left.

The trail climbs and then descends and winds through the low hills. An unusual building then comes into view atop a hill to your right (east). Agua Verde Castle (aka Dunham Castle) is a private home built by Duane Dunham for his wife, Ginny, as a wedding gift. The Dunhams have lived here since the late 1970s, and the castle has intrigued passersby ever since. The property has an observatory, a swimming pool, and a small railroad track that goes around the top of the hill.

The trail curves to cross a canyon at 2.5 miles and then crosses a wash and gas line road before heading north. In 0.3 mile the trail makes a curve to the right (northeast) to switchback up the hill and cross under power lines. At 3.0 miles from the trailhead, the trail trends to the northeast. After it crosses

Spotlight: Saguaro Cactus

An icon of the Southwest, the saguaro cactus (*Carnegiea gigantea*) grows only in the Sonoran Desert of southern Arizona and the western part of the Mexican state of Sonora. It grows just 1–1.5 inches in its first eight years. You can find smaller specimens under sheltering "nurse trees" such as mesquite and palo verde. Saguaros generally don't grow their first arm until they are 50–70 years old; they can live to be 150–175 years old and weigh 6 tons or more, reaching a possible height of 50 feet. Crested, or cristate, saguaros have a rare fanlike mutation; you can see two cristate saguaros on Hike 12, Gila River Canyons (see page 114).

The saguaro has a woody skeleton made up of ribs; the folds allow it to expand and contract as it stores water. Woodpeckers create nests by pecking holes, which then scar over to form a permanent cavity, or boot. Other birds, such small owls or songbirds, use the nesting cavities after the woodpeckers leave.

The saguaro bloom is the state flower; blooming season is April–June, but alas, the flowers themselves last only one day. Pollinators include bees, birds, and bats.

Saguaros bear fruit just before the start of the monsoon season in late June/early July, providing an important food source for birds and animals. The fruit—green and red on the outside, its bright red pulp dotted with black seeds—is also culturally significant to the Indigenous Tohono O'odham people of the area, who call the saguaro *Ha:sañ* (pronounced ha-shawn) and the fruit *bahidaj*. They use it as food and medicine and ferment it to make a ceremonial wine. The flavor has been described as figlike, with a hint of strawberry; the nutty-tasting seeds can be eaten out of hand or baked into breads and muffins.

When a saguaro eventually dies, it falls over and the pulp rots away, leaving behind the woody skeleton and the boot. The woody ribs have been used throughout history to construct houses, furniture, and artwork.

a couple of small ravines, the trail climbs to cross a fence line marking Colossal Cave Mountain Park in 0.6 mile and passes Dunham Castle.

You're aiming for the saddle ahead—a low point between two hills. The trail winds its way up the hill, reaching the hike's high point in 0.6 mile (3,654'). You have a view into Colossal Cave Mountain Park and its La Posta Quemada Ranch below, with the Rincons in the distance.

Continue through the saddle, and in 0.5 mile the trail makes a wide switchback west as it descends toward the ranch. Reach the turnoff for the ranch at 4.8 miles at a sign with a knife and fork and an arrow. Take the spur trail to the left (north), and switchback down the hill to cross Aqua Verde Canyon. In 0.2 mile cross the creekbed, and then go through a fence line to reach an AZT kiosk sign.

Clockwise from top left: Saguaro cactus in bloom, saguaro with fruit, saguaro fruit, and saguaro bloom (Arizona's state flower)

Go through the trees and the picnic area to reach the Cowboy Parking Lot at La Posta Quemada Ranch (3,370'). The ranch house is located 0.1 mile to your right (east). **At 5.1 miles, this is the end of the one-way hike, with 567 feet of elevation gain.**

If you're doing the 10.2-mile out-and-back, return the way you came, making a right (west) at the spur trail junction to rejoin the AZT. The hike back to the Gabe Zimmerman Memorial Trailhead has a much more wide-open feel to it. The Empirita Mountains are ahead to the south, the Santa Rita Mountains are to the southwest (right), and the Whetstones to the southeast (left).

At 9.1 miles the trail leaves the utility corridor and turns right (south)—if you reach a metal gate, you've missed the turn. In 0.5 mile cross Cienega Creek and then go right (south) to leave the creek and enter a side canyon. Stay to the right (west) side of the canyon for 0.1 mile; the trail then leaves the canyon and ascends the hill. After climbing out of Cienega Creek, reach a junction and take the trail to the right, signed TO GABE ZIMMERMAN DAVIDSON CANYON TRAILHEAD, to complete the 10.2-mile out-and-back.

Gateway Community: VAIL *(see page 69)*

DISTANCE FROM TRAILHEAD: 6.0 miles **POPULATION:** 10,208 **ELEVATION:** 3,235'

Getting There

COWBOY TRAILHEAD, COLOSSAL CAVE MOUNTAIN PARK (HIKE END):
N32° 03.021' W110° 38.265', elevation 3,370'

ROAD CONDITIONS: All vehicles; graded dirt for 0.2 mile

FACILITIES: Toilets, picnic benches, grills, no water

GABE ZIMMERMAN MEMORIAL TRAILHEAD (HIKE START AND PARKING FOR OUT-AND-BACK HIKE): N32° 00.832' W110° 38.848', elevation 3,446'

ROAD CONDITIONS: All vehicles; paved

FACILITIES: Shaded picnic bench at trailhead, a bike rack in the form of a snake, and (as of this writing) a portable toilet

DIRECTIONS *Hike end:* From downtown Tucson (Congress Street and I-10), take I-10 East for 20.7 miles to Exit 279 for Colossal Cave Road/Wentworth Road, and turn left (north). In 2.1 miles turn right (east) onto Colossal Cave Road, and drive 4.2 miles to Old Spanish Trail. Turn right (southeast) at the stop sign, go 1.0 mile to a junction, and veer right (southeast) through Colossal Cave Mountain Park's entrance station, following the signs for the picnic areas and La Posta Quemada Ranch. In 0.2 mile pass a left turn for the picnic areas and overnight camping, and in 1.1 miles turn left (east) into La Posta Quemada Ranch; then, in another 0.2 mile, turn right (south) into the Cowboy Parking Lot. (**Note:** The parking lot gates are locked daily at 5 p.m.) If you're doing the hike as a point-to-point, leave a shuttle vehicle here, drive back out of the park to I-10, and follow the directions below.

Hike start: Take I-10 East to Exit 281 for AZ 83 South (Sonoita/Patagonia). In 0.4 mile turn left (north) at the stop sign. Cross back over the freeway and, in 0.2 mile, turn right (northeast) at the sign that says FRONTAGE ROAD TO MARSH STATION ROAD; then, in 0.1 mile, turn right (southeast) onto Marsh Station Road. In 3.3 miles turn right (east) into the Gabe Zimmerman Memorial Trailhead. Please leave the gravel side of the parking lot open for horse trailers.

Molino Basin to West Spring

Switchbacks and expansive views

7

SCENERY: ★★★★
TRAIL CONDITION: ★★
CHILDREN: ★★★
(short hike)
DIFFICULTY: ★★★
SOLITUDE: ★★

Blooming feather dalea on the Bellota Trail

DISTANCE & CONFIGURATION: 4.8-mile out-and-back

ACCUMULATED ELEVATION GAIN: 1,350'

SHORT HIKE OPTION: 2.0-mile out-and-back to valley overlook (600' elevation gain)

OUTSTANDING FEATURES: Views of the Rincon Mountains, juniper–oak grasslands

LAND-MANAGEMENT AGENCY: Coronado National Forest, Santa Catalina Ranger District, 520-749-8700, fs.usda.gov/coronado

MAPS: USGS 7.5' *Agua Caliente Hill, AZ*

AZT PASSAGE: 10/Redington Pass, aztrail.org/explore/passages/passage-10 -redington-pass

ANCESTRAL LANDS: Tohono O'odham, Pascua Yaqui

SEASON: Winter, spring, fall

ACCESS: No fees or permits; open 24-7 year-round

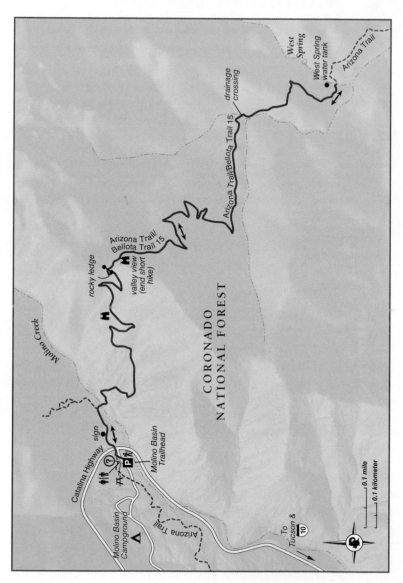

Overview

This hike on the Arizona National Scenic Trail (AZT) climbs to a saddle with expansive views across the Agua Caliente Valley, overlooking the Rincon Mountains. The second section descends into the valley to West Spring, a water tank. The trail switchbacks across the hillside, zigzagging as it gains and loses elevation.

The hike described below was my introduction to the AZT in the early 2000s. Back then I never considered that one day I would walk the entire AZT twice and write this guidebook. If you're just starting out, the short option to the valley overlook is a great payoff for the climb.

This part of the AZT is popular with mountain bikers; see "Sharing the Trail" (page 16) for more information about trail etiquette. An interpretive sign at the trailhead tells about the relationship between elevation and vegetation in the Sky Islands; see "Elevation Is Everything" (page 16) for more information about life zones.

On the Trail

To find the start of the trail, face the bathrooms and look right (northeast) for the continuation of the parking lot loop. Take this and immediately look right (northeast) for a kiosk with signs about the Catalinas, the Molino Basin Trailhead, and the Bellota Trail in 100 feet. Take the rock-lined path past the kiosk to the Catalina Highway crossing. A sign lists mileages for Bellota Trail 15. Look both ways before carefully crossing Catalina Highway at the crosswalk, and pass a small metal AZT sign at 300 feet.

The trail squeezes between some boulders put there to deter vehicles and reaches a big metal AZT sign on your left (north); labeled MOLINO BASIN TRAILHEAD, it has a map of the AZT through the area. Continue northeast on a gravel trail above the streambed; in winter and spring, you may see pools of water or even a full flow. In 0.1 mile pass another small metal AZT sign, marking a turn to your right (southeast) to cross the creek.

At the intersection just beyond the metal sign, look to your right (southeast) for another metal sign across the creek that marks the continuation of the

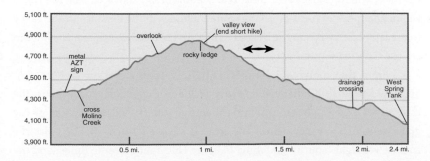

trail. The trail that goes straight ahead (northeast) is not the AZT—your trail curves to the right (south) and switchbacks left (northeast), ascending on gravel tread interspersed with rock steps. Vegetation in this stretch includes different varieties of agave, such as shindaggers, beargrass, sotol, and Spanish bayonet. Oaks, junipers, acacias, and manzanitas line the trail, along with prickly pear cactus. In 0.1 mile at a curve to the right, pass an alligator juniper on your right (west), and you can see how it gets its name. During my research for this hike, I saw two different sets of white-tailed deer bounding across the slopes.

In 0.2 mile Airmen Peak comes into view to the northwest. The trail curves right (east) and continues to climb rocky steps and switchback up the hill. In 0.2 mile there is a small overlook to your left (west) as the trail makes a curve to the right (east). You can see down into Molino Basin and onto Catalina Highway. Across the basin to the west, on the left side of the canyon, the north-bound AZT is visible on the hills past the campground. Rocky steps make a turn to the right (south) at a big oak tree in 0.1 mile, and the trail switchbacks right (east) with the saddle you are heading toward in front of you.

Just before the saddle, you make a short descent and, in 0.1 mile, come to a rocky ledge to your left with good seating and views of the basin. Go just a bit farther beyond the saddle for fantastic views to the south and east. From the ledge turn right (east) toward a fence line at the saddle. Here you find, from left to right, a combination bike crossing, pedestrian crossing, and equestrian crossing. The pedestrian path weaves through the barbed wire fence in the middle, and the AZT curves around to the right (south). **The short hike ends at rocks just past the high point at the small metal AZT sign (4,813'), at 1.0 mile and 600 feet of elevation gain.**

Have a seat on the rocks and enjoy the views, with the Rincon Mountains framing the AZT way down in the Agua Caliente Valley. Mica Mountain, with the rocky outcrop of Helen's Dome, is to the southeast, and Agua Caliente Hill is the smaller peak in front of it. The white buildings in the distance in the valley to the left (east) make up the Bellota Ranch. To the east, past the ranch, you can see the Galiuro Mountains.

From this spot it's 1.4 miles and 775 feet of elevation loss to West Spring—keep in mind that you'll have to tackle that uphill on your way out. The trail curves to the right (south) and is benched into the side of the hill, giving great views of the valley below. The tread is steep and rocky. In 0.2 miles the trail curves right (south), and Agua Caliente Hill, Tanque Verde Ridge, and the

Santa Rita Mountains come into view. The Santa Ritas are another Sky Island traversed by the AZT (see Hike 4, page 59), with Mount Wrightson the tallest peak in the range (9,456'). The vegetation is a little different on this side of the hill, with spiny stalks of ocotillo and more mesquite trees and cactus. Continue following the switchbacks back and forth, losing elevation and reaching a ridgeline in 0.5 mile. Wood-and-stone steps lead down the ridgeline, and the AZT stays on the right (north) side of the canyon as it descends into the valley.

In 0.3 mile the trail begins to curve to the right (southeast) to cross the drainage we've been following. The drainage is a wetter environment than the ridge, with larger oak and cottonwood trees. This drainage may also have water in it during wetter times of year. Cross the drainage in 0.2 mile; just after you cross, there are some rocks to sit on to your right (west) before you pass a large oak tree.

The trail descends, flattens, and then begins to climb just past another large oak tree, curving to the right (south) in 0.1 mile. The AZT curves to the left (east) and starts a descent through tight switchbacks with rock-and-wooden steps for 0.2 mile. West Spring Tank, a tall, round concrete holding tank, becomes visible in the valley to your left (southeast).

Reach the canyon bottom at 2.4 miles. Cross the canyon straight ahead (east), and make a right (southeast) to reach West Spring Tank (4,038'). The area around West Spring is quite pretty; there may be water running in the creek, and cottonwood, ash, mesquite, and juniper trees grow nearby. You can have a seat near the tank or on some rock ledges just beyond the tank in the creek to the south. The water in the tank is hard to access so don't count on it as a water source. You may see some of Bellota Ranch's horses if you're lucky.

Go back the way you came, taking your time on the return trip and enjoying the views of where you've been.

Gateway Community: TUCSON

DISTANCE FROM TRAILHEAD: 10.0 miles **POPULATION:** 535,677 **ELEVATION:** 2,389'

The second largest city in Arizona and the largest Gateway Community of the AZT, Tucson is surrounded by five mountain ranges. The AZT passes through three of them: the Santa Catalina Mountains to the north (Hikes 7–10, starting on page 79), the Rincon Mountains to the east, and the Santa Rita Mountains to the south (see Hike 4, page 59).

Opportunities for recreation are plentiful in town. Pima County has a 131-mile multiuser path called **The Loop** that's great for walking, biking, or running. It connects many local parks, restaurants, hotels, and more and is decorated with artwork from murals to mosaics to sculpture gardens. **Saguaro National Park,** which showcases its namesake giant cacti, has two sections on the east and west sides of town. The park's West District is also close to the **Arizona-Sonora Desert Museum,** a combination zoo–botanical garden that educates visitors about the unique qualities of the Sonoran Desert.

Tucson, the first city in the U.S. to be named a UNESCO World City of Gastronomy, prides itself on restaurants, gardens, and farmers' markets that use locally sourced ingredients and heritage techniques for cultivating, harvesting, and preparing food. Some of the places that exemplify this artisanal approach include **Cafe Poca Cosa**, **Mission Garden** (a living agricultural museum featuring local native plants), and **Barrio Bread**.

Although the Sonoran hot dog was born in Hermosillo, Mexico, it has found popularity in Tucson, and many restaurants around town offer a bacon-wrapped grilled hot dog on a roll with pinto beans, onions, tomatoes, jalapeño sauce, and mayonnaise. **El Güero Canelo** was nominated for a James Beard Award, and **BK Carne Asada & Hot Dogs** has made several national best-of lists, including *The New York Post*'s 10 Best Hot Dogs in America and *National Geographic*'s Best Places to Eat and Drink in Tucson. After your hike, you can cool down like a local with an **Eegee's** frozen slush, made with shaved ice and bits of fruit.

Rincon Mountain view with the AZT visible in the valley below

Historic Fourth Avenue and Downtown Tucson are home to bars, concert venues, museums and historical sites, restaurants, and local festivals. The University of Arizona has frequent sporting events and entertainment.

Tucson offers a range of lodging options, from chain hotels to Airbnb properties, resorts, and guest ranches. Camping is available in Coronado National Forest on Mount Lemmon at Molino Basin and Gordon Hirabayashi Campgrounds at lower elevations and General Hitchcock, Spencer Canyon, and Rose Canyon Campgrounds at higher elevations. Free dispersed (primitive) camping is available seasonally along Mount Bigelow and Bear Wallow Roads. For last-minute items, Summit Hut, a local favorite, has two locations in town, and there's an REI in Tucson Mall.

THE LOOP: Consists of 131 miles of multiuse trail throughout Pima County; 520-724-5000, webcms.pima.gov/government/the_loop

SAGUARO NATIONAL PARK: Eastern District, 3693 S. Old Spanish Trail, 520-733-5153; Western District, 2700 N. Kinney Rd., 520-733-5158; nps.gov/sagu. Admission: Week-long passes cost $25/vehicle, $20/motorcycle, or $15/pedestrian or bicyclist. Open daily, sunrise–sunset (vehicles) or 24-7 year-round (pedestrians and bicyclists); visitor centers open daily, 9 a.m.–5 p.m. except December 25.

ARIZONA-SONORA DESERT MUSEUM: 2021 N. Kinney Road, 520-883-2702, desert museum.org. Admission: $21.95 adults, $19.95 ages 65+, $9.95 ages 3–12, free ages 2 and younger. *March–September:* Open daily, 7:30 a.m.–5 p.m. *October–February:* Open daily, 8:30 a.m.–5 p.m.

CAFE POCA COSA: 110 E. Pennington St., 520-622-6400, cafepocacosatucson.com. Open Tuesday–Saturday, 11 a.m.–9 p.m.

MISSION GARDEN: 946 W. Mission Lane, 520-955-5200, tucsonsbirthplace.org. Suggested donation, $5; call ahead for tours. Open Wednesday–Saturday, 8 a.m.–12 p.m.; October–March, 8 a.m.–2 p.m.; closed major holidays.

BARRIO BREAD: 18 S. Eastbourne Ave., 520-327-1292, barriobread.com. Open Tuesday–Friday, 9 a.m.–5 p.m.; Saturday, 9 a.m.–2 p.m.

EL GÜERO CANELO: 2480 N. Oracle Rd. (plus two other locations in town), 520-882-8977, elguerocanelo.com. Open Monday–Thursday, 10 a.m.–10 p.m.; Friday and Saturday, 10 a.m.–midnight; Sunday, noon–8 p.m.

BK CARNE ASADA & HOT DOGS: 2680 N. First Ave., 520-207-2245; 5118 S. 12th Ave., 520-295-0105; bktacos.com. Open Sunday–Thursday, 9 a.m.–11 p.m.; Friday and Saturday, 9 a.m.–midnight.

EEGEE'S: 6810 E. Tanque Verde Rd. (plus 24 other locations in town), 520-885-1803, eegees.com. Open daily, 9:30 a.m.–11 p.m.

HISTORIC FOURTH AVENUE: University Avenue south to Ninth Street, 520-624-5004, fourthavenue.org

DOWNTOWN TUCSON: 520-268-9030, downtowntucson.org

UNIVERSITY OF ARIZONA: Located about 1 mile northeast of downtown Tucson, 520-621-2211, arizona.edu

CORONADO NATIONAL FOREST CAMPING: Call 520-749-8700 or see fs.usda.gov /activity/coronado/recreation/camping-cabins for details. The closest campground to this hike, **Molino Basin,** has a few dozen campsites southwest of the trailhead parking area and restrooms. A camp host is across the road from the campground sign. Open October–April; rates are $10–$20/night for single tent sites, $50–$100 for group sites (prices vary seasonally). Trailers and RVs under 22' are permitted; no hookups. For reservations, call 877-444-6777 or go to recreation.gov/camping/campgrounds/233223.

SUMMIT HUT: Eastside, 5251 E. Speedway Blvd., 520-325-1554; Northwest, 7745 N. Oracle Rd., 520-888-1000; summithut.com. Open Monday–Friday, 9 a.m–8 p.m.; Saturday, 9 a.m.–6:30 p.m.; Sunday, 9 a.m.–5 p.m.

REI: 160 W. Wetmore Road, 520-887-1938, rei.com/stores/tucson. Open Monday–Friday, 10 a.m.–9 p.m.; Saturday, 10 a.m.–8 p.m.; Sunday, 10 a.m.–6 p.m.

Getting There

MOLINO BASIN TRAILHEAD: N32° 20.240' W110° 41.457', elevation 4,330'

ROAD CONDITIONS: All vehicles; paved

FACILITIES: Restrooms but no water

DIRECTIONS *From Tucson:* Take I-10 East or West to Exit 256, and turn east onto Grant Road. In 6.8 miles turn left (northeast) onto Tanque Verde Road, and drive 2.1 miles. Turn left (north) onto Catalina Highway, drive 4.2 miles to the Coronado National Forest boundary, and zero your odometer. At milepost 5.7, turn left (west) after passing a sign for Molino Basin. On your left (southeast) is the AZT parking area, directly across from the restrooms, with seven spots labeled NO FEE REQUIRED. A kiosk has information about passes, but no day-use fee is required if you're only hiking the AZT.

An accessible parking spot is to the right (northeast) of the bathrooms, and additional parking is located to the left (southwest). There are several canopy-covered picnic tables and some with no shade. Picnic sites are day-use only and have grills.

From the south and east: Take I-10 West to Exit 275 and go right (north) on Houghton Road. In 15.0 miles, turn right (northeast) onto Catalina Highway, and follow the directions above.

8 Gordon Hirabayashi Campground to Sycamore Canyon Dam

Desert views and a tribute to a human rights trailblazer

SCENERY: ★ ★ ★ ★ ★
TRAIL CONDITION: ★ ★ ★ ★
CHILDREN: ★ ★ ★ ★ ★
(short hike)
DIFFICULTY: ★ ★ ★
SOLITUDE: ★ ★

A view of Sabino Basin from Shreve Saddle. (*Note:* Dogs are not allowed in Pusch Ridge Wilderness beyond the saddle.)

DISTANCE & CONFIGURATION: 6.0-mile out-and-back

HIKING TIME: 3–5 hours

ACCUMULATED ELEVATION GAIN: 1,025'

SHORT HIKE OPTION: 2.8-mile out-and-back to Shreve Saddle (300' elevation gain)

OUTSTANDING FEATURES: Historical background of the former prison camp, views of the Sabino Basin, Sycamore Canyon Reservoir

LAND-MANAGEMENT AGENCY: Coronado National Forest, Santa Catalina Ranger District, 520-749-8700, fs.usda.gov/coronado

MAPS: USGS 7.5' *Agua Caliente Hill, AZ*

AZT PASSAGE: 11/Santa Catalina Mountains, aztrail.org/explore/passages/passage-11 -santa-catalina-mountains

ANCESTRAL LANDS: Tohono O'odham, Pascua Yaqui

SEASON: Winter, spring, fall

ACCESS: Open 24-7 year-round, but the campground is closed and gated May– September; dogs prohibited beyond Shreve Saddle in Pusch Ridge Wilderness

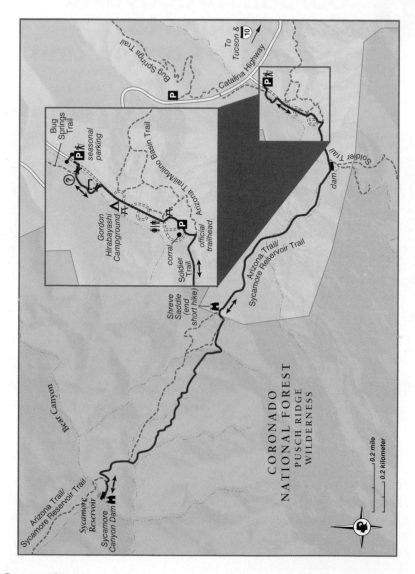

Overview

The Catalina Federal Honor Camp was established in 1937 to house federal prisoners who supplied the labor to build an access road up the Catalina Mountains. During World War II, it also housed Gordon Hirabayashi (1918–2012), a Seattle-born sociology student who was resisting discrimination against Americans of Japanese descent in the wake of the attack on Pearl Harbor in 1941. In 1942

President Franklin D. Roosevelt enacted Executive Order 9066, which ordered the evacuation and internment of more than 100,000 Japanese, including both recent immigrants and American-born citizens, in camps around the western United States. (Some 13,000 Americans of German and Italian descent were interned as well.)

In 1942 Hirabayashi turned himself in to the FBI rather than report for relocation, and he was sentenced to 90 days in the Catalina Federal Honor Camp. He later served a year in a Washington state prison as a conscientious objector.

In 1987 a federal commission determined that Executive Order 9066 had been motivated by racism and wartime fearmongering, and Hirabayashi's conviction was overturned. In 1988 President Ronald Reagan signed the Civil Liberties Act, acknowledging the injustice and apologizing for the internment.

In 1999 the Catalina Federal Honor Camp was renamed after Hirabayashi and repurposed as a U.S. Forest Service recreation site and campground. Hirabayashi attended the dedication ceremony.

On this hike you will see remnants of the old camp buildings, foundations, and infrastructure on your way to Sycamore Canyon Dam, whose reservoir provided water for the camp.

Note: This hike description includes the interpretive path and a walk through the campground to reach the official trailhead, which is open October 1–April 30. If you prefer to park at the official trailhead, park at the seasonal trailhead to do the interpretive trail to your right (north) past the gate, walk 0.1 mile back to your vehicle after crossing the second bridge, and drive the remaining 0.3 mile through the campground to park. This will shorten the total hike distance by 0.6 mile. Make sure to take the time to do the interpretive trail, as it provides a very interesting history and context for the hike.

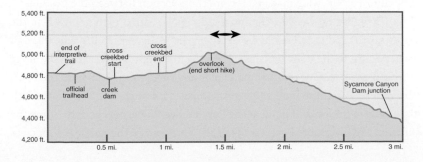

On the Trail

Cross the bridge near the parking area gate (4,885'), and reach a kiosk at the junction for Molino Basin Trail 11 and Bug Springs Trail to the right (north) in 100 feet. Bug Springs Trail serves as the AZT Wilderness Bypass—bikes are prohibited in Pusch Ridge Wilderness, and this bypass allows them to take a different route up Mount Lemmon.

A paved path goes left toward a stone foundation with stairs and reaches a kiosk with information about Gordon Hirabayashi, Japanese interment during World War II, and the history of the former Catalina Federal Honor Camp. In 200 feet pass the stone structure, turn left (south) to continue on the paved path, and then pass another structure on your left (east). Past a couple of benches on your left (east), the trail continues to curve left (southeast) down stairs and crosses a second bridge at 0.1 mile.

Turn right (southeast) and walk the road through Gordon Hirabayashi Campground; the sites have grills, fire pits, picnic tables, and bear boxes. The restrooms are on the right (west) at 0.25 mile. Go left (south) at the junction in the parking lot, pass a picnic table and corral, and reach the official AZT trailhead (4,854') in the south corner of the parking lot in 0.1 mile. Take the trail uphill to reach a junction with a metal AZT sign in 100 feet, and go right (west).

The trail follows a closed road that descends on rocky tread toward another, smaller metal AZT sign in 0.1 mile. Reach a junction with Soldier Trail 706, and cross the creekbed at a rock dam past yet another small AZT sign. The trail is flat on the north side of the creek, where junipers and oaks grow, and then crosses back and forth in the sandy drainage. Pass some metal scraps and, in 0.3 mile, stay on the wide path when there is another trail coming in from the left. Cross a metal pipe and a concrete pipe in 0.2 mile, and the trail curves left (west) and begins the climb to the saddle ahead. Past another metal pipe, the AZT climbs on the wide road bed toward the low point between the two hills.

There is a brown AZT sign on a metal pole, with a path going off to the right (north) and concrete blocks—stay on the main trail. In 0.1 mile the trail makes a turn to the right (northwest) on the final approach to the saddle along the rocky road, passing another metal pipe and small metal AZT sign. You reach Shreve Saddle and the high point of the hike at 1.4 miles (5,024'). Go through the saddle to the lookout point at the Pusch Ridge Wilderness boundary and the junction with Sycamore Reservoir Trail 39. Northeast of the saddle is a concrete foundation from the old prison camp. **This is the turnaround for the short hike, at 1.4 miles and 300 feet of elevation gain. Dogs not allowed beyond this point.**

You can see the trail heading down toward Sycamore Dam on the slopes to your left (west). From the saddle, you see, from left to right, the sheer cliff in Bear Canyon, which has Sycamore Reservoir at its base, followed by the East and West Forks of Sabino Canyon, the path that the AZT takes on its way to Romero Pass.

Cathedral Rock, the highest point in the front range (7,957') rises above Romero Pass straight ahead (northwest), and above that is the ridge that leads to the top of Mount Lemmon. The Ravens, Rappel Rock, and the summit towers are visible to the right (north-northwest). To the southeast are views of pointy Rincon Peak and Mica Mountain.

Sycamore Reservoir Trail 39 continues through the saddle to the left (southwest) and descends. You will pass several areas with rock pillars and concrete that were once part of the camp. The trail curves right (west) in 0.4 mile, then veers left (southwest) and crosses a ravine in 0.2 mile. Past stone steps, you traverse to the northwest for 0.1 mile. Curve left (southwest) and cross another ravine in 0.1 mile. The AZT makes a couple of short switchbacks and then curves right (west) to cross another ravine in 0.2 mile.

To the right (northeast) as you descend, you can see General Hitchcock Highway above. As you travel northwest you can see the wall of the canyon getting closer. In 0.4 mile turn right (northwest), cross a small drainage, and ascend to the right (north). In 0.1 mile, go straight (north) through a flat area and ignore a trail coming in from the right (east).

You can see large trees—cottonwoods, sycamores, alders, and ash—in Sycamore Canyon below. This area is especially pretty during fall-color season, which can be as late as November in this region and elevation. In 0.1 mile curve right (northwest) and switchback left (southwest), reaching a trail junction in 0.1 mile. The AZT continues to the right (northeast), but you're going to Sycamore Canyon Dam, so turn left (west). This trail runs along the canyon bottom, crossing a stone wall and reaching a concrete foundation and overlook for the Sycamore Canyon Dam in 0.1 mile. This is both the end of the hike, at 3.0 miles, and the low point, at 4,327 feet.

The water here, colored brown by natural organic compounds called tannins, is often referred to by locals as "Catalina tea." Steps lead up to a thin use path on the left (south) side of the canyon that goes 50 feet to a spot where you can look back upstream at the water flowing over the dam. The peak that you can see from here, called Thimble Peak after the sewing implement, is the tallest point in the Sabino Basin (5,322'). You may hear the goatlike calls of the canyon tree frog.

Go back the way you came, making a right (southeast) at the AZT junction, and immediately start ascending the hill toward Shreve Saddle. Make sure to go straight ahead (south) through the flat area in 0.3 mile instead of taking the path to your left (east).

Gateway Community: TUCSON (see page 83)

DISTANCE FROM TRAILHEAD: 12.0 miles **POPULATION:** 535,677 **ELEVATION:** 2,389'

Getting There

GORDON HIRABAYASHI CAMPGROUND TRAILHEAD: N32° 20.168' W110° 43.191', elevation 4,854'

ROAD CONDITIONS: All vehicles; paved

FACILITIES: Restrooms and picnic tables but no water. Gordon Hirabayashi Campground consists of 12 campsites and is open October–April. Single site: $20, with $10 Golden Age/Access or Interagency Senior/Access pass. Group site: $50 plus $10 per vehicle. Payable with cash or check. Trailers and RVs under 22' permitted; no hookups.

DIRECTIONS *From Tucson:* Take I-10 East or West to Exit 256, and turn east onto Grant Road. In 6.8 miles turn left (northeast) onto Tanque Verde Road, and drive 2.1 miles. Turn left (north) onto Catalina Highway, drive 4.2 miles to the Coronado National Forest boundary, and zero your odometer. At milepost 7, turn left (southwest). If the campground gate is unlocked (October–April), do the interpretive trail (see note on page 89), and then continue through the campground 0.3 mile and turn right (north) at the junction. Past a corral and picnic tables, you'll find parking in several different areas for cars—please leave the turnaround open for people hauling trailers. The trailhead is in the south corner of the parking lot.

From the south and east: Take I-10 West to Exit 275 and go right (north) on Houghton Road. In 15.0 miles, turn right (northeast) onto Catalina Highway, and follow the directions above.

Marshall Gulch–Aspen Loop
Sublime Sky Island saunter

SCENERY: ★★★★
TRAIL CONDITION: ★★★★
CHILDREN: ★★
DIFFICULTY: ★★★
SOLITUDE: ★★

Viewpoint on the Aspen Loop

DISTANCE & CONFIGURATION: 3.7-mile loop

HIKING TIME: 2–4 hours (due to high elevation)

ACCUMULATED ELEVATION GAIN: 1,000'

SHORT HIKE OPTION: 2.4-mile out-and-back to Marshall Saddle (500' elevation gain)

OUTSTANDING FEATURES: Seasonal creek, wildflowers, mountain views, fall colors

LAND-MANAGEMENT AGENCY: Coronado National Forest, Santa Catalina Ranger District, 520-749-8700, fs.usda.gov/coronado

MAPS: USGS 7.5' *Mount Lemmon, AZ*

AZT PASSAGE: 11/Santa Catalina Mountains, aztrail.org/explore/passages/passage-11 -santa-catalina-mountains

ANCESTRAL LANDS: Tohono O'odham and Pascua Yaqui

SEASON: Spring, summer (be careful of monsoons; see page 35), fall

ACCESS: Trailhead parking requires a day-use pass ($5/day or $20/year); open 24-7 year-round, but the road to the trailhead is closed seasonally (generally mid-December–March, adding 0.5 mile each way to the hike)

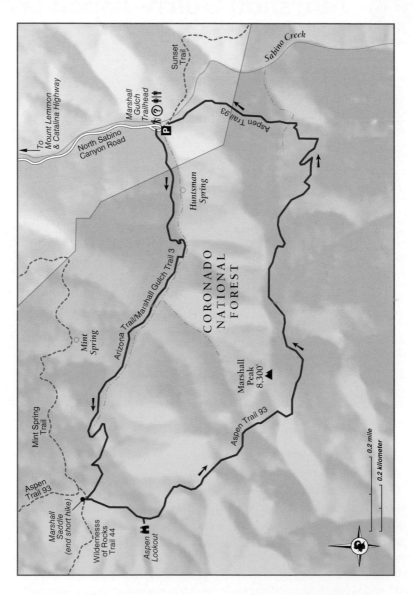

Advisory

At the time of this writing, Marshall Gulch and Aspen Trails are scheduled to open November 1, 2020, after the June 2020 Bighorn Fire, which was ignited by a lightning strike and burned 119,978 acres in the Santa Catalina Mountains. Go to the passage page at aztrail.org/explore

/passages/passage-11-santa-catalina-mountains or Coronado National Forest fs.usda.gov/coronado for updates.

Overview

Though this hike is in southern Arizona, the Arizona National Scenic Trail (AZT) along Marshall Gulch ranges from 7,500 to 8,000 feet in elevation, making it a perfect summer outing with lots of trees. A seasonal creek runs through Marshall Gulch, and both summer wildflowers and fall colors are spectacular on both the AZT and the Aspen Trail, which you'll use to make a loop back to the trailhead.

Note: From July to September, be aware of monsoon storm activity (see page 35 for more information). Also be aware that the road to the Marshall Gulch Trailhead is closed seasonally after the first large snow or from December 15 to April 1. In winter, vehicle access is gated 0.5 mile from the trailhead, but you can still walk in. For current road conditions, call the Pima County Department of Transportation road-closure hotline at 520-547-7510, or check the Coronado National Forest website (fs.usda.gov/coronado) for closure information.

On the Trail

From the trailhead take the AZT, signed here as Marshall Gulch Trail 3, to the right (north) of the bathrooms. (Another trail is right next to the bathrooms, but that is not the official AZT.) The tread is rocky and ascends immediately into the forest. The primary rock type here is granite gneiss, a metamorphic rock that has quartz inclusions and sparkly flakes of silver mica; you'll pass some in the trail tread 500 feet from the trailhead.

There are many types of trees at this elevation, known as the Canadian Zone (see "Elevation Is Everything," page 16, for a discussion of life zones).

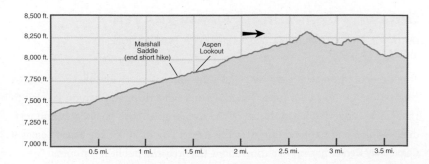

In addition to aspen and ponderosa pine, you'll find Douglas-fir and white fir, Gambel and silverleaf oak, and the beautiful red-bark Arizona madrone.

The trail climbs and contours above the canyon past a small metal AZT sign. At 0.5 mile the trail levels somewhat and then descends to cross the creek twice, 0.1 mile apart. Look for yellow columbine near the stream in the summer. Start a steeper ascent and the canopy opens up. This area was heavily impacted by the human-caused Aspen Fire of 2003, which burned 84,750 acres and destroyed 340 homes and businesses and much of Summerhaven. Sadly, at the time of this writing, the Bighorn Fire—ignited in June 2020 by a lightning strike—has surpassed the Aspen Fire with 120,000 acres burned. This time, firefighters were able to save Summerhaven and there was no loss of life or structures.

Cross the creek two more times and, at 1.0 mile, switchback up through the pines. Pass another metal AZT sign to reach Marshall Saddle (7,949')—**this is the turnaround spot for the short hike, at 1.2 miles and 500 feet of elevation gain.** This junction has four trails leading off from it. The AZT continues on the Wilderness of Rock Trail, which is not covered in this book. Instead, you go left (south) to join Aspen Trail 93 and make a loop back to the trailhead.

In 0.2 mile, take a right (west) on a small spur trail 50 feet to some boulders. This is a great spot for a break, with expansive views of the Catalina Mountains and the Tucson basin. Cathedral Rock (7,957') is the tallest peak to your right. (*Babad Do'ag,* which translates to "Frog Mountain," is the local Indigenous Tohono O'odham name for the Catalina Mountains.)

Climb to a saddle in 0.4 mile, and the trail levels and then descends. In 0.4 mile the trail makes a series of brief climbs. Reach the high point of this hike at a saddle in 0.3 mile (8,127'). The trail switchbacks downhill, and in 0.8 mile you encounter a series of small ups and downs before one final descent into Marshall Gulch Trailhead, closing the loop at mile 3.7.

Gateway Community: SUMMERHAVEN

DISTANCE FROM TRAILHEAD: About 1 mile north **POPULATION:** 40
ELEVATION: 8,000'

This tiny community is very hiker-friendly and offers several places to spend time before or after your hike. The AZT runs right through town on its way to the Oracle Ridge Trailhead. Much of the community, both businesses and residences alike, had to be rebuilt after the Aspen Fire of 2003. The **Mount Lemmon Community Center** has information about the area and public bathrooms.

Spotlight: Quaking Aspen

The namesake trees of the Aspen Loop are quaking aspens (*Populus tremuloides*), which grow well in soil disturbed by fires. They proliferate in sunny areas and are resistant to subsequent fires. The tree puts out lateral roots with shoots that are a clone of those of the parent plant. This means that tree clusters will have similar physical characteristics and will all change color at the same time in the fall. Clusters can range from less than 1 acre to more than 100 acres. The leaves quake, or flutter, in the wind due to their stem structure, making a lovely sound. On the AZT, quaking aspens are seen in southern Arizona on the tops of Sky Islands, above the Mogollon Rim, and on the Kaibab Plateau at elevations from 7,000 to 9,000 feet. (Hikes 2, 21, 25, 28, and 29 also feature them.)

Stop in the **Mt. Lemmon Cookie Cabin** for one of their namesake giant treats, along with pizza and ice cream; you may also find a food truck parked in town. **The Living Rainbow** sells unique gifts. The **Mt. Lemmon General Store** has a trail register for AZT hikers to sign and a gift shop with AZT merchandise; they also sell delicious fudge along with a selection of groceries and camping items. **Sawmill Run** restaurant has a full bar and patio.

There are several Airbnb and VRBO properties on the mountain as well as the **Mount Lemmon Cabins** (reservations recommended). The **Mount Lemmon Hotel,** an all-cabin resort, was scheduled to open in 2020 but may be delayed due to the Bighorn Fire (see mtlemmonhotel.com for more information). There are also several campgrounds on Mount Lemmon (no RV hookups), along with free primitive camping (no facilities) along Bear Wallow Road and near Mount Bigelow. The **Palisades Visitor Center** at milepost 19.9 on the Catalina Highway, has a small gift shop and information desk; they also sell daily and yearly passes for U.S. Forest Service (USFS) fee-charging areas. The **Palisades Ranger Residence Cabin** is available for rent through recreation.gov as part of the USFS's Rooms with a View program.

Tucson and the University of Arizona are important centers for astronomy, and the **Mt. Lemmon SkyCenter,** at the 9,157-foot summit, offers day tours with solar viewing as well as the SkyNights StarGazing Program with 24-inch and 32-inch telescopes. All tours are by reservation only.

MOUNT LEMMON COMMUNITY CENTER: 12949 N. Sabino Canyon Pkwy., 520-724-5000. Open Friday–Sunday, 8 a.m.–5 p.m.

MT. LEMMON COOKIE CABIN: 12781 N. Sabino Canyon Pkwy., 520-576-1010, thecookiecabin.org. Open daily, 11 a.m.–5 p.m.

THE LIVING RAINBOW GIFT SHOP: 12789 N. Sabino Canyon Pkwy., 520-576-1519. Open daily, 10:30 a.m.–4:30 p.m.; hours can vary, so check ahead to confirm.

MT. LEMMON GENERAL STORE & GIFT SHOP: 12856 N. Sabino Canyon Pkwy., 520-576-1468, mtlemmon.com. Open daily, 10 a.m.–6 p.m.

SAWMILL RUN: 12976 N. Sabino Canyon Pkwy., 520-576-9147, sawmillrun.com. Open Monday–Thursday, 10:30 a.m.–4 p.m.; Friday and Saturday, 10:30 a.m.–8 p.m.

MOUNT LEMMON CABINS: 520-576-1455 (reservations by phone only)

PALISADES VISITOR CENTER: 11301 Catalina Hwy. (milepost 19.9), 520-576-6626, tinyurl.com/palisadesvisitorcenter. Open daily, 8 a.m.–5 p.m.

PALISADES RANGER RESIDENCE CABIN: East Organization Ridge Road, next to the Palisades Visitor Center; tinyurl.com/palisadesrangercabin (reservations: 877-444-6777, recreation.gov/camping/campgrounds/250033). Nightly rate: $125 for up to four people.

MT. LEMMON SKYCENTER: 520-626-8122, skycenter.arizona.edu. Office hours are Wednesday–Sunday, 9 a.m.–4 p.m.

Getting There

MARSHALL GULCH TRAILHEAD: N32° 25.688' W110° 45.355', elevation 7,465'

ROAD CONDITIONS: All vehicles; paved

FACILITIES: Restrooms and picnic tables but no water

DIRECTIONS *From the north:* Take I-10 East or West to Exit 256, and turn east onto Grant Road. In 6.8 miles turn left (northeast) onto Tanque Verde Road, and drive 2.1 miles. Turn left (north) onto Catalina Highway and drive 4.2 miles to the Coronado National Forest boundary. The Catalina Highway winds 26.0 miles farther up the mountain and through the Gateway Community of Summerhaven to the Marshall Gulch Trailhead, at the end of the road. Parking is limited, so it may be necessary to park at one of the lots down the street.

It's said that driving from the bottom to the top of Mount Lemmon is equivalent to driving from Mexico to Canada due to the many biotic communities, or life zones, found on the way up the mountain. In the Sky Islands as well as the rest of Arizona, the type of vegetation and temperature is dependent on the elevation, and a drive up the mountain is a fantastic illustration of that. Make sure to pack appropriately, as temperatures at the top of the mountain can be as much as 20°–30° cooler than at the base. See page 17 for more information on life zones.

From Tucson: Drive to the intersection of Grant and Tanque Verde Roads, and follow the directions above.

From the south and east: Take I-10 West to Exit 275 and go right (north) on Houghton Road. In 15.0 miles turn right (northeast) onto Catalina Highway, and follow the directions above.

10

American Flag Ranch Trailhead to Oracle Ridge

Historic ranches, scenic ridges

SCENERY: ★★★★
TRAIL CONDITION: ★★★
CHILDREN: ★★★
DIFFICULTY: ★★★
SOLITUDE: ★★★

The main building at High Jinks Ranch was constructed in 1928.

DISTANCE & CONFIGURATION: 6.8-mile out-and-back

HIKING TIME: 3–5 hours

ACCUMULATED ELEVATION GAIN: 1,077'

SHORT HIKE OPTION: 4.0-mile out-and-back to High Jinks Ranch (620' elevation gain)

OUTSTANDING FEATURES: Historical sites, valley and ridge vistas

LAND-MANAGEMENT AGENCY: Coronado National Forest, Santa Catalina Ranger District, 520-749-8700, fs.usda.gov/coronado

MAPS: USGS 7.5' *Campo Bonito, AZ*

AZT PASSAGE: 12/Oracle Ridge, aztrail.org/explore/passages/passage-12-oracle-ridge

ANCESTRAL LANDS: Apache

SEASON: Winter, spring, fall

ACCESS: No fees or permits; open 24-7 year-round

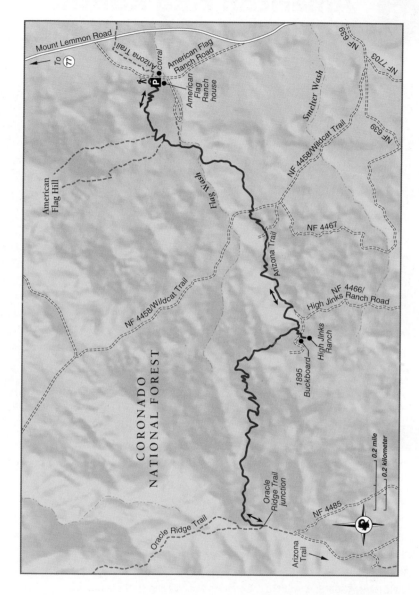

Overview

This hike on the Arizona National Scenic Trail (AZT) is steeped in history: at the trailhead is the American Flag Ranch house, thought to be the oldest territorial post office building still standing in Arizona. The Cody Trail is named after Buffalo Bill Cody—military scout, showman, and hunter—who staked the High

Jinks gold-mining claim on which the historic High Jinks Ranch was later built. Though celebrated in the West, Cody helped lead federal efforts against the area's Indigenous population through his participation in the Indian Wars.

On the Trail

This hike is the one that started my obsession with the AZT. Back in May 2007, I went to Oracle looking for a day hike, and locals suggested the AZT. I had a great time, and when I came back to the trailhead, I saw a big metal sign with a map that spurred my imagination because it crossed all of these wonderful places I wanted to visit. The trail was still incomplete at the time, but the sign noted that it was eventually going to connect from Mexico to Utah. I thought, "How on Earth could anyone hike across Arizona? There's no water!" That led me to do some research about long-distance hiking, and before long I was hooked. I made a plan to start hiking the AZT the following year, and the rest is history. For the full story of my love affair with the AZT, see page 4.

From the trailhead go 250 feet south on the road to visit a piece of territorial Arizona history at American Flag Ranch. The ranch house was built by Isaac Laurin in 1877 and was designated as the post office in 1880 to support the local mining claims that had sprung up in the area. The post office was open for only 10 years before the mining claims played out. The ranch is on the National Register of Historic Places and is thought to be the oldest territorial post office building still standing in Arizona. Inside the ranch is a museum that is open by appointment with the Oracle Historical Society; it contains artifacts from the original post office and of area mining and ranching.

Take the AZT southbound (west) through the portal labeled THE ARIZONA TRAIL; a smaller sign reads SANTA CATALINA MOUNTAINS SEGMENT, DEDICATED MAY 20, 1989. The sign across the way that simply says THE ARIZONA

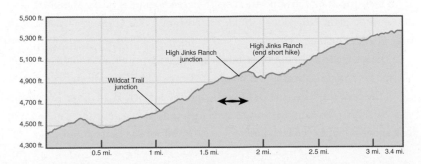

TRAIL marks the northbound AZT toward Oracle State Park (4,408'; see next hike). Another sign reads CODY TRAIL #9 and lists mileages.

The trail curves to the left (south) past the wooden corral and switchbacks up the grassy hill. As you gain elevation, views open to the east toward the San Pedro River Valley and the Galiuro Mountains. In 0.3 mile reach a small plateau and curve through the flats; then resume climbing.

Start descending into the wash at a switchback to the left (south). You can see Oak Creek Ranch across the way on top of the hill, but not High Jinks Ranch. The mountains you see in the distance to the east are the Rincons. In 0.2 mile the descent ends and the trail crosses a small, sandy wash.

The trail then descends to parallel the wash briefly and follows it through red-barked manzanita and oak trees. This part of the trail is often shady. The AZT follows the left (east) side of the wash and makes a turn to the left (southeast) in 0.2 mile to resume climbing away from the wash to the south. Cross beneath two sets of power lines. To your right (north) is American Flag Hill. The boulder formations for which Oracle is known start to appear. Continue through the grasses and oaks and climb to a dirt road, Wildcat Trail, in 0.4 mile.

Heads-Up: Look across the road and to your right (north) to see the continuation of the trail just beyond the dip in the road. Turn right (north) and descend just past the bottom of the dip; then, when the road begins to climb, look to your left (west) to continue on the AZT.

Switchbacks climb a low hill, and the trail crosses another set of power lines and then a dirt road. The trail continues climbing to the west, with the last switchback in 0.4 mile. The trail makes a turn to the right (west), ascending below a grassy ridge.

Here you pass large, serrated-leaved sotol plants, which may have gigantic stalks protruding from them. The plant sends up a stalk that can be as tall as 15 feet; the stalk falls and then scatters seeds, perpetuating the plant. The nonserrated plants that look similar are beargrass. Pass through an area with large granite boulders.

Heads-Up: In 0.2 mile the trail makes a turn to the right (north)—*do not take the use path going straight.* A brown AZT carsonite sign indicates the turn.

The trail curves to the left (west), and the historic High Jinks Ranch can be seen across the canyon. Locate the large, gray slab across the canyon, and look above it and to the left. Look for the turnoff for the ranch in 0.1 mile.

Curve around the head of the canyon and reach a junction with a metal sign that says ARIZONA TRAIL, UTAH 602/MEXICO 199 and another sign pointing to High Jinks Ranch. This is the turnoff to visit the second historic site on this hike. You'll be returning here after your visit to the ranch for the long and short versions of the hike.

From the junction, take a left (southwest). The access trail makes a short climb and then goes through a portal that reads HIGH JINKS. There are two driveways in front of you: Oak Creek Ranch is to the right, and High Jinks Ranch is to the left. A sign reads NATIONAL HISTORIC SITE.

Reach the High Jinks sign, water spigot, and sheds, along with a gate signed RING BELL, PRIVATE RESIDENCE. **This is the turnaround for the short hike, at 2.0 miles and 620 feet of elevation gain (4,954').**

In 1912, Buffalo Bill Cody came to Arizona to stake a gold-mining claim he called the High Jinks Mine. His foster son, Johnny Baker, built the main house on the property in the 1920s, complete with a crow's nest third-floor bedroom with windows that afford views of more than 180 degrees. Over the years, more buildings were added to the property.

In 1975, Dean Prichard bought the ranch, spent years restoring it and turned it into living spaces and a common spot for parties. Dean was a founding member of the Arizona Trail Association, so when they were laying out the path that the AZT would take near Oracle, he routed it right past the High Jinks Ranch. This was also one of Dale Shewalter's favorite places to visit on the AZT.

In the driveway of the ranch are historical parts of movie sets, including an 1895 buckboard wagon that was used in the 1987 TV movie *Poker Alice,* starring Elizabeth Taylor and very loosely based on the life of Alice Ivers (1851–1930), an English-born gambler, brothel owner, and rancher. The ranch offers water for travelers from a spigot in the driveway—drink your fill and enjoy the views, but please respect the signs for private property.

After Prichard's passing in 2007, the ranch lay vacant for several years. Dan Blanco, an astronomer and artist, restored it and set up several of its buildings to accommodate AZT travelers. Blanco owned and operated High Jinks from 2011 until his death in 2016. At the time of this writing, the ranch is for sale and access may change in the future. Respect signs for public property.

When you're done visiting High Jinks, cross the road. The portal that says TO THE ARIZONA TRAIL makes a great photo op. For the shorter version of this hike, make a right at the junction to go back the way you came. Make sure to pay attention to navigation at the two spots you passed on the way in (see **Heads-Up** on pages 102–103).

Back to the AZT, go straight (north) at the junction. The trail traverses through boulders; crosses a power line; and, in 0.3 mile, curves into a canyon, then descends to cross it. Begin switchbacking up the grassy hill. The trail traverses another shady, boulder-lined part of the trail and then continues climbing to the southwest past the Oak Creek Ranch. This land was part of the original 10.5 acres that made up the High Jinks property. The trail switchbacks and ascends the hill.

In 0.3 mile turn right (west) into a small side canyon and continue climbing. Take a breather to enjoy great views of the boulders, the sotol and beargrass, and the San Pedro River Valley with the Galiuro Mountains to the east.

Continue climbing and switchback past some boulder formations; then, in 0.3 mile, cross the top of the ravine. The trail continues climbing and turns right (west). Just before the junction, the trail curves south, reaching the junction with Oracle Ridge Trail 1 and the high point of the hike, at 3.4 miles (5,353').

As you crest the ridge, the futuristic domes of Biosphere 2 are visible in the valley, and the small, pointy mountain in the distance to the northwest is Picacho Peak. Biosphere 2 was designed to develop technology for colonizing space by mimicking seven different environments on Earth. There were two missions with eight Biospherian scientists each: one from 1991 to 1993 and one from March to September in 1994. Biosphere 2 has been administered by the University of Arizona since 2011 and is open for tours daily.

The AZT continues southbound on Oracle Ridge Trail 1 to the left, past Apache and Rice Peaks on its way to the Gateway Community of Summerhaven (8,000'; see page 96). Take a break, take it all in, and then return to the trailhead the way you came, enjoying the expansive views of the San Pedro River Valley on your way down.

Note: On your return, make sure to take a right (south) and join the road up to the top of the hill and then take a left (east) back onto the singletrack AZT at the point noted in **Heads-Up,** page 102).

Gateway Community: ORACLE

DISTANCE FROM TRAILHEAD: 4.0 miles **POPULATION:** 20,837 **ELEVATION:** 4,524'

This eclectic artists' community is set among the boulders of the Catalina Mountain foothills. The **Oracle Visitor Center** is a good place to stop for information.

Though there are many places around town where you can eat after your hike, one of my favorites is the **Oracle Patio Cafe**, where you can top off your meal with a slice of their legendary pie. They also have a market with a selection of groceries, baked goods, and sandwiches, and they own the **Oracle Cook Shack** across the street, serving burgers, hot dogs, and chili. **Casa Rivera** and its quick-service **Taco Express** are great for Mexican favorites or a trail burrito to go.

Several guest ranches offer overnight stays, such as **El Rancho Robles, 3C Ranch,** and **Triangle L Ranch;** you can also stay at one of the quirky A-frames of the **Chalet Village Motel.** Marney and Jim, who run the Chalet Village, are legendary AZT trail angels who have provided support for many hikers and mountain bikers over the years.

Developed camping is available at **Peppersauce Campground,** 4.2 miles from the trailhead, and **Arizona Zipline Adventures** (see below); dispersed (primitive) camping is available throughout Coronado National Forest.

If you'd like to learn more about Oracle after seeing the historic ranches on this hike, visit the **Oracle Historical Society** and **Acadia Ranch Museum** on your way back to town.

The night skies are really something to see, and **Oracle State Park** was designated an International Dark Sky Park in 2014. If you're looking for something with a little more adrenaline involved, **Arizona Zipline Adventures** is located 2.5 miles south on Mount Lemmon Road from American Flag Ranch Trailhead and also serves food daily. Or tour the University of Arizona's **Biosphere 2** and learn about the research being done to better understand the intricate biomes of Earth.

HIGH JINKS RANCH: 33550 South Highjinks Road, facebook.com/HighJinksRanch

ORACLE VISITOR CENTER: 1470 W. American Ave., 520-896-3300, visitoracle.org. Open daily, 9 a.m.–4 p.m.

THE ORACLE PATIO CAFE AND MARKET: 300 W. American Ave., 520-896-7615, oracle patiocafe.com. Café open Tuesday–Sunday, 7 a.m.–3 p.m.; market open until 6 p.m.

ORACLE COOK SHACK: 405 E. American Ave., 520-225-0005, theoraclecookshack.com. Open Monday–Friday, 11 a.m.–7 p.m.

CASA RIVERA AND TACO EXPRESS: 1975 W. American Ave., 520-896-3747, tinyurl .com/casariveraoracle. Open Sunday–Friday, 6:30 a.m.–8:30 p.m.

EL RANCHO ROBLES: 1170 N. Rancho Robles Rd., 520-896-7651, elranchorobles.com. Rooms and house rentals available.

3C RANCH: 36033 S. Mount Lemmon Rd., 520-896-2372, 3cranchaz.com. Rooms and house rentals available. Bar open Friday, 8 a.m.–7 p.m.; Saturday and Sunday, 11 a.m.–7 p.m.

TRIANGLE L RANCH: 2805 N Triangle L Ranch Rd., 520-623-6732, trianglelranch.com

CHALET VILLAGE MOTEL: 1245 W. American Ave., 520-896-9171

PEPPERSAUCE CAMPGROUND: Forest Service Road 38, 6.0 miles southeast of Oracle. 17 tent/RV sites plus 1 group site for up to 35 people; first come, first served. Water and vault toilets but no hookups. RVs must be 22' or shorter; trailers are discouraged as the sites are small and there are no pull-throughs. Nightly rates: $15 for single sites, $50 for group site. For more information about developed and dispersed camping in Coronado National Forest, call 520-749-8700 or see fs.usda.gov/activity/coronado/recreation/camping-cabins.

ORACLE HISTORICAL SOCIETY AND ACADIA RANCH MUSEUM: 825 E. Mount Lemmon Hwy., 520-896-9609, oraclehistoricalsociety.org. Free admission; open Thursday, 4–6 p.m.; Saturday, 1–4 p.m. Or call/email to schedule a tour.

ORACLE STATE PARK: 3820 Wildlife Dr., 520-896-2425, azstateparks.com/oracle. Admission: $7/vehicle, $3/pedestrian or bicyclist. The park is open October–May, daily, 8 a.m.–5 p.m., and May-October, daily, 7 a.m.–4 p.m.; the trailhead parking area on American Avenue is always open (with no fee) to accommodate hikers and after-hours use by stargazers. See page 111 of the next hike for more information.

Winter snow blankets the American Flag Ranch Trailhead.

ARIZONA ZIPLINE ADVENTURES: 35406 S. Mount Lemmon Rd., 520-308-9350, zip arizona.com. Zipline tours: $79 and up; nightly camping rates: $15 tent sites and cabins, $20 RV sites (no hookups), hot showers $3. Open Tuesday–Friday, 10 a.m.–5 p.m.; Saturday and Sunday, 8 a.m.–5 p.m.

BIOSPHERE 2: 32540 S. Biosphere Rd., 520-621-4800, biosphere2.org. Admission: $21 adults; $19 ages 62+, $14 ages 5–12. Open daily, 9 a.m.–4 p.m., except Thanksgiving and December 25.

Getting There

AMERICAN FLAG RANCH TRAILHEAD: N32° 34.851' W110° 43.225', elevation 4,408'

ROAD CONDITIONS: All vehicles; graded dirt for 0.4 mile

FACILITIES: None

DIRECTIONS *From Tucson:* Take I-10 East or West to Exit 256, and turn east onto Grant Road. To turn onto Oracle Road/AZ 77 northbound, go through the intersection in 1.0 mile and make a U-turn, then go right (north) onto Oracle Road. In 22.0 miles, veer right (northeast) at the Y-intersection with AZ 79 to continue on AZ 77. In 9.1 miles take a right (southeast) at the western turnoff for Oracle, marked with visitor center signs, onto American Avenue. Drive 2.4 miles, and turn right (southeast) onto Mount Lemmon Highway. In 3.5 miles, pass the entrance for Oracle State Park (see next hike).

In 2.0 miles, the highway splits—take the right fork to go south. In 0.6 mile, turn right onto American Flag Ranch Road, marked by a small, square AZT sign. This graded dirt spur will take you 0.4 mile to trailhead parking on both sides just north of American Flag Ranch. This hike starts from the trail with the large metal AZT map, on your right as you drive in; the next hike starts from the trailhead across the road, which goes toward Oracle State Park.

From Phoenix Sky Harbor Airport: Follow the signs for AZ 202 East, and take it 3.6 miles to AZ 101 Loop South. In 3.1 miles take Exit 55 A/B onto US 60 East; drive 36.0 miles, and take Exit 212 onto AZ 79 South. Drive 58.0 miles, and then veer left (northeast) at the Y-intersection onto AZ 77. In 9.1 miles take a right (southeast) at the western turnoff for Oracle, marked with visitor center signs, onto American Avenue. Drive 2.4 miles, and turn right (southeast) onto Mount Lemmon Highway. In 3.5 miles pass the entrance for Oracle State Park, and then proceed to the trailhead as above.

Oracle State Park

11

Windmill wandering

An ancient grinding hole with a view: this mortar would have been used with a pestle, or pounding rock, for processing grains.

DISTANCE & CONFIGURATION: 8.8-mile out-and-back

HIKING TIME: 4–6 hours

ACCUMULATED ELEVATION GAIN: 1,100'

SHORT HIKE OPTION: 4.0-mile out-and-back to Oracle State Park boundary (310' elevation gain)

OUTSTANDING FEATURES: 360-degree Sky Island views, Oracle State Park, windmill and picnic area

LAND-MANAGEMENT AGENCIES: Coronado National Forest, Santa Catalina Ranger District, 520-749-8700, fs.usda.gov/coronado; Oracle State Park, 520-896-2425, azstateparks.com/oracle

MAPS: USGS 7.5' *Campo Bonito, AZ*

AZT PASSAGE: 13/Oracle, aztrail.org/explore/passages/passage-13-oracle

ANCESTRAL LANDS: Apache

SEASON: Winter, spring, fall

ACCESS: This hike visits Oracle State Park, which charges an admission fee ($7/vehicle, $3/pedestrian or bicyclist) at the main entrance. No fee is necessary to enter the park from the American Flag AZT trailhead, from which this hike starts.

Overview

This hike on the Arizona National Scenic Trail (AZT) weaves in and out of drainages on its way to Oracle State Park—the only state park on the AZT and a designated International Dark Sky Park—and a windmill with picnic benches. The ridgetops afford 360-degree views of the surrounding Sky Island mountain ranges.

On the Trail

From the parking area, pass through the signed gate reading THE ARIZONA TRAIL (4,408'). Another ARIZONA TRAIL sign across the way has a smaller sign reading SANTA CATALINA MOUNTAINS SEGMENT, DEDICATED MAY 20, 1989; this marks the beginning of the previous hike, American Flag Ranch Trailhead to Oracle Ridge. Carefully continue east, cross the fence line, and curve left (north) in 100 feet. The trail curves right (east) past a pile of boulders and goes northeast through a fence line at 500 feet. The trail then descends with views of the Galiuro Mountains and American Flag Hill to your left (west). In 0.2 mile, Mount Lemmon Highway is visible, and the trail turns right (east).

Carefully continue east across Mount Lemmon Highway on the AZT. The trail curves left (northeast) and climbs a small hill in 0.2 mile. Views spread in every direction, combined with the boulder formations that Oracle is known for. To the north are the Pinal Mountains, in the distance to the east are the Galiuros, to the south are Apache and Rice Peaks, and to the southeast are the Santa Catalina and Rincon Mountains. Plant life includes yucca, mesquite, and prickly pear and barrel cactus.

In 0.2 mile the trail makes a curve to the left (northwest) and passes some rock pinnacles. Go through a fence line with a gate and a rollover bicycle ramp in 0.1 mile. Flip a small lever to use the gate.

The tread on this part of the trail consists of gravel and dirt. Descend and, in 0.2 mile, cross a doubletrack dirt road to the northwest. The trail curves right (north) and crosses a small wash in 0.3 mile, then gradually climbs and crosses another small, sandy wash in 0.2 mile. Look for boulders on both sides of the trail in 0.2 mile; to the right (east), at the base of the mesquite tree, is an ancient grinding hole, or metate. The Apache who lived in this area before colonization used it to grind mesquite beans (seed pods) and corn.

The trail meanders in the desert, reaching the Webb Road AZT Super Gate in 0.2 mile; close the gate behind you, and cross the road to the north.

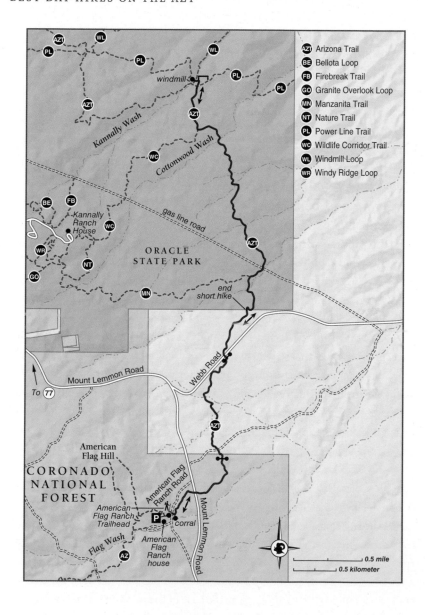

The trail makes a couple of curves and resumes a northeast track. In 0.4 mile (2.0 total miles), the AZT joins a doubletrack road. Turn left (north) toward the AZT Super Gate that marks the Oracle State Park boundary, and sign in at the register. **This is the end of the short hike, at 2.0 miles and 310 feet of elevation gain.**

Spotlight: Oracle State Park

This 4,000-acre state park in the foothills of the Santa Catalina Mountains is an International Dark Sky Park, a designation awarded to public and private parklands that are exceptionally conducive to stargazing due to their lack of light pollution. The park holds special Star Night Parties in partnership with local astronomers and science centers; go to azstateparks.com/oracle and click "Dark Skies" for more information.

Before or after your hike, drive into the park and take a self-guided tour of the **Kannally Ranch House.** Listed in the National Register of Historic Places, this Mediterranean Revival–style house was built from 1929 to 1932 by the Kannally family and displays original artwork, historical photos, and more. Oracle State Park's visitor center and gift shop are also located here.

The park and ranch house have several picnic areas, along with two group day-use areas available by reservation. Hikers can choose from 15 miles of trails in an oak-woodland environment.

The park is open October–May, daily, 8 a.m.–5 p.m., and May-October, daily, 7 a.m.–4 p.m., with an admission fee of $7/vehicle, $3/pedestrian or bicyclist at the main entrance. The American Avenue trailhead access is always open (with no fee) to accommodate hikers and stargazers.

The AZT curves right (northeast) after the gate, then heads north. In 0.2 mile curve left (west) and descend to cross two small washes. Reach a junction with the Manzanita Trail in 0.2 mile, and turn right (northeast). Cross a gas line road in 0.1 mile; the AZT climbs and curves left (northwest), reaching the top of the climb in 0.3 mile at a small saddle with a juniper tree and 360-degree views. Descend to another wash crossing in 0.1 mile; the trail climbs steeply out the other side and then descends and turns right (north) in 0.1 mile.

Enter a sandy drainage in 0.2 mile. The AZT joins the wash for 100 feet, then exits out the right (north) side, marked with a wooden post. The trail

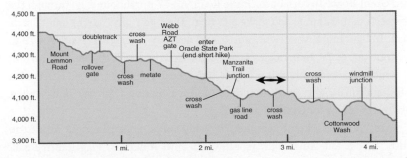

climbs and curves right (northeast), then descends to cross a drainage in 0.1 mile. It climbs out to the north and makes a left (northwest) and then a right (north). In 0.2 mile the trail switchbacks uphill to a ridgetop before descending northeast to cross a wash. Reach a junction with Cottonwood Wash and a gas line road in 0.2 mile. The AZT climbs out to the northwest and curves left (west). Reach the top of the climb in 0.3 mile.

The trail descends southwest to the Wildlife Corridor Trail junction and then turns right (north) at a sign noting that a windmill is 0.3 mile away. Descend to the northwest; in 0.2 mile the AZT curves right (northeast), and you can see the windmill in the valley below. Switchback left (west) for a final descent into the canyon and the low point of the hike (3,967'). There is a bench to the right (north). Cross the wash directly ahead to the right of the sign that reads WINDMILL LOOP.

There are two picnic tables to the left (south), and the windmill is to the right (north). This is a wonderful place for a break and a snack, but there is no shade. Possible shady areas can be found back in the wash.

Return the way you came. For information about American Flag Ranch at the trailhead, see the previous hike.

Gateway Community: ORACLE *(see page 104)*

DISTANCE FROM TRAILHEAD: 4.0 miles **POPULATION:** 20,837 **ELEVATION:** 4,524'

Getting There

AMERICAN FLAG RANCH TRAILHEAD: N32° 34.851' W110° 43.225', elevation 4,408'

ROAD CONDITIONS: All vehicles; graded dirt for 0.4 mile

FACILITIES: None

DIRECTIONS *From Tucson:* Take I-10 East or West to Exit 256, and turn east onto Grant Road. To turn onto Oracle Road/AZ 77 northbound, go through the intersection in 1.0 mile and make a U-turn, then go right (north) onto Oracle Road. In 22.0 miles, veer right (northeast) at the Y-intersection with AZ 79 to continue on AZ 77. In 9.1 miles take a right (southeast) at the western turnoff for Oracle, marked with visitor center signs, onto American Avenue. Drive 2.4 miles, and turn right (southeast) onto Mount Lemmon Highway. In 3.5 miles, pass the entrance for Oracle State Park.

In 2.0 miles Mount Lemmon Highway splits—take the right fork to go south. In 0.6 mile turn right (southwest) onto American Flag Ranch Road, marked by a small, square AZT sign. This graded dirt spur road will take you 0.4 mile to trailhead parking on both sides just north of American Flag Ranch. This hike starts from the trail on your left (east) as you drive in; the previous hike starts from the trailhead across the road with the large metal AZT map.

From Phoenix Sky Harbor Airport: Follow the signs for AZ 202 East, and take it 3.6 miles to AZ 101 Loop South. In 3.1 miles take Exit 55 A/B onto US 60 East; drive 36.0 miles, and take Exit 212 onto AZ 79 South. Drive 58.0 miles, and then veer left (northeast) at the Y-intersection onto AZ 77. In 9.1 miles take a right (southeast) at the western turnoff for Oracle, marked with visitor center signs, onto American Avenue. Drive 2.4 miles, and turn right (southeast) onto Mount Lemmon Highway. In 3.5 miles pass the entrance for Oracle State Park, and then proceed to the trailhead as above.

A double rainbow arches over an AZT Super Gate. These distinctive gates are designed by Tucson artist Rob Bauer.

Central (Hikes 12–19)

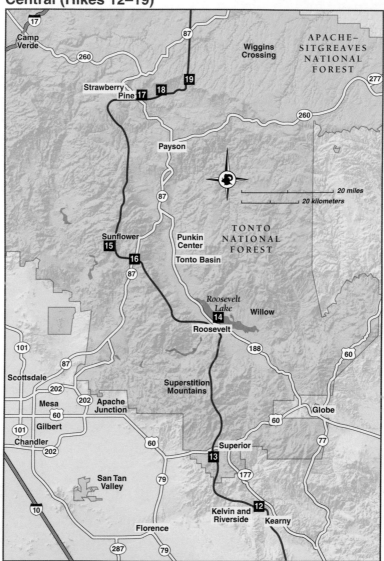

Gateway Communities are highlighted in yellow.

CENTRAL

Fall colors brighten Sycamore Canyon (see Hike 16, page 145). Photo: Patrick Fuchs

12

Gila River Canyons

Splendid Sonoran Desert river

SCENERY: ★★★★
TRAIL CONDITION: ★★★
CHILDREN: ★★★
DIFFICULTY: ★★
SOLITUDE: ★★★

Wildflowers and fall colors at the same time in December

DISTANCE & CONFIGURATION: 6.2-mile out-and-back

HIKING TIME: 2–4 hours

ACCUMULATED ELEVATION GAIN: 910'

SHORT HIKE OPTION: 4.6-mile out-and-back to completion marker/580' elevation gain

OUTSTANDING FEATURES: Gila River, riparian streamside habitat, AZT completion marker

LAND-MANAGEMENT AGENCY: Bureau of Land Management, Gila District, Tucson Field Office, 520-258-7200, blm.gov/office/tucson-field-office

MAPS: USGS 7.5' *Kearny* and *Grayback, AZ*

AZT PASSAGE: 16/Gila River Canyons, aztrail.org/explore/passages/passage-16 -gila-river-canyons

ANCESTRAL LANDS: Akimel O'odham, Apache

SEASONS: Winter, spring, fall

ACCESS: No fees or permits; open 24-7, year-round

Overview

This passage of the Arizona National Scenic Trail (AZT) was the final section to be built, completely connecting the trail from Mexico to Utah, in 2011 and marked by a "Golden Spike." It's a great spot for both spring wildflowers, which peak in February or March, and fall colors, which often don't reveal themselves until December due to the low elevation. This day hike showcases the riparian environment of the Gila River with gorgeous Sonoran Desert vegetation, including two rare crested saguaros.

On the Trail

From the parking lot, turn left (west) at the first intersection toward a gate with an AZT emblem on it. The trail heads west on a closed roadbed, paralleling the Gila River. Railroad tracks belonging to the Copper Basin Railway come into view.

In 0.3 mile the AZT turns right (north) and away from the railroad tracks between some boulders and past a trail register. The trail then curves right (northeast); climbs next to a wash; and, in 0.2 mile, turns west and continues to climb. Cross the wash that you've been following and turn left (south). Shortly afterward, the Gila River comes into view once again.

The trail curves to the right (north), climbs along the ridge, and then contours and climbs on the side of the ridge. The open-pit Ray Mine is visible to the northeast. This area has had mining claims for copper, silver, gold, lead, and zinc since the 1870s.

Switchback at 1.0 mile and the trail resumes heading northwest. Cross a couple of small side canyons; then, in 0.5 mile, turn west and descend to cross another side canyon. Continue climbing and the trail turns briefly to the east in 0.3 mile.

Now 225 feet above the river where you started, you get a great view. Fall colors at this low elevation often don't occur until mid-December and into early January. The cottonwoods in the river corridor turn it into a swath of gold. In 0.1 mile the trail makes a turn to the right (west), paralleling the river while high above it.

The trail reaches a high point in 0.3 mile (2,106') and starts a series of switchbacks down the hill. Just as you start to descend, the completion marker of the AZT, aka the "Golden Spike," is close to the ground to your right in a pile of rocks and easy to miss. A round, gray concrete survey marker rather than an

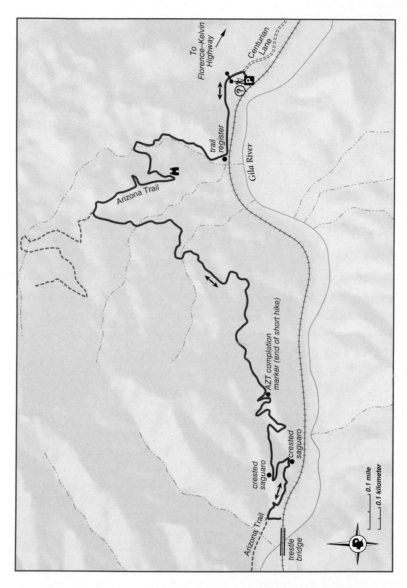

actual golden spike, it's marked with the letters DS in honor of Dale Shewalter, the "Father of the Arizona Trail" (see "One Man's Vision: How the AZT Came to Be," page 1).

The trail was connected from Mexico to Utah at this very spot, and the marker was placed in a ceremony on December 16, 2011. I was part of the crew that built the ceremonial last stretch of trail, and it was an incredibly special day. Dale passed away after a battle with cancer in 2010, but his memory will always live on in the form of this trail that brings joy to so many. Thanks, Dale, for such a wonderful vision!

From the completion marker, you have fantastic views of the S-curve of the Gila River and the trestle bridge across it; the rugged, saguaro-studded slopes; and A-Diamond Ranch in the distance, with a backdrop of the Tortilla Mountains. **This is the turnaround for the short hike option, at 4.6 miles round-trip and 580 feet of elevation gain.** If you decide to continue to the trestle bridge, be aware that it's a 350-foot drop in elevation that you'll need to make up on your way back.

The trail begins a series of switchbacks, every one of them bringing you closer to the river. The path is steep and gravelly in short stretches. In 0.7 mile pass a rocky outcropping; then the trail curves into a small side canyon and crosses it.

In 0.2 mile start looking for the first of two crested saguaros on the hill to your right (north). The best angle is just as the bridge comes back into view at 2 o'clock—if you reach the switchback, you've gone too far for the good view of the crest, but you can see the back of it looking north up the hill. Crested, or cristate, saguaros are very rare and something of a botanical mystery (see page 75). Scientists don't know for certain what causes the fanlike growths at the plant's main stem and/or arms.

In 0.2 mile, just after the trail switchbacks to follow the river toward the bridge again, the second crested saguaro comes into view to the left (south), just as the trail makes a curve to the right (west); the crest has five small arms. In 0.1 mile start the final descent, with a view of the railroad tracks, cottonwoods, and more saguaros. The trail then follows a fence line at the bottom of the descent.

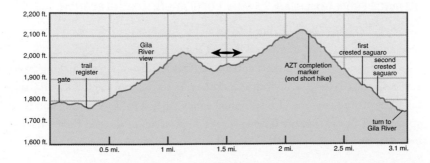

119

In 0.1 mile turn off to the left (south) to visit the trestle bridge. The eco-system in this area is called a mesquite bosque, or woodland, and is typical of the flats near streams and rivers. These bosques provide a habitat for many birds, mammals, reptiles, and insects. The mesquite trees here are in the same family as the mesquites whose wood is used for grilling food. If you reach a metal AZT gate, you've gone too far.

Take a left (south) on a well-worn path and go less than 0.1 mile to a view of the railroad tracks and the bridge. Please respect private property and DO NOT TRESPASS signs, and keep a safe distance—**do not ascend to the railroad tracks.** The river can also be accessed at this point underneath the bridge. (The flow in the Gila River varies based on how much water is let out of Coolidge Dam at San Carlos Lake on the San Carlos Apache Reservation. The water even gets "shut off" at certain times of the year—this doesn't dry up the river completely, but it does decrease its flow considerably.) This is the low point of the hike, at 1,740 feet.

> **BONUS WILDFLOWER WALK** Continue on the Florence–Kelvin Highway to the Florence–Kelvin Trailhead, a dirt pull-off 1.5 miles south and west of this hike on the left (south) side of the road. (Google Maps labels this as "Arizona Trail Kelvin Parking." **GPS:** N33° 05.341' W110° 59.412'.) The flowers are usually best in the first 0.5 mile southbound past the big metal AZT sign and along the slopes of the hills on the trail northbound across the highway. Hike out-and-back as far as you like, but please stay on the trails to avoid damaging the wildflowers.

Go back to the junction and turn right (east) to go back the way you came, for a total distance of 6.2 miles round-trip and 910 feet of elevation gain. If you missed the completion marker on your way out, you can find it again on the left side of the trail, just before you reach the hike's high point.

Gateway Community: KEARNY

DISTANCE FROM TRAILHEAD: 7.5 miles **POPULATION:** 2,095 **ELEVATION:** 1,680'

Kearny calls itself "The Friendliest Town on the Arizona Trail" for good reason—it prides itself on going above and beyond to take care of trail users.

Gary and Lorraine Birkett at **Old Time Pizza** are legendary for making trail-side deliveries to the Kelvin bridge; visit them in town after your hike, and Gary might even sing you one of his original songs. They have beer on tap and two special AZT pizzas. **Buzzy's Drive-In** serves diner-style meals, and **Norm's Hometown Grocery** has daily specials at the deli.

A rare cristate saguaro near the trestle bridge

Lodging is available at the **General Kearny Inn,** which also has a full bar, as well as the **free campground** at **Kearny Lake City Park,** which has shaded picnic benches and grills; a toilet is on-site, but there are no RV hookups.

OLD TIME PIZZA: 370 Alden Rd., 520-363-5523, facebook.com/oldtimepizza. Open daily, 11 a.m.–9 p.m.

BUZZY'S DRIVE-IN: 111 Tilbury Dr., 520-363-7371, tinyurl.com/buzzysdriveinkearny. Open Monday–Saturday, 10 a.m.–8 p.m.

NORM'S HOMETOWN GROCERY IGA: 345 Alden Rd., 520-363-5595, norms.igaarizona .com. Open Monday–Saturday, 7 a.m.–8 p.m.; Sunday, 8 a.m.–7 p.m.

GENERAL KEARNY INN: 301 Alden Rd., 520-363-5505, generalkearnyinn.com. Lounge open Monday–Thursday, 10 a.m.–10 p.m., Friday and Saturday, 10 a.m.–11 p.m. (call ahead to confirm hours).

KEARNY LAKE CAMPGROUND: Kearny Lake City Park, 520-363-5547, townofkearny .com/attractions.html. From AZ 177, take Hartford Road west 0.4 mile to Wanda Dalton Road; then turn right (north) at the brown campground sign. Just ahead, after a saguaro cactus on your left, make a left into the campground.

Getting There

CENTURIAN TRAILHEAD: N33° 06.393' W110° 58.752', elevation 1,783'

ROAD CONDITIONS: All vehicles; graded dirt road for 0.5 mile

FACILITIES: None

DIRECTIONS *From Phoenix Sky Harbor Airport:* From East Sky Harbor Boulevard, take AZ 143 South to I-10 and Exit 1A for AZ 60 East. Go 54.0 miles to the town of Superior, and turn right (south) onto AZ 177 on the east end of town. In 16.0 miles, turn right (southwest) onto the Florence–Kelvin Highway just north of the railroad tracks, just after the green sign for Kelvin and Riverside. In 1.1 miles, reach an unsigned road—labeled on online maps as Centurian Lane—branching to the right (southwest) past a maintenance yard, just before the Florence–Kelvin Highway crosses the Gila River on the Jake Jacobson Bridge of Unity, which opened in 2018 (see box below).

In about 0.1 mile, turn right just past a group of mailboxes, and the road curves to the right (north). In 1.3 miles, past a DEAD END sign, the road turns to graded dirt. Curve to the left (south) to cross Mineral Creek, and the road climbs away from the river. In 1.5 miles, pass some houses; then, just before the road ascends and curves to the right (north), look for a dirt road to the left (west) marked by a brown AZT carsonite sign: this is the continuation of Centurian Lane. Follow Centurian 0.2 mile to the trailhead driveway; then turn left (west) into the trailhead parking lot.

> **THE JAKE JACOBSON BRIDGE OF UNITY** in Kelvin/Riverside honors Stephani Yesenski, a resident of the town of Riverside who passed away in 1999 at age 20 after the community rallied to help her get treatment for cancer. L. S. "Jake" Jacobson, the president and CEO of the Copper Basin Railway, pledged to build a new two-lane bridge over the Gila River in her memory; the old one-lane bridge remains as the pedestrian crossing of the AZT over the river.

From Tucson (Congress Street and I-10): Take I-10 West to Exit 256, and turn right (east) onto Grant Road. To turn onto Oracle Road/AZ 77 northbound, go through the intersection in 1.0 mile and make a U-turn, then go right (north) onto Oracle Road. In 22.0 miles, veer right (northeast) at the Y-intersection to continue on AZ 77. Drive 46.0 miles to Winkleman; then, at another Y-intersection, turn left (northwest) onto AZ 177. Go north for 16.0 miles; then turn left (southwest) onto the Florence–Kelvin Highway just north of the railroad tracks, just after the green sign for Kelvin and Riverside, and proceed to the trailhead as directed above.

Picketpost

Mountain vistas and sweet Sonoran Desert

13

SCENERY: ★ ★ ★ ★ ★
TRAIL CONDITION: ★ ★ ★ ★
CHILDREN ★ ★ ★ ★ ★
(short hike)
DIFFICULTY: ★ ★
SOLITUDE: ★ ★

Dark skies at the Picketpost Trailhead make for a great star show.

DISTANCE & CONFIGURATION: 7.2-mile out-and-back

HIKING TIME: 3–4 hours

ACCUMULATED ELEVATION GAIN: 900'

SHORT HIKE OPTION: 3.6-mile out-and-back to rest stop and overlook/400' elevation gain. But any length of time you spend going out and back will have spectacular views.

OUTSTANDING FEATURES: Views of Picketpost and the Superstition Mountains; saguaro cactus

LAND-MANAGEMENT AGENCY: Tonto National Forest, Globe Ranger District, 928-402-6200, fs.usda.gov/tonto

MAPS: USGS 7.5' *Picketpost, AZ*

AZT PASSAGE: 17/Alamo Canyon, aztrail.org/explore/passages/passage-17-alamo-canyon

ANCESTRAL LANDS: Apache, Akimel O'odham

SEASON: Winter, spring, fall

ACCESS: No fees or permits; open 24-7, year-round

123

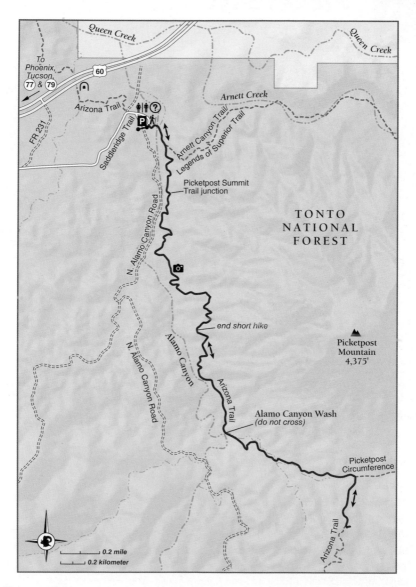

Overview

This passage of the Arizona National Scenic Trail (AZT) is great for all skill levels and is located just an hour's drive east of Phoenix. The AZT goes through classic Sonoran Desert: towering saguaro cacti, rugged mountain views, and the possibility of seeing a spectacular sunset. The trail has a gentle uphill grade, weaving in and out of the drainages that descend from Picketpost Mountain.

Note: This passage of the AZT is very popular with hikers, mountain bikers, and equestrians, so please observe proper trail etiquette. Horses have the right-of-way—if you see horses on the trail, pull off to the side of the trail and greet the rider so the horse understands that you're a human and not a predator. Mountain bikers yield to both hikers and horses. For more on trail etiquette, see "Sharing the Trail," page 16.

On the Trail

A metal AZT sign with a map greets you at the Picketpost Trailhead (2,392')—sign in at the register. From the trailhead, the AZT proceeds southwest and, in 150 feet, curves and reaches a cairn and a wash (seasonal creek) crossing signed DO NOT ENTER WHEN FLOODED. Descend and cross the wash heading west; then curve to the right (southeast) and cross two more washes before exiting the other side.

The trail curves right (south) and ascends past lichen-coated rock formations. At 0.2 mile reach a junction with Arnett Canyon Trail coming in from the left (east). The Arnett Canyon Trail is part of the Legends of Superior Trails (LOST) and is the first trail built to connect a Gateway Community to the AZT. The trail crosses two small canyons with Alamo Wash to your right (west).

Picketpost Mountain (4,375'), an eroded volcanic vent topped with lava flows, is approximately 18 million years old. Much of the exposed rock is consolidated ash, or volcanic tuff, but there is also schist, rhyolite, conglomerates, and you might also see some quartz. The Superstition Mountains are visible to the north, and Weavers Needle is the spire to the left (west). Picketpost got its

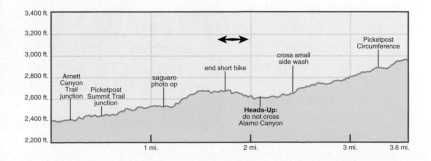

name from a historic Army outpost and a heliograph station on the peak that used mirrors to send messages.

Cross another small wash, and the trail climbs to a signed intersection at 0.5 mile for the Picketpost Summit Trail, a wide trail coming from the left (east). The Summit Trail is poorly marked, requires scrambling (pulling yourself up by your hands), and is a much tougher challenge than the AZT hike—I don't recommend it unless you've done your research. The AZT continues south and climbs at a gentle grade. In 0.3 mile, the trail curves into a larger side canyon with great views. Descend to cross the canyon and climb out the other side.

At 1.0 mile the trail goes into another side canyon, which is more open and flat than previous ones. The trail meanders south and goes through some boul-

ders. Make a turn to the left (east) in 0.2 mile, and you will find a perfect saguaro with boulders to frame it with Picketpost behind it; this would make a great photo opportunity. Curve right past a large yellow boulder to cross another drainage and then a ridge. Continue climbing and, in 0.3 mile, the AZT turns right to trend south.

At 1.8 miles you'll find a nice spot with some rocks to sit on and an excellent view of the Superstition Mountains to the north and Picketpost to the east (2,647'). **This is the turnaround for the short hike, at 3.6 miles round-trip and 400 feet of elevation gain.**

From the rest spot with the sitting rocks, the trail curves to cross several small drainages and then, in 0.4 mile, descends to briefly parallel Alamo Canyon on the left (east) side, then leaves the wash and ascends. The terrain opens a

An equestrian and her dog ride beneath a saguaro photo spot.

bit, crosses a ravine, and stays above the small tributary to your right (west). In 0.2 mile cross another ravine.

Heads-Up: At 2.5 miles reach Alamo Canyon wash again. **Do not cross this wash straight ahead**—instead, the crossing is to your left (north), across the small tributary coming in from the left that feeds into Alamo Canyon.

In 0.2 mile turn left (north) to cross the head of the ravine and climb; then curve right (east) at the nose of the ridge. The trail contours above the right side of the canyon to the east. The trail dips to cross a brown, sandy wash and then switchbacks to the left (north) to climb out, now trending west.

At mile 3.0, cross another wash, then join it briefly and exit the right (south) side again; then cross the wash to the left (north) side. The trail climbs and switchbacks in 0.1 mile before crossing a couple of drainages. The trail is once again out in the open and crosses a ravine in 0.25 mile. It parallels the drainage and then crosses it in 0.2 mile.

Heads-Up: The trail climbs and, at a curve to the right (south) in 0.2 mile, you reach a junction for a hiking and equestrian route that goes into Telegraph Canyon and around Picketpost to your left (east). That hike is beyond the scope of this book; see hikearizona.com for more details on the Picketpost Circumference. The AZT curves to the right (south) at the switchback. Shortly afterward you'll see a brown carsonite sign confirming that you're on the AZT.

The trail goes through several clearings, then climbs toward a small saddle. The cliffs of the Apache Leap are visible to the left (east). The legend of Apache Leap says that during a battle with the American cavalry, the Apache people were trapped between the troops and a large escarpment of cliffs. The remaining Apache chose to leap to their deaths off the cliffs rather than surrender to the troops. The small, black, marblelike obsidian pebbles found in the area are known as Apache tears.

Switchback to the right (west) and arrive at the aforementioned saddle, which has a steep hill to the right and a small hill to the left. A stately saguaro looks into a wide valley with a large rounded hill to the left, a rocky-topped hill in the middle, and a rounded peak to your right across the valley.

Go left (east) and pick your way through the cactus to climb the small hill to the east for the best view. There is abundant quartz on top of the hill as well; unfortunately, there isn't much in the way of rocks to sit on.

This is the end of the hike, at 3.6 miles and 2,942 feet of elevation. Return the way you came to the Picketpost Trailhead.

Gateway Community: SUPERIOR

DISTANCE FROM TRAILHEAD: 6.0 miles **POPULATION:** 2,895 **ELEVATION:** 2,888'

Superior was the first Gateway Community to build a connector trail from the AZT. The **Legends of Superior Trail (LOST)** goes east through Arnett Canyon 0.3 mile south of the Picketpost Trailhead; it connects all the way through town from Passage 17 through the airport to the east side of Superior and continues to the old US 60 tunnel.

Main Street has charming shops and galleries and a perfect photo op at the WELCOME TO SUPERIOR mural. The newly renovated **Hotel Magma** (built in 1912) has **The Ladle Restaurant,** which serves breakfast daily. **The Superior Barmacy** uses a renovated historical theater and old pharmacy building to administer food and drink and live music. Enjoy a burger and a beverage on the patio at **Porter's Cafe and Spirits,** Asian fusion at **Jade Grill,** or Mexican favorites at **Los Hermanos** (*pro tip:* pick up a burrito to go for your hike). Stop in at **Felicia's Ice Cream Shop** for a cone or shake. The **Buckboard City Cafe & Saloon** on US 60 is also home to the World's Smallest Museum. The **Boyce Thompson Arboretum,** a world-class facility founded in the 1920s, highlights the fascinating plants of the world's deserts.

Hikers have several options for camping in the area. **Box 8 Ranch** is on the west end of town, and the free **Oak Flat Campground,** with world-class climbing and bouldering nearby, is a short distance east on US 60; dispersed (primitive) camping is also available along dirt roads on Tonto National Forest land. **Note:** Camping is not allowed at the Picketpost Trailhead.

LEGENDS OF SUPERIOR TRAILS: superioraztrails.com

FELICIA'S ICE CREAM SHOP: 329 Main St., 520-689-1940. Open Monday–Saturday, noon–6 p.m.

HOTEL MAGMA/THE LADLE RESTAURANT: 100 W. Main St., 520-689-2300, hotelmagma superior.com (call for restaurant hours)

THE SUPERIOR BARMACY: 101 W. Main St., 480-636-6965, tinyurl.com/thesuperior barmacy. Open Tuesday–Saturday, 11:30 a.m.–8 p.m.; Sunday, 11:30 a.m.–4 p.m.

PORTER'S CAFE AND SPIRITS: 695 Main St., 520-689-5003, facebook.com/portersaz. Open Monday–Wednesday, 11 a.m.–8 p.m.; Thursday, 11 a.m.–10 p.m.; Friday and Saturday, 8 a.m.–10 p.m.; Sunday, 8 a.m.–9 p.m.

JADE GRILL: 639 W. AZ 60, 520-689-2885, facebook.com/jadegrillaz. Open Wednesday–Sunday, 11:30 a.m.–2:30 p.m. (lunch), 5–7:30 p.m. (dinner).

LOS HERMANOS: 835 W. AZ 60, 520-689-5465, tinyurl.com/loshermanossuperior. Open daily, 5:30 a.m.–9:30 p.m.

BUCKBOARD CITY CAFÉ & SALOON/WORLD'S SMALLEST MUSEUM: 1107 W. US 60, 520-689-5800, buckboardcitycafe.com. Open Wednesday–Friday, 7 a.m.–2 p.m.; Saturday and Sunday, 7 a.m.–3 p.m.

BOYCE THOMPSON ARBORETUM: 37615 AZ 60, 520-689-2811, btarboretum.org. Admission: $15 adults, $5 ages 5–12. *October–April:* Open 8 a.m.–5 p.m. *May–September:* Open 6 a.m.–3 p.m. *June–September:* Open Wednesday–Monday only; hours are daily the rest of the year.

BOX 8 RANCH: 226 S. Smith Dr., 602-625-6567, box8ranch.com

OAK FLAT CAMPGROUND: East Oak Flats Road, 4.0 miles east of Superior on US 60; 928-402-6200, tinyurl.com/oakflatcampground. Picnic tables, fire pits, and toilets but no water.

WELCOME TO SUPERIOR MURAL: Historic Main Street at Lobb Avenue

Getting There

PICKETPOST TRAILHEAD: N33° 16.317' W111° 10.577', elevation 2,392'

ROAD CONDITIONS: All vehicles; graded dirt for 1.1 miles

FACILITIES: Toilets, no water

DIRECTIONS *From Phoenix Sky Harbor Airport:* From East Sky Harbor Boulevard, take AZ 143 South to I-10 and Exit 1A for US 60 East. In 53.8 miles, or 9.4 miles past a junction with AZ 79 to the south, turn right (south) onto Forest Service Road 231. (At the time of this writing, there is a PICKETPOST TRAILHEAD/ARIZONA NATIONAL SCENIC TRAIL sign just before the turn.) Take this graded dirt road 0.4 mile to a T-intersection, turn left (east), and go 0.7 mile; then turn right and drive 0.1 mile to the trailhead.

From Tucson (Congress Street and I-10): Take I-10 West to Exit 256, and turn right (east) onto Grant Road. To turn onto Oracle Road/AZ 77 northbound, go through the intersection in 1.0 mile and make a U-turn, then go right (north) onto Oracle Road. In 22.0 miles, veer left (northwest) at the Y-intersection onto AZ 79 toward the Gateway Community of Florence. In 58.0 miles, take the exit for US 60 East toward Globe. In 9.4 miles, turn right (south) onto FR 231, and proceed to the trailhead as directed above.

14 Vineyard Trailhead to Mills Ridge *Steep trail, spectacular views*

SCENERY: ★★★★★
TRAIL CONDITION: ★★
CHILDREN: ★
DIFFICULTY: ★★★★
(point-to-point)/
★★★★★ *(out-and-back)*
SOLITUDE: ★★★

Theodore Roosevelt Lake and Bridge

DISTANCE & CONFIGURATION: 6.25-mile point-to point, 12.5-mile out-and-back

HIKING TIME: 4–6 hours point-to-point, 7–9 hours out-and back

ACCUMULATED ELEVATION GAIN: 2,188' ascent/740' descent (reverse if hiking downhill) point-to-point, 2,930' out-and-back

SHORT HIKE OPTION: 1.4-mile out-and-back to lake overlook/530' elevation gain

OUTSTANDING FEATURES: Views of Theodore Roosevelt Lake, Bridge, and Dam; Apache; Four Peaks

LAND-MANAGEMENT AGENCY: Tonto National Forest, Tonto Basin Ranger District, 602-225-5395, fs.usda.gov/tonto

MAPS: USGS 7.5' *Theodore Roosevelt Dam, AZ*

AZT PASSAGE: 20/Four Peaks, aztrail.org/explore/passages/passage-20-four-peaks

ANCESTRAL LANDS: Yavapai–Apache, Western Apache

SEASON: Winter, spring, fall

ACCESS: No fees or permits; open 24-7, year-round

Advisory

National forests sometimes close due to fire danger, so check before you go. The Vineyard Trailhead is scheduled to open March 1, 2021, after the 193,455-acre Bush Fire, which started in June 2020 by a vehicle fire on the roadside. Go to the passage page at aztrail.org/explore/passages/passage-20-four-peaks for updates.

Overview

This hike on the Arizona National Scenic Trail (AZT) has incredible views of Theodore Roosevelt Lake and Bridge, Apache Lake, and the Four Peaks, Sierra Ancha, and Mazatzal ranges. It can be done point-to-point, in an uphill or downhill direction, if you have two vehicles for a shuttle, or out-and-back if you don't. Portions of this hike are steep, loose, and rocky; hiking poles and caution are recommended.

On the Trail

Theodore Roosevelt Dam was completed on the Salt River in 1911, and the reservoir it created is Arizona's largest lake lying completely within its borders. The dam is 357 feet tall; the bridge across the lake, constructed in 1990, stretches 1,080 feet and ranks as the longest two-lane, single-span, steel-arch bridge in North America. The construction of the dam and subsequent filling of Roosevelt

Spotlight: Salado Culture and Tonto National Monument

Just 3.9 miles south of the Vineyard Trailhead, Tonto National Monument tells the story of the Indigenous Salado culture that occupied the basin from 1250 to 1450 CE. The name *Salado* comes from the Spanish word for "salty," a reference to the Salt River. According to the national monument's website, "*Salado* describes the prehistoric cultural group living in the Tonto Basin between 1250 CE and 1450 CE, but also encompasses a particular group of artifacts, architectural styles, and a belief system exemplified by Salado symbols and images (iconography)."

Tonto National Monument preserves two cliff dwellings. The trail to the Upper Cliff Dwelling (3 miles out-and-back, 600' elevation gain) requires a reservation for a free guided tour (November–April only; call 928-467-2241 to reserve). The Lower Cliff Dwelling, open year-round, is reached on a paved, self-guided, 1.0-mile out-and-back hike with 400 feet of elevation gain. A museum displays colorful polychrome pottery, textiles, and other artifacts from the Salado culture.

Admission to the park costs $10 per person; the visitor center is open daily, 8 a.m.–5 p.m., except December 25. Visitors must start the self-guided hike to the Lower Cliff Dwelling by noon June–August or by 4 p.m. the rest of the year.

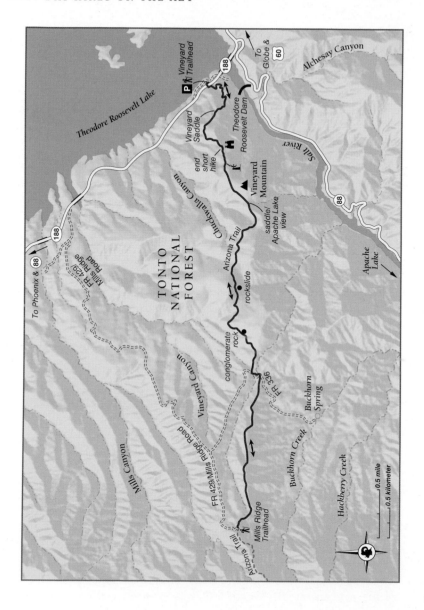

Lake inundated many archaeological sites of the cultures who inhabited the area, though cliff dwellings such as those found at Tonto National Monument remain. The area was inhabited by the Yavapai and Western Apache tribes before colonization of their lands.

The hike described here heads uphill and east–west from the Vineyard Trailhead to the Mills Ridge Trailhead. There is a metal AZT sign in the parking area (2,192') with the bridge behind it—a perfect photo opportunity. Walk 70 feet to the end of the guard rail, turn left (west) to carefully cross AZ 188 and turn left (south) immediately. The trail is between the guard rail and the hill. Pass a sign that says JUNCTION ARIZONA 88—½ MILE. Then, 300 feet from the trailhead, reach a sign that says VINEYARD TRAIL #131 and make a right (southwest).

The tread is rocky, and parts are covered in small gravel. The AZT climbs, crosses a small ravine, and curves left (east). Dutchwoman Butte is the prominent sloped peak across the lake. The trail levels, and a small spur to the left (north) has an interpretive sign for O'Rourke's Camp. Go back to the trail and take a left (south) to continue. You have a great view of the bridge as the trail ascends. The AZT switchbacks up the hill and goes through a saddle in 0.5 mile.

In wildflower season, you might see pink and white fairy dusters, yellow brittlebush, orange Mexican poppies, white mariposa lilies, fuchsia blooming hedgehog cactus, and purple scorpionweed and lupine. Small *Dudleya* agaves send up colorful orange, red, and yellow stalks.

A short spur trail curves to the right along the base of a cluster of rocks to reach a nice sitting area with fantastic views of the lake and the bridge. **This is the turnaround point for the short hike option, at 1.4 miles round-trip and 530 feet of elevation gain.**

The trail continues ascending to the west after a brief level section, and the views of the lake just keep getting better and better. In 0.2 mile the trail curves to the left (northwest), and views open toward the Mazatzal (MAH-zat-zal or Madda-ZELL) Mountains beyond the lake. Spiky jatropha trees appear, along with serrated-leaved sotol. Ocotillo looks like a spiky bundle of sticks and may or may not bear small leaves depending on how recently it has rained.

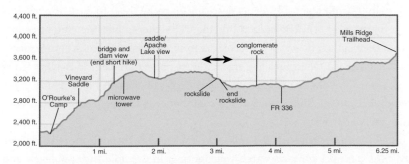

133

In 0.1 mile the AZT turns left (west), descends briefly, and then resumes climbing. Notice the big grayish-green blobs on the rocks and soil to your left (east)—this is called cryptobiotic crust, and it's a very important part of the environment in the desert. It helps stabilize the soil and takes many thousands of years to generate, so take care when stepping off the trail to let people pass, take photos, or go to the restroom. (See "Desert Hiking Tips and Tricks," page 28, for more information.)

The climb curves south and steepens as it heads for the ridgetop ahead. The good news is that there are great views to look at while you stop to catch your breath. In 0.2 mile go through a small saddle, and go another 0.1 mile to get the best view of the dam and bridge at a turn to the right (west).

The trail curves right and climbs to the northwest, then west. On top of the hill, a microwave tower with a large rectangular panel on it comes into view. The trail climbs toward the tower and passes it in 0.2 mile. While researching this hike, I had a very high-speed plane fly right over me. The AZT curves to the left (west) and the Four Peaks come into view. The trail levels out with commanding views of the Four Peaks and Buckhorn Mountain.

The trail contours below the ridge and, in 0.3 mile, turns southwest with views of Apache Lake and the Superstition Mountains beyond. Descend toward a saddle and reach it in 0.2 mile to enjoy views of the Apache Trail (AZ 88), Apache Lake, and the Superstitions. In 0.1 mile the view of the lake goes away, and the trail climbs the side of the ridge. Look for banana yuccas, which grow waxy white flowers on a stalk in the spring. In 0.3 mile go west through a saddle and pass a low structure to your right (south). The trail stays fairly level, and Mills Ridge Road comes into view as the trail approaches the saguaro-studded cliff. This passage is the northernmost reach of the saguaro cactus on the AZT (see page 75 for more information).

In 0.4 mile the trail steeply descends on rocky tread to cross the hillside. Big, fuzzy teddy bear cholla cacti line the trail—there's nothing cute or cuddly about their spines, however, so make sure to avoid them and watch out for pieces that might have fallen into the tread. The segments are very loosely attached and come off at the slightest touch. Many desert hikers carry a comb for cholla removal: if you get stuck, you place the comb between the segment and your skin, then pull to detach.

Cross a rockslide in 0.2 mile. The trail passes through more rockslides over the next 0.1 mile, so watch your footing. In 0.2 mile the trail levels and heads southwest, then west. In 0.2 mile the trail curves around the hill to head southwest, climbing gradually. In 0.2 mile pass rocks made of an interesting conglomerate on both sides of the trail.

In 0.3 mile the trail turns west and begins descending toward a dirt road. In 0.2 mile you come to a sign that reads VINEYARD TRAIL #131 LEFT, FOREST SERVICE ROAD 336 LEFT AND RIGHT. Look to your left (west) for a brown carsonite AZT sign, and take this road for a little less than 0.2 mile.

The road curves south, crossing a low point in 0.1 mile, then climbs to the southeast for less than 0.1 mile. Another brown sign marks a turn off the road as it curves right (south). Look to your right (west) for a line of rocks with a trail sign behind them; then reach the rocks and the sign for Vineyard Trail in 0.1 mile. The trail heads west along the ridge and reaches the crest in 0.4 mile.

The AZT rides the top of the ridge for a short distance and then descends. In 0.1 mile the trail turns right (northwest) after passing a stand of saguaros to steeply climb to the top of the ridge ahead. Cross the ridge and continue gradually climbing to the west.

In 0.4 mile the trail steepens and curves to the right (northwest); then, in 0.1 mile, reach the top of the hill and continue west on top of the ridge. The Mills Ridge Trailhead is visible ahead. The trail descends gradually, passing a water-catchment system with a metal top in 0.3 mile; in another 0.1 mile, it turns right (northwest) for a short descent and then the final steep climb to the Mills Ridge Trailhead (3,640'), 0.25 mile ahead. This marks the end of the point-to-point hike or the turnaround for the out-and-back. Your total mileage to this point is 6.25 miles, with a total ascent of 2,188 feet and a descent of 740 feet.

If you didn't leave a shuttle vehicle at the Mills Ridge Trailhead, go back the way you came (downhill and west–east) to the Vineyard Trailhead for a total of 12.5 miles and 2,930 feet of elevation gain.

Gateway Community: ROOSEVELT
DISTANCE FROM TRAILHEAD: 2.0 miles **POPULATION:** 28 **ELEVATION:** 2,208'

Gateway Community: TONTO BASIN
DISTANCE FROM TRAILHEAD: 16.0 miles **POPULATION:** 2,230 **ELEVATION:** 2,238'

Gateway Community: PUNKIN CENTER
DISTANCE FROM TRAILHEAD: 18.0 miles **POPULATION:** 1,424 **ELEVATION:** 2,238'

The town of Roosevelt was created for the workers who were building the dam. The **Roosevelt Lake Visitor Center,** administered by Tonto National Forest, is a great source of information about the area, with a bookstore and restroom on-site. Nearby, **Roosevelt Lake Marina** has a store that carries basic camping items, food, and beverages; the selection is geared to car campers and boaters. An outdoor barbecue grill is on the large patio overlooking the lake. The marina also provides pontoon, kayak, and ski boat rentals, along with shoreline camping and a restaurant.

U.S. Forest Service campgrounds are located on the shore of Roosevelt Lake along AZ 188. Free dispersed (primitive) lakeside camping is available at **Bermuda Flat.** Paved loops with facilities and shade structures are located at **Cholla Campground,** one of the largest solar-powered campgrounds in the United States. It has RV and tent-only sites, along with potable water, restrooms, showers, playgrounds, and a paved boat launch. **Roosevelt Resort Park,** a private lodging complex 11 miles south of the Visitor Center, has RV sites with hookups, a motel, and cabin and mobile home rentals, along with a restaurant and bar.

The town of Tonto Basin, 16.0 miles north of the trailhead, has the **Tonto Basin Inn** for accommodations. For a posthike meal, there's the **Butcher Hook,** a combination restaurant, bar, grocery, convenience store, and gas station; **Big Daddy's**

Apache Lake and the scenic Apache Trail (AZ 88). This passage is the farthest north that saguaro cacti grow on the AZT.

Pizza; and **Tonto Basin Marketplace,** which stocks camping supplies and has a full grocery store with a deli that serves breakfast, lunch, and dinner. A couple of miles north of Tonto Basin is Punkin Center, home of **M&M Reno Creek Cafe.**

ROOSEVELT LAKE VISITOR CENTER: Milepost 242.8 on AZ 188, 602-225-5395, tinyurl .com/rooseveltlakevisitorcenter. Open daily, 8 a.m.–4:30 p.m. (closed federal holidays).

ROOSEVELT LAKE MARINA: 28085 North AZ 188, 602-977-7170, rlmaz.com. Day-use parking costs $6 per vehicle; developed shoreline camping costs $8 per night for cars and $48 per night for RVs. (A $4 fee is added to both day-use and camping fees for vehicles towing trailers.) Sites are first come, first served; pets require a $15 permit and proof of current vaccination. Store open daily, 7 a.m.–7 p.m.; boat rental hours: 8 a.m.–3 p.m. Call for restaurant and bar hours.

CHOLLA CAMPGROUND: AZ 188, 6.0 miles north of Roosevelt Visitor Center, 602-225-5395, tinyurl.com/chollacampground. Nightly rates: $25 for single sites, $50 for doubles. Availability is first come, first served and by reservation; odd-numbered sites can be reserved November–April by calling 877-444-6777 or visiting recreation.gov.

ROOSEVELT RESORT PARK: 358 N. Stagecoach Trail, 928-467-2276, rooseveltresortpark.com

TONTO BASIN INN: Milepost 260.0 on AZ 188, 928-479-2891, tontobasininn.com

BUTCHER HOOK: Milepost 259.0 on AZ 188, 928-479-2226, tinyurl.com/butcherhookaz. Open daily; call or check website for hours, which vary throughout the week.

BIG DADDY'S PIZZA: 100 Salado Trail, 928-479-3223, tinyurl.com/bigdaddyspizzaaz. Open Tuesday–Thursday, 11 a.m.–7 p.m.; Friday and Saturday, 11 a.m.–8 p.m.

M&M RENO CREEK CAFE: 270 Old AZ 188, 928-479-2710, facebook.com/mandmreno creekcafe. Open Monday–Thursday, 7 a.m.–8 p.m., Saturday and Sunday, 7 a.m.–9 p.m.; call for summer hours.

Getting There

VINEYARD TRAILHEAD (UPHILL START/DOWNHILL END): N33° 40.616' W111° 09.657', elevation 2,192'

ROAD CONDITIONS: All vehicles; paved

FACILITIES: None

DIRECTIONS *From Phoenix Sky Harbor Airport:* Follow the signs to get onto AZ 202 Loop East, and in 7.1 miles take Exit 13 left (north) onto Country Club Drive (AZ 87). In 57.5 miles reach a junction and make a sharp right onto AZ 188, heading southeast. Drive through the Gateway Communities of Punkin Center and Tonto Basin, and in 31.0 miles the trailhead will be on your left (east).

From Globe/US 60: From the intersection of US 60 and AZ 188, go north onto AZ 188 for 30.0 miles. The trailhead will be on your right (east), shortly after you cross the Roosevelt Lake Bridge.

MILLS RIDGE TRAILHEAD (DOWNHILL START/UPHILL END):

N33° 40.304' W111° 14.451', elevation 3,642'

ROAD CONDITIONS: All vehicles; 5.1 miles of graded dirt. *Note:* There are steep drop-offs on the sides of road in sections where it follows the ridgetop.

FACILITIES: None

DIRECTIONS *From Phoenix Sky Harbor Airport:* Follow the directions above to reach the junction of AZ 87 and AZ 188, and turn right (southeast) onto AZ 188. Drive through the Gateway Communities of Punkin Center and Tonto Basin, and in 29.0 miles the turnoff for Forest Service Road 429 (Mills Ridge Road) will be on your right (west)—if you reach the Vineyard Picnic Area on your left (east), you've missed the turn.

Zero your odometer when you turn onto FR 429. At mile 0.4, you'll see a ROAD CLOSED sign straight ahead—turn left (west) to continue on FR 429. The road climbs, with a short descent at mile 1.3. The road reaches the first ridgetop at mile 2.6 and then, at mile 3.0, turns right (west). At mile 3.5 you reach another section on the ridgetop and make a steep ascent. At mile 3.8, FR 336 comes in from the left (southeast). You drive a long stretch of road on the ridgetop until mile 4.7, followed by a steep descent to the Mills Ridge Trailhead at mile 4.9.

FR 429 dead-ends at the Mills Ridge Trailhead at mile 5.1; Vineyard Trail 131 is on your left (south) across the parking lot from the metal AZT sign and Tonto National Forest information board, heading downhill. Four Peaks Trail 130 is north behind the AZT sign going uphill—this section of the trail is not covered in this book, but the next hike, Four Peaks, travels part of it higher up the mountain.

Via Globe/AZ 60 from Phoenix Sky Harbor: Follow signs for Loop 202 East and take it 3.6 miles to Loop 101 South. In 3.1 miles take the exit for AZ 60 East toward Globe. In 70.8 miles, reach AZ 188, turn left and go north 32.0 miles. The turn for FR 429 is on your left (west), 2.0 miles after you cross the Roosevelt Bridge and pass the Vineyard Trailhead on your right (east)—look for the turnoff just after the sign for the Vineyard Picnic Area, after you cross another small bridge. Zero your odometer at the turnoff, and follow the directions above to the Mills Ridge Trailhead.

Point-to-point shuttle: Use the GPS coordinates to plan your trip. For the uphill (east–west) route described, leave a car at the Mills Ridge Trailhead on FR 429, then drive back to the Vineyard Trailhead on AZ 188 to start the hike; do the reverse for the downhill (west–east) route.

Four Peaks

High-country traverse

SCENERY: ★ ★ ★ ★ ★
TRAIL CONDITION: ★ ★ ★
CHILDREN: ★ ★
DIFFICULTY: ★ ★ ★
SOLITUDE: ★ ★ ★

Four Peaks Wilderness spans 60,740 acres, and Brown's Peak is the highest in the range, at 7,657 feet.

DISTANCE & CONFIGURATION: 7.6-mile out-and-back

HIKING TIME: 4–6 hours

ACCUMULATED ELEVATION GAIN: 1,670'

SHORT HIKE OPTION: 3.8-mile out-and-back to Four Peaks Trail junction/ 670' elevation gain

OUTSTANDING FEATURES: Views of the Four Peaks Wilderness and Roosevelt Lake

LAND-MANAGEMENT AGENCY: Tonto National Forest, Tonto Basin Ranger District, 928-402-6200, fs.usda.gov/tonto

MAPS: USGS 7.5' *Four Peaks, AZ*

AZT PASSAGE: 20/Four Peaks, aztrail.org/explore/passages/passage-20-four-peaks

ANCESTRAL LANDS: Western Apache, Yavapai–Apache

SEASON: Winter (check for snow conditions), spring, fall

ACCESS: No fees or permits; open 24-7, year-round

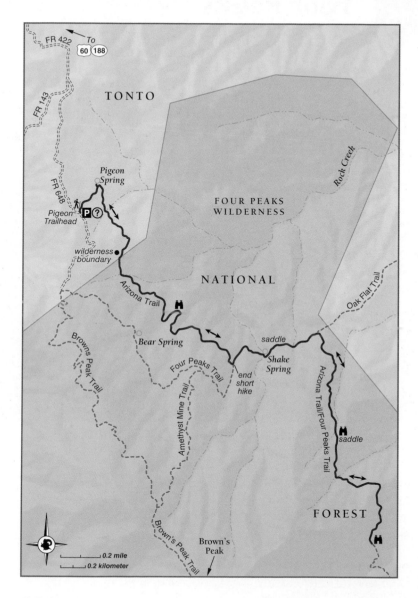

Advisory

National forests sometimes close due to fire danger, so check before you go. At the time of this writing, the Pigeon Trailhead is scheduled to open March 1, 2021, after the 193,455-acre Bush Fire, which started in June 2020 by a vehicle fire. Go to the passage page at aztrail.org/explore/passages/passage-20-four-peaks for updates.

Overview

This hike on the Arizona National Scenic Trail (AZT) traverses the high country of the Four Peaks Wilderness. Fantastic views of Roosevelt Lake and the Sierra Ancha and Mazatzal Mountains take center stage as the trail winds through ponderosa pine, oak, and alligator juniper. The fall-color season showcases bigtooth maple.

On the Trail

From the Pigeon Trailhead (5,577'), pass a metal AZT sign and information board, and go left (north). The trail descends to the northeast through ponderosa pine, oak, and alligator juniper. The tread is alternately gravelly and rocky. In 0.2 mile reach a sign for Pigeon Spring. To visit the spring, turn left (west) and follow a short trail just 20 feet.

Back on the AZT, continue downhill. The trail curves to the right (south) and affords great views of Brown's Peak, highest in the range at 7,657' elevation. The crest of the Four Peaks is made up of 1.5-billion-year-old Mazatzal (MAH-zat-zal or Madda-ZELL) quartzite. The red-barked trees are manzanitas, whose name means "little apple" in Spanish; they have pink and white blooms in the spring and their fruits look like mini apples.

In 0.2 mile the trail begins to climb. Reach the Four Peaks Wilderness boundary sign in 0.1 mile. If you're lucky, you may see hummingbirds and hear their trilling song in this passage.

From the boundary the trail descends to the south, curves left (southeast), and switchbacks to the right (south). In 0.2 mile there are some pretty boulders to your right (west). Pass through some large trees, and the trail goes southeast.

In 0.3 mile the trail starts descending to the right (south) for 0.1 mile, then begins climbing. In 0.2 mile descend to cross a drainage, which may have water

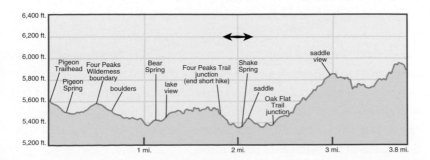

141

seasonally. Bear Spring is nearby, though there is no sign on the AZT—the spring, 0.3 mile southwest, is not part of this hike.

In 0.1 mile get an amazing view of Roosevelt Lake and the Sierra Ancha Mountains. The trail curves right (southwest) into the canyon and climbs to cross the drainage above some rocks. If you're here at the right time during the snow-melt, you may find a waterfall at this crossing. In 0.2 mile cross the boulder-filled drainage and continue climbing.

The trail levels and begins a descent for 0.1 mile; the tread here is cut into the hillside, and the drop-offs can be steep at times. The AZT crosses the ravine and continues to climb. In 0.3 mile descend to cross another drainage; just after crossing it, reach the junction for Four Peaks Trail 130.

Turn left (northeast) and join the Four Peaks Trail (5,455'). The right (south) turn goes uphill to Lone Pine Saddle Trailhead in about 2 miles. **This junction marks the turnaround for the short hike option, at 3.8 miles out-and-back and 670 feet of elevation gain.**

Continuing on the AZT, the Four Peaks Trail descends to the northeast and then curves right (east). In 0.2 mile cross the low point of this hike at a drainage, and reach a sign for Shake Spring (5,332'). The spring box is just behind the sign, but at the time of this writing it was completely overgrown. The trail climbs steeply uphill from the spring to a small saddle with a campsite in 0.1 mile. The trail levels briefly on its way to the junction with Oak Flat Trail 123, heading northeast and reaching this junction in 0.3 mile—turn right (east) to stay on the Four Peaks Trail.

The trail steeply climbs to the south on loose rocks. Join the drainage, continue climbing, and cross it in 0.6 mile. Reach a saddle with an amazing view of Roosevelt Lake and Four Peaks in 0.1 mile. The trail turns right (south) and descends on the hillside. Cross a drainage in 0.2 mile, and the trail stays gener-ally level. Go through a saddle at 0.4 mile, and the trail starts a steep climb for 0.2 mile. You then reach a view of a rocky outcrop with Roosevelt Lake in the background—this is the hike's high point, at 5,864 feet. Then descend 100 feet to a small clearing and the end of the hike (see photo on page 144 for view).

On your return, there are views of the Mazatzal Mountains—Mount Ord with towers on top, Mazatzal Peak, and beyond that the Mogollon Rim. Take care to stay left (southwest) at the junction with Oak Flat Trail and go right (southwest) at the Four Peaks Trail junction.

Gateway Community: ROOSEVELT *(see page 135)*

DISTANCE FROM TRAILHEAD: 23.0 miles **POPULATION:** 28 **ELEVATION:** 2,208'

Gateway Community: TONTO BASIN *(see page 135)*

DISTANCE FROM TRAILHEAD: 5.0 miles **POPULATION:** 2,230 **ELEVATION:** 2,238'

Gateway Community: PUNKIN CENTER *(see page 135)*

DISTANCE FROM TRAILHEAD: 7.0 miles **POPULATION:** 1,424 **ELEVATION:** 2,238'

Getting There

PIGEON TRAILHEAD: N33° 42.651' W111° 20.183', elevation 5,577'

ROAD CONDITIONS: No low-clearance vehicles; graded dirt for 10.5 miles

FACILITIES: None

TRAVEL NOTE: The driving directions described below are for passenger vehicles. Another route, Four Peaks Road (Forest Service Road 143), leads to the trailhead from AZ 87, but it requires a high-clearance vehicle, experience driving these kinds of roads, and a lot of patience—you'd be jostled about on a very bumpy dirt road for 20.0 miles. Instead, I recommend coming in from AZ 188 and El Oso Road. This road is also dirt but is maintained regularly to service the communications towers on the ridge. (*El Oso* means "the bear" in Spanish and refers to the black bears that inhabit the Four Peaks range.)

DIRECTIONS *From Phoenix Sky Harbor Airport:* Follow the signs to get onto AZ 202 Loop East, and in 7.1 miles take Exit 13 left (north) onto Country Club Drive (AZ 87). In 57.5 miles reach a junction and make a sharp right onto AZ 188, heading southeast. Drive through the Gateway Communities of Punkin Center and Tonto Basin, and in 20.6 miles turn right (southwest) onto El Oso Road. *Zero your odometer here.* Be aware of other drivers on the road ahead of you—there are pullouts for yielding. Note that this area gets off-road-vehicle traffic on weekends.

El Oso Road makes a hard turn to the left (south) and passes a sign that says PIGEON TRAILHEAD 11 MILES. The road is steep but suitable for passenger cars, and there are mileage markers every mile.

At mile 2.0 get wonderful views of Roosevelt Lake. At mile 3.6 the road is cut into the hillside with a drop-off to the left (southeast). At mile 4.3 the road reaches a small hill, makes a sharp curve, and turns right (west); it also goes around the hill for vehicles that need the space to turn. The road is steep and makes another sharp turn to the left (south) 0.2 mile ahead, then ascends to a small saddle at mile 4.7 and makes a sharp right turn (northwest).

Miles 5.0–6.0 are not as exposed or steep. After a short descent at mile 6.3, the road resumes climbing steeply. After mile 7.0, the trees get larger above 5,000 feet elevation and include alligator junipers and oaks. Reach the communications towers at mile 8.3.

At mile 8.5 reach Forest Service Road 422 and turn left (southeast), following the sign that says PIGEON TRAILHEAD 2 MILES. (The northbound AZT follows FR 422, but this section is not in the book.) At 9.6 miles (5,716'), reach a junction with FR 648 and go left (southeast). The road descends to the south, reaching a sign for the Pigeon Trailhead with an arrow pointing left (northeast) at 10.5 miles. Look for a very small parking area on the left side of the road; there's also room for several cars to park along the shoulder.

On your return, turn right (northeast) back onto El Oso Road and remember that all the elevation you gained must now be lost—take your time on the steep sections, and give yourself plenty of time.

From Globe/US 60: From the intersection of US 60 and AZ 188, take a sharp right to head north on AZ 188 for 30.0 miles, past the Roosevelt Lake Visitor Center. In 12.7 miles reach El Oso Road, turn left (southwest), and pick up the directions above.

End-of-hike view of Theodore Roosevelt Lake with a backdrop of the Sierra Ancha Mountains

Sycamore Canyon

Riparian ramble

16

Seasonal water in Boulder Canyon

DISTANCE & CONFIGURATION: 9.4-mile out-and-back

HIKING TIME: 5–7 hours

ACCUMULATED ELEVATION GAIN: 1,150'

SHORT HIKE OPTION: 4.6-mile out-and-back to Sycamore Creek/600' elevation gain

OUTSTANDING FEATURES: Riparian vegetation, seasonal creek, mountain views

LAND-MANAGEMENT AGENCY: Tonto National Forest, Payson Ranger District, 928-474-7900, fs.usda.gov/tonto

MAPS: USGS 7.5' *Boulder Mountain, AZ*

AZT PASSAGE: 21/Pine Mountain, aztrail.org/explore/passages/passage-21-pine-mountain

ANCESTRAL LANDS: Yavapai–Apache, Akimel O'odham

SEASON: Winter, spring, fall

ACCESS: No fees or permits; open 24-7, year-round

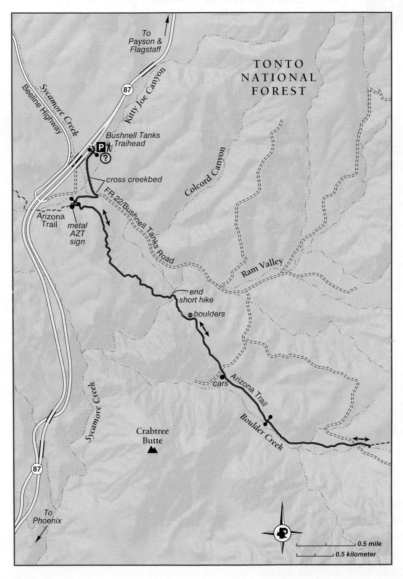

Advisory

National forests sometimes close due to fire danger, so check before you go. The Bushnell Tanks Trailhead is scheduled to open March 1, 2021, after the 193,455-acre Bush Fire, which started in June 2020 by a vehicle fire on the roadside. Go to aztrail.org/explore/passages/passage-21-pine-mountain for updates.

Overview

This passage of the Arizona National Scenic Trail (AZT) crosses beautiful Sycamore Canyon and Boulder Creek, riparian areas with large trees. This is a great spot for wildflowers and cactus blooms in the spring months as well as fall color around November. You'll also enjoy views of the rugged Mazatzal (MAH-zat-zal or Madda-ZELL) Mountains and the foothills of the Four Peaks.

On the Trail

From the parking area, head south toward the gate and go through the space on the left (east) side (3,439'). The sign to the right (west) says, "Bushnell Tanks area closed temporarily due to vegetation rehabilitation and stream crossing hazards; unauthorized entry prohibited." This prohibition applies only to vehicles, however. The closure for habitat restoration became necessary after the area was damaged by overuse. This area is full of grasses that can get into your shoes and socks, so I recommend wearing gaiters, which go over your shoes and socks to keep gravel and grasses out of the top of the shoes.

In 100 feet, come to an AZT kiosk signed BUSHNELL TANKS TRAIL-HEAD; a second panel on the kiosk illustrates best practices on sharing the trail with horses and mountain bikes. Continue down the closed road as it curves to the left (south) at 0.1 mile, then crosses a creekbed at 0.2 mile. Along with the canyon's namesake sycamores, you can see juniper, acacia, and cottonwood trees. The fall color is great here, but it doesn't arrive until November.

Heads-Up: At 0.3 mile the road curves to the left (east) at a brown sign with two hikers and an arrow pointing right (south). Take this trail down into the creekbed of Sycamore Canyon, and keep your eyes open for signs leading you across. The creek floods and the paths change from time to time, so you may have to do a little searching around.

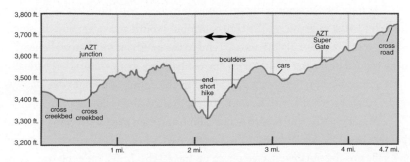

In 0.1 mile come to a sign that reads ACCESS TO ARIZONA TRAIL with an arrow. (There is another sign pointing the way that you just came.) Turn right (west) to join the creekbed. There should be a cairn (a stack of rocks) marking the turn, but these sometimes get washed away. In 300 feet the trail leaves the creekbed to the left (south) at another ACCESS TO ARIZONA TRAIL sign.

Follow the trail west beneath the canopy of sycamore trees. At 0.5 mile there is another cairn and brown carsonite sign. The trail curves right (west) to parallel Sycamore Creek, then crosses it; the crossing is just downstream of a concrete square. When the creek has water, you'll need to walk parallel to it until it reaches a spot where you can cross on rocks and keep your feet dry. During higher flows, dry crossings may not be possible.

Look across the creek to the south and up the hill for a trail ascending out of the canyon with a brown carsonite sign pointing right. Cross the second arm of the creek wherever you can, and take the trail up to the sign (3,382').

At 0.6 mile turn right (west) and follow the cairns as the trail curves to the right (south). Go up two switchbacks, and climb to a cowboy gate, remembering to leave the gate the way you found it (see page 13 for more information).

In 0.1 mile come to a signed junction. One sign reads SUNFLOWER TRAIL #344, LITTLE SADDLE TRAIL #244, 5½ MILES. The other sign says BOULDER CREEK TRAIL #73, JUNCTION ROAD 22 AHEAD, ½ MILE, JUNCTION ROAD 422 RIGHT, 2.7 MILES. Make a left (east) to follow the Boulder Creek Trail and pass a large metal AZT sign. The trail curves into a small drainage, climbs out of it, and then switchbacks to the right (southeast) at 0.75 mile.

Switchback left (north) and the trail turns right (southeast). Mount Ord is visible with the towers on top to the northeast, as well as the parking area to the east across Sycamore Canyon. The trail climbs above the canyon and then levels out at mile 0.9.

At mile 1.0 Sycamore Canyon comes into view, with Boulder Mountain to the right. In 0.2 mile you see the trail continuing south and traversing the slope.

Cross two side canyons, and ascend to the south on rocky tread beneath a rocky topped peak. The bushes with the red bark are manzanitas; there are also sugar sumac bushes, beargrass, and sotol. In the spring you might see *Dudleya* agave, small succulents with flowers on red, orange, and yellow stalks.

At mile 1.6 the trail makes a short climb and then takes a sweeping curve to the right (east). Saddle Mountain, also on the AZT, can be seen across the highway and valley to the northwest (see photo on page 115). In 0.2 mile, the trail turns left (northeast), then right (south), and then does a series of switchbacks as it descends to the southeast.

In 0.2 mile a rocky peak comes into view on the right as the trail descends into the valley, and the AZT turns right (south). In 0.1 mile the trail curves to the left (east) and continues descending; then, in 0.1 mile, it climbs and again curves to left (northeast). Descend to the northeast on some rock steps to a creek crossing at mile 2.3. **This is the turnaround for the short hike option, at 4.6 miles round-trip, a total ascent and descent of 600 feet.** To your right (south) is a small, sandy beach and rocks to sit on (3,315').

Continuing on the AZT, you may have to hunt around for the best spot to rock-hop across the creek. Pick up the trail on the other side and turn right to parallel the creek, following cairns. The AZT leaves the creek on the left (east) in 0.1 mile. It climbs and makes a few tight switchbacks out of the creek, then curves right to climb to the south. The trail goes through an area with chunks of white milky quartz in 0.1 mile. Then you make a steep 0.2-mile climb to a saddle, and the AZT curves east (right) past some beautiful boulders.

The trail turns right (south) and climbs. In 0.2 mile go through a flat area at a saddle, heading southeast. At mile 3.0, reach a view into the valley of Boulder Creek below.

The trail descends to cross a creekbed in 0.2 mile, then crosses a degraded old roadbed. Soon afterward you come upon several old, rusty, shot-up cars to your right (south). The AZT travels southeast through the wide valley and crosses the northern arm of the creek in 0.1 mile.

In 0.1 mile the trail makes a short ascent and then levels to continue along the ridge. The trail stays above the left (northeast) side of the canyon and reaches an AZT Super Gate. The trail, now somewhat level with the canyon, continues southeast for 0.7 mile.

Cross two forks of the creek in 0.1 mile; the trail then climbs out of the creek and switchbacks to the right (south). The AZT runs above Boulder Canyon again on the left (north) side and heads east. Cross a doubletrack road in 0.5 mile, and the trail comes close to Boulder Creek in 0.1 mile.

Take a right (south) toward the creek, and in 50 feet there's seating on white and brown rock outcrops on either side of the creek to the right (west) of a juniper (3,700'). If the trail begins to climb away from the creek and you see large black rocks across the creek, you've gone too far. Go back to where the trail is flat for the easiest access.

There is little shade here, but there may be seasonal water—the sound of which is one of the sweetest sounds in the desert. On one hike, I also saw big, showy, yellow-and-black tiger swallowtail butterflies. Enjoy your break on the rocks, then return the way you came.

On your return you'll have views of Saddle Mountain, Sheep Mountain, Mount Peeley, and Mazatzal Peak to the northwest. At the Sunflower Trail junction, turn right (northeast) and pass through the gate. Look for signs beneath a large sycamore that indicates a turn to the left (north) out of the creek. Join the road and turn left (west), and now you're on the closed road back to the trailhead.

Gateway Community: PAYSON

DISTANCE FROM TRAILHEAD: 32.0 miles **POPULATION:** 15,710 **ELEVATION:** 5,003'

Though the community of Sunflower is marked on the map, you'd be sorely disappointed if you wanted to chow down on a posthike burger here, as there are no services—the closest Gateway Community is Payson. It's also one of the larger Gateway Communities, with a full range of services and plenty of places to stay, shop, and eat. You can stay at a chain hotel, or you can rent a cabin, Airbnb, or vacation home.

AZT Super Gate in Boulder Canyon

Ayothaya Thai Cafe serves both Thai and Chinese dishes and has lunch specials. Check out **La Sierra** for Mexican food, or visit **Crosswinds Grille** at the airport, which boasts, in their words, a "million-dollar view" of the Mogollon Rim. **Fargo's Steakhouse** has outdoor seating, along with vegetarian and fish options in addition to steaks.

Nearby campgrounds include **Houston Mesa** and **Flowing Springs,** both north of town. Free dispersed (primitive) camping is available along the many roads in Tonto National Forest. **Green Valley Park** is a great spot for a walk, a picnic at one of the small lakes, or a visit to the **Rim Country Museum and Zane Grey Cabin.** Many of Western author Zane Grey's works were set in and inspired by the Mogollon Rim country.

Local attractions include **Tonto Natural Bridge State Park,** where you can visit what is believed to be the largest natural travertine bridge in the world: 183 feet high, 400 feet long, and 150 feet across at its widest point. The park has hiking trails, four overlooks that can be seen from the parking lot, a small store, and the historic 10-bedroom Goodfellow Lodge (available for group rentals only).

Visit the **Shoofly Village Archaeological Site** for a look at more than 80 rooms built by the Mogollon Culture that were occupied between 1000 and 1250 CE. There are interpretive signs along the wheelchair-accessible 0.3-mile loop trail.

AYOTHAYA THAI CAFÉ: 404 E. AZ 260, 928-474-1112, ayothayathaicafe.com. Open daily, 11 a.m.–8 or 9 p.m. (call to confirm hours).

LA SIERRA: 800 N. Beeline Hwy., 928-468-6711, facebook.com/lasierrapaysonaz. Open Monday–Friday, 11 a.m.–9 p.m.; Saturday and Sunday, 10 a.m.–9 p.m.

CROSSWINDS GRILLE: 800 W. Airport Rd. B, 928-474-1613, facebook.com/crosswinds rest. Open daily, 6 a.m.–8 p.m.

FARGO'S STEAKHOUSE: 620 East AZ 260, 928-474-7455, fargossteakhouse.com. Open Monday–Thursday, 11 a.m.–9 p.m.; Friday and Saturday, 11 a.m.–10 p.m.; Sunday, 11 a.m.–8 p.m.

GREEN VALLEY PARK: 1000 W. Country Club Dr., 928-472-5111, paysonrimcountry .com/parks. Open daily, 6 a.m.–10:30 p.m.

RIM COUNTRY MUSEUM AND ZANE GREY CABIN: 700 S. Green Valley Pkwy., 928-474-3483, rimcountrymuseum.org. Admission: $5 adults, $4 seniors ages 55 and older, $3 students (ages 12–18), free for kids under age 12. Open Wednesday–Saturday, 10 a.m.–4 p.m.

HOUSTON MESA CAMPGROUND: Houston Mesa Road (Forest Service Road 199), 928-474-7900, tinyurl.com/houstonmesa. From AZ 260 in Payson, go 2.0 miles north on AZ 87, then 0.1 mile east on Houston Mesa Road; the campground is on the left (north) side of the road. There are 74 wheelchair-accessible campsites for tents, RVs (no hookups), and equestrians, along with coin-operated showers and flush toilets. Nightly rates: $19–$26; reserve by calling 877-444-6777 or visiting recreation.gov/camping/campgrounds/232355.

FLOWING SPRINGS CAMPGROUND: Forest Service Road 272, 928-474-7900, tinyurl .com/flowingsprings. From AZ 260 in Payson, go 3.0 miles north on AZ 87; then, near milepost 257.0, just south of the East Verde River, turn right (east) onto FR 272 and drive 0.5 mile farther. The campground is on the left (north) side of the road. Free; vault toilet but no other facilities on-site.

TONTO NATURAL BRIDGE STATE PARK: FR 583, 928-476-4202, azstateparks.com /tonto. From AZ 260 in Payson, go 10.3 miles north on AZ 87; then turn left (west) onto FR 583, and drive 1.8 miles to the visitor center. Admission: $7 adults, $4 ages 7–13, free ages 6 and younger. Open daily, 9 a.m.–5 p.m.; Thanksgiving and December 24, 9 a.m.– 2 p.m.; closed December 25. Pets prohibited on trails.

SHOOFLY VILLAGE ARCHAEOLOGICAL SITE: About 5 miles north of Payson on Houston Mesa Road (FR 199). **GPS:** N34° 17.432' W111° 17.093'.

Getting There

BUSHNELL TANKS TRAILHEAD: N33° 52.140' W111° 27.906', elevation 3,439'

ROAD CONDITIONS: All vehicles; paved with dirt parking lot

FACILITIES: None

DIRECTIONS *From Phoenix Sky Harbor Airport:* Follow the signs to get onto AZ 202 Loop East, and in 7.1 miles take Exit 13 left (north) onto Country Club Drive (AZ 87). In 42.0 miles, past milepost 281.0 in Sunflower, turn right (east) onto Forest Service Road 22, signed for Bushnell Tanks. A gate and parking area are located 500 feet down the road; please keep the turnaround open for people pulling trailers.

From Flagstaff via Lake Mary Road: Take Lake Mary Road south for 54.0 miles, and turn right (southwest) onto AZ 87. In 36.0 miles take the second exit off the roundabout onto Beeline Highway (AZ 87); then, in 0.6 mile, take the second exit off the second roundabout to stay on AZ 87. In 34.0 miles, turn left (east) onto Bushnell Tanks Road (FR 22).

From Flagstaff via I-17 and AZ 260: Take I-17 South for 52.0 miles to Exit 287, and go left onto AZ 260 East; then take the second exit off the round-about to continue east on AZ 260. In 34.0 miles turn right (southwest) to stay on AZ 260/AZ 87, and drive 24.0 miles through the Gateway Communities of Strawberry and Pine. Then take the second exit off the roundabout onto Beeline Highway (AZ 87) in Payson, and proceed as directed in the previous paragraph.

17

Highline: PINE TRAILHEAD TO RED ROCK SPRING

Pine forests, rim and mountain views

SCENERY: ★ ★ ★ ★
TRAIL CONDITION: ★ ★ ★ /
★ ★ ★ ★ *(full hike/Pine Loop)*
CHILDREN: ★ ★ ★ ★ ★
(Pine Loop)
DIFFICULTY: ★ ★ ★ ★ /★ ★
(full hike/Pine Loop)
SOLITUDE: ★ ★

The Arizona Trail contours beneath Milk Ranch Point on the Mogollon Rim.

DISTANCE & CONFIGURATION: 8.8-mile out-and-back

HIKING TIME: 4–6 hours

ACCUMULATED ELEVATION GAIN: 1,450'

SHORT HIKE OPTION: 2.7-mile Pine Loop/360' elevation gain

OUTSTANDING FEATURES: Ponderosa pine forest, vistas of the Mogollon Rim and mountains; Pine Loop good for beginners and children

LAND-MANAGEMENT AGENCY: Tonto National Forest, Payson Ranger District, 928-474-7900, fs.usda.gov/tonto

MAPS: USGS 7.5-minute *Pine, AZ*

AZT PASSAGE: 26/Highline, aztrail.org/explore/passages/passage-26-highline

ANCESTRAL LANDS: Apache, Yavapai–Apache, Hopi

SEASON: Spring, summer, fall

ACCESS: No fees or permits; open 24-7, year-round

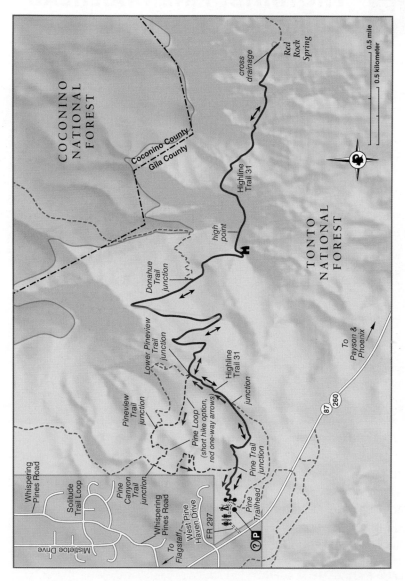

Overview

The Mogollon (MO-go-yawn) Rim is an escarpment up to 1,000 feet high that forms the edge of the Colorado Plateau. This is a major transitional area on the Arizona National Scenic Trail (AZT). North of the Mogollon Rim, the AZT changes to much more flat hiking through ponderosa pine forests, versus the mountainous and rugged terrain in the southern part of the state. This hike and the next two in the book travel part of the Highline National Recreational Trail, sections of which follow the path of an ancient route and historical wagon road.

On the Trail

Note: The mileages listed on the signs may be a bit off. Extensive trail work has added a bit of length to the AZT in this area, which makes for a much better hiking experience.

This hike starts at the east end of the parking lot, at a hiker sign and trail register (5,394'). Sign in and go between signs for the Pine Trailhead/Highline Trail 31 and a big metal AZT sign.

The Highline Trail was first established in the 1870s as a path for transportation between homesteads beneath the Mogollon Rim. Many parts of the current 55.0-mile Highline National Recreational Trail have been rerouted from the original roadbed to provide a better user experience on foot, bicycle, and horseback.

In 100 feet there is a bike-access ramp to your left and then an AZT Super Gate to your right. Go through the gate and reach a U.S. Forest Service sign; the trail then curves left (northeast). In 200 feet reach an AZT metal mileage sign that reads UTAH 337, MEXICO 465. The trail switchbacks up the hill and, at 0.25 mile, reaches a junction with Pine Canyon Trail 26 to your left (north)—continue straight (east) on the AZT.

The trail curves through a drainage and then heads south. Alligator juniper, ponderosa pine, manzanita, holly scrub oak, and live oak line the trail. This region is part of the largest ponderosa pine forest in the entire world, stretching all the way north to Flagstaff and east along the Mogollon Rim. In 0.3 mile the

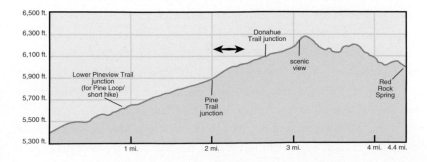

trail curves to the northeast and climbs; then, in 0.1 mile, it levels and descends to a junction with a trail coming in from the right (south)—go left (northeast) to stay on the combined Highline Trail/AZT.

The trail crosses a drainage and continues northeast. The Highline Trail/AZT is marked by signage and white diamond blazes on the trees. The AZT goes through the canopy of trees, passing some bigtooth maples to your left (southwest) in the next drainage. The trail climbs out of the drainage and turns to the right (east), then left (north). In 0.3 mile continue northeast to a junction with the Lower Pineview Trail to your left (west). Two trails go right—take the hard right (east) to stay on the Highline to Red Rock Spring. **Or if you're looking for a shorter hike, this is the junction to turn for the Pine Loop (see next page for description).**

Descend and cross the drainage, and you will see a wooden AZT sign and white diamond to the east. The trail switchbacks to the left (northeast) and then right (south), and in 0.2 mile the trail curves into more open terrain with views of Milk Ranch Point to the northeast. The trail continues switchbacking up the hill; the tread in this passage is dirt with rocky sections.

In 0.4 mile, you can catch glimpses of the Pine–Strawberry valley to your right (west), with Deadman Mesa to the southwest. In 0.3 mile get sweeping views of the valley all the way to the south in the Mazatzal Mountains.

The AZT gradually curves northeast and continues climbing. In 0.5 mile the trail curves right (southeast) at a flat wooded area. In 0.4 mile reach a junction with Donahue Trail 27—the Highline Trail continues straight (southeast) at a sign that says GERONIMO TRAILHEAD LEFT, PINE TRAILHEAD RIGHT. The AZT climbs and traverses a drainage into an area with red soil in 0.4 mile. Then, in 0.1 mile, the trail makes a hard turn to the left (northeast) and passes through a flat area with a campsite and logs to sit on to the right (southeast).

After the saddle, views open of the Mogollon Rim stretching out to the east, the town of Payson and the mesas north of it, and the Sierra Ancha range in the distance to the south. The rim is composed of cream-colored Coconino sandstone and red Supai Group rock. Go northeast up the hill on the red-rock steps, continuing a steep climb for 0.2 mile, and then reach the hike's high point at 6,290 feet. The vegetation opens, and you can see Four Peaks, Mount Ord, and the Mazatzal Mountains (pronounced MAH-zat-zal or Madda-ZELL).

The trail descends and contours to the southeast, then to the northeast. In 0.3 mile the AZT bears right (southeast), descends, and crosses a drainage. In

0.1 mile switchback right (southeast), and the climb becomes less steep, flattens in 0.1 mile, and then descends on red-rock steps for 0.3 mile to a drainage crossing. The trail climbs back out of the drainage to the east for 0.1 mile, then descends to cross another drainage that may have water in it. Pass through a camping area with good spots for sitting and taking a break; 50 feet past the camping area is Red Rock Spring, which is piped into a concrete tank. It might not look like much, but water sources and seasonal springs like this are very important for AZT hikers. This is the turnaround for the main hike, at 4.4 miles and 6,000 feet.

Short Hike Option: Pine Loop

From the AZT/Lower Pineview Trail junction, the trail descends to the west and curves north, and the Lower Pineview meets the Pineview Trail #28 in 0.4 mile. Take a left (west) to continue to the Pine Trailhead. In 0.1 mile the trail switchbacks to go down the hill, and in 0.2 mile it curves north into a drainage, then continues to the southwest.

Reach the junction with the Pine Canyon Trail #26 in 0.1 mile and take a left (south) to go toward the Highline Trail—a sign says 0.7 MILE, PINE TRAILHEAD 1 MILE LEFT. In 0.1 mile, the trail curves left (southeast) toward a drainage and descends, then turns east to cross a drainage and makes a hard right (southwest). The trail ascends, curves into another drainage, and switchbacks up the hill to the west for 0.3 mile. The trail heads south and levels out, and buildings and the Pine Trailhead come into view on the right (west) in 0.1 mile.

The trail turns left (southeast) in 0.2 mile just before the Highline junction. Turn right (west) to close the loop and return to the Pine Trailhead in 0.3 mile. Switchback down the hill on the piece of AZT that you took at the beginning of the hike.

Gateway Community: PINE

DISTANCE FROM TRAILHEAD: 1.0 mile **POPULATION:** 1,963 **ELEVATION:** 5,367'

Gateway Community: STRAWBERRY

DISTANCE FROM TRAILHEAD: 4.0 miles **POPULATION:** 961 **ELEVATION:** 5,889'

Beneath the cliffs of the Mogollon Rim are the Gateway Communities of Pine and Strawberry, separated by 3.0 miles on AZ 87/AZ 260.

The closest restaurant to the Pine Trailhead is **That Brewery and Pub,** where you can get a delicious meal and pair it with an Arizona Trail Ale. A portion of the proceeds from the sale of the ale goes right back into the AZT via a donation to the Arizona Trail Association, so you can enjoy a beer and help the trail at the same time! Catch live music on the patio in the summertime.

Old County Inn has wood-fired pizzas with gluten-free options and a full bar. The **Early Bird Cafe** has fantastic burritos and a breakfast platter big enough for even a thru-hiker's appetite.

Pine Creek Cabins, the **Beeline Guest House,** and the **Strawberry Inn** have accommodations and there are many cabins, guest houses, and rooms for rent on Airbnb.

Local attractions include **Tonto Natural Bridge State Park,** where you can visit what is believed to be the largest natural travertine bridge in the world: 183 feet high, 400 feet long, and 150 feet across at its widest point. The park has hiking trails, four overlooks that can be seen from the parking lot, a small store, and the historic 10-bedroom Goodfellow Lodge (available for group rentals only). No pets are allowed on the trails at the park.

If you're looking for camping options, there are plenty of dispersed (primitive) camping spots on dirt roads in Tonto and Coconino National Forests. Nearby **U.S. Forest Service** campgrounds include **Houston Mesa** and **Flowing Springs,** both just north of Payson.

THAT BREWERY AND PUB: 3270 AZ 87, 928-476-3349, thatbrewery.com. Open Monday and Tuesday, 11 a.m.–7 p.m.; Friday and Saturday, 11 a.m.–8 p.m.; Sunday, 11 a.m.–7 p.m.

OLD COUNTY INN: 3502 AZ 87, 928-476-6560, oldcountyinn.com. Open Sunday and Wednesday, 11 a.m.–9 p.m.; Thursday, 11 a.m.–10 p.m.; Friday and Saturday, 11 a.m.–11 p.m. Bar closes an hour before the restaurant.

EARLY BIRD CAFE: 3618 AZ 87, 928-476-4092, facebook.com/theearlybirdcafepine. Open Sunday–Thursday, 6:30 a.m.–2 p.m.; Friday, 6:30 a.m.–7 p.m.; Saturday, 6:30 a.m.–3 p.m.

PINE CREEK CABINS: 3901 AZ-87, 928-970-9511, pinecreekcabinsaz.com

BEELINE GUEST HOUSE: 4042 AZ 87 #150, 928-476-6515, beelineguesthouse.com

STRAWBERRY INN: 5073 AZ 87, 928-202-7790, thestrawberryinn.com

TONTO NATURAL BRIDGE STATE PARK: Forest Service Road 583, 928-476-4202, azstateparks.com/tonto. From AZ 260 in Payson, go 10.3 miles north on AZ 87; then turn left (west) onto FR 583, and drive 1.8 miles to the visitor center. Admission: $7 adults, $4 ages 7–13, free ages 6 and younger. Open daily, 9 a.m.–5 p.m.; Thanksgiving and December 24, 9 a.m.–2 p.m.; closed December 25. Pets prohibited on trails.

HOUSTON MESA CAMPGROUND: Houston Mesa Road (FR 199), 928-474-7900, tinyurl.com/houstonmesa. From AZ 260 in Payson, go 2.0 miles north on AZ 87, then 0.1 mile east on Houston Mesa Road; the campground is on the left (north) side of the road. There are 74 wheelchair-accessible campsites for tents, RVs (no hookups), and equestrians, along with coin-operated showers and flush toilets. Nightly rates: $19–$26; reserve by calling 877-444-6777 or visiting recreation.gov/camping/campgrounds/232355.

FLOWING SPRINGS CAMPGROUND: FR 272, 928-474-7900, tinyurl.com/flowingsprings. From AZ 260 in Payson, go 3.0 miles north on AZ 87; then, near milepost 257.0, just south of the East Verde River, turn right (east) onto FR 272 and drive 0.5 mile farther. The campground is on the left (north) side of the road. Free; vault toilet but no other facilities on-site.

Getting There

PINE TRAILHEAD: N34° 22.459' W111° 26.591', elevation 5,394'

ROAD CONDITIONS: All vehicles; paved except last 0.2 mile of graded dirt leading to the trailhead

FACILITIES: Restrooms 0.1 mile west of trailhead parking

DIRECTIONS *From Phoenix Sky Harbor Airport:* Follow the signs to get onto AZ 202 Loop East, and in 7.1 miles take Exit 13 left (north) onto Country Club Drive (AZ 87). In 74.7 miles, go through the Gateway Community of Payson, taking the second exit off both roundabouts in town to stay on AZ 87. The Pine Trailhead is 12.6 miles north. Turn right (east) and pass a restroom in 0.1 mile, and the road ends in 0.2 mile at the Pine Trailhead, which has a large parking area for vehicles and a turnaround circle for trailers (please don't block this).

From Flagstaff: Take Lake Mary Road south for 54 miles, and turn right (southwest) onto AZ 87. Go 23.5 miles through the Gateway Communities of Pine and Strawberry, and turn left (east) at the PINE TRAILHEAD sign. The parking area is 0.2 mile ahead.

If you're lucky, you may see some elks or hear them bugling during your hike.

Highline: GERONIMO TRAILHEAD TO BRAY CREEK

Red-rock rim views

SCENERY: ★ ★ ★ ★ ★
TRAIL CONDITION: ★ ★ ★
CHILDREN: ★ ★
DIFFICULTY: ★ ★ ★/★ ★ ★ ★
(short hike/full hike)
SOLITUDE: ★ ★ ★

The AZT winds beneath the colorful Coconino sandstone of the Mogollon Rim.

DISTANCE & CONFIGURATION: 7.2-mile out-and-back

HIKING TIME: 4–6 hours

ACCUMULATED ELEVATION GAIN: 1,290'

SHORT HIKE OPTION: 3.6-mile out-and-back to rim view/700' elevation gain

OUTSTANDING FEATURES: Mogollon Rim views, seasonal creek

LAND-MANAGEMENT AGENCY: Tonto National Forest, Payson Ranger District, 928-474-7900, fs.usda.gov/tonto

MAPS: USGS 7.5' *Kehl Ridge, AZ*

AZT PASSAGE: 26/Highline, aztrail.org/explore/passages/passage-26-highline

ANCESTRAL LANDS: Apache, Hopi

SEASON: Spring, summer, fall

ACCESS: No fees or permits; open 24-7, year-round

Overview

This hike on the Arizona National Scenic Trail (AZT) follows the Highline National Recreational Trail, which uses parts of an old wagon road and ancient route that connects areas underneath the Mogollon (MO-go-yawn) Rim. It climbs to spectacular views of red rock and pinnacles on the Mogollon Rim on its way to seasonal Bray Creek.

On the Trail

This trail winds in and out of the canyons that drain the Mogollon Rim, an escarpment that forms the edge of the Colorado Plateau. In places where the trail is singletrack, the tread is generally good. In some areas, the trail uses the old wagon road, and those sections are more rocky, steep, and loose.

The Highline Trail, which runs 50.0 miles beneath the rim, used to be an old wagon road that served the area. From the trailhead (5,431'), switchback up the hill on red dirt and rock. In 0.25 mile the path briefly descends and you see the beautiful striped red and white rock of the Mogollon Rim. Resume climbing through alligator juniper, ponderosa pine, oak, and red-barked manzanita. In 0.3 mile reach a junction with an old roadbed, and turn right (northeast).

Cross a metal pipe, and the trail crosses the creek, leaves the road, and curves to the right (southwest). Pass a sign that says #31 straight ahead, and the trail begins climbing in 0.1 mile. The brown AZT carsonite signs are co-marked with the white diamond of the Highline National Recreation Trail; the white diamonds are also blazed on the trees.

In 0.2 mile you descend to cross the drainage; then the AZT climbs steeply through a series of short switchbacks. In 0.4 mile descend and climb out of three drainages over the next 0.2 mile. The canopy opens in 0.3 mile, with views of the pinnacles on the rim. In 0.1 mile the trail curves right (north) to a camping area with rocks for sitting on your left (west). There are spectacular views to the south of the Mazatzal Mountains (MAH-zat-zal or Madda-ZELL), Mount Ord, and the Four Peaks in the distance. **This is the end of the short hike option, at 1.8 miles and 700 feet of elevation gain.**

To continue on the AZT, curve right (northeast) and descend on a rocky roadbed for 0.2 mile; then go in and out of small drainages for the next 0.2 mile. The trail heads south through a flat, wooded area with a campsite and reaches a junction with the BSA Trail to the left (north). Stay on the combined Highline Trail/ AZT as it climbs south, then levels out. In 0.2 mile descend briefly and then start a climb to the north to a saddle; in 0.1 mile make a steep descent to cross a drainage. After a brief flat area, the trail resumes climbing for 0.1 mile to the small saddle.

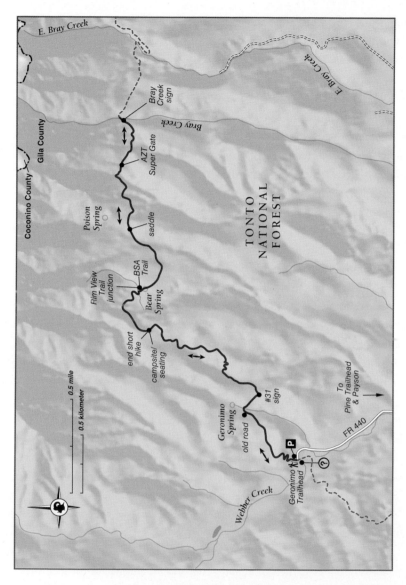

The AZT curves in and out of a small drainage beneath sandstone pillars. In 0.4 mile descend to cross another drainage; then switchback and continue climbing to a high point of 6,224 feet. The trail is benched into the side of the hill and you get fantastic views of the surrounding area. Reach a saddle and a turn to the left (east) in 0.2 mile. The AZT rolls through some short, steep hills with exposed areas of red slickrock, then curves left (north) to cross the drainage in 0.1 mile.

Go through an AZT Super Gate and descend, curving left (northeast). In 0.1 mile reach a sign that says BRAY CREEK 90 FEET TO THE RIGHT, UNTREATED SPRING WATER 60 FEET TO THE LEFT, and lists mileages: 482 to Mexico and 343 to Utah.

This is the end of the hike, at 3.6 miles and 6,208 feet of elevation. Return the way you came.

Gateway Community: STRAWBERRY *(see page 157)*

DISTANCE FROM TRAILHEAD: 12.0 miles **POPULATION:** 961 **ELEVATION:** 5,889'

Gateway Community: PINE *(see page 157)*

DISTANCE FROM TRAILHEAD: 10.0 miles **POPULATION:** 1,963 **ELEVATION:** 5,367'

Getting There

GERONIMO TRAILHEAD: N34° 24.051' W111° 21.945', elevation 5,431'

ROAD CONDITIONS: All vehicles; gravel for 7.3 miles

FACILITIES: None

DIRECTIONS *From Pine Trailhead (see page 159 for GPS coordinates and driving directions):* Turn left (south) onto AZ 87; then go 1.6 miles to the junction with Control Road 64, and go left (east). In 5.5 miles reach Forest Service Road 440, and turn left (northeast), then in 0.2 mile turn left (northwest). Take FR 440 1.6 miles, and the parking area is on your right (west).

From Payson (junction of AZ 87 and AZ 260): Go 12.0 miles north to Control Road 64, and turn right (east). Then proceed as directed above.

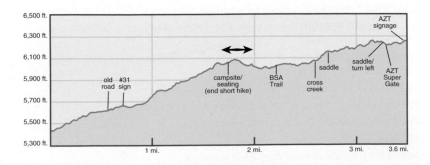

Highline: WASHINGTON PARK TRAILHEAD TO GENERAL SPRINGS CABIN *From river to rim*

19

SCENERY: ★★★★
TRAIL CONDITION: ★★★/
★★★★ (full hike/short hike)
CHILDREN: ★/★★★★
(full hike/short hike)
DIFFICULTY: ★★★★/★★
(full hike/short hike)
SOLITUDE: ★★

A small cascade on the East Verde River

DISTANCE & CONFIGURATION: 6.9-mile out-and-back to General Springs Cabin with Tunnel Trail

HIKING TIME: 4–6 hours

ACCUMULATED ELEVATION GAIN: 1,800'

SHORT HIKE OPTION: 2.2-mile out-and-back to road junction/350' elevation gain

OUTSTANDING FEATURES: East Verde River, historical railroad tunnel and fire lookout cabin, Mogollon Rim views

LAND-MANAGEMENT AGENCY: Tonto National Forest, Payson Ranger District, 928-474-7900, fs.usda.gov/tonto

MAPS: USGS 7.5' *Kehl Ridge, AZ*

AZT PASSAGE: 26/Highline, aztrail.org/explore/passages/passage-26-highline

ANCESTRAL LANDS: Apache, Yavapai–Apache, Hopi

SEASON: Spring, summer, fall

ACCESS: No fees or permits; open 24-7, year-round

Overview

This hike on the Arizona National Scenic Trail (AZT) consists of two parts. The first meanders back and forth, crossing the East Verde River on picturesque bridges through shady forest. The second climbs to visit an abandoned railroad tunnel on the way to the top of the Mogollon (MO-go-yawn) Rim. The hike ends above the rim at General Springs Cabin, a historical fire lookout. The full hike has a very loose and steep approach to the tunnel that is not recommended for children.

On the Trail

From the trailhead (6,048'), pass the big metal AZT sign to your left (west). In 100 feet you come to a message board and an AZT sign with maps and history of Washington Park and information about sharing the trail. White diamonds on the trees mark the Highline National Recreation Trail. In 300 feet reach a bridge over the East Verde River. An equestrian bypass takes off to the left (west), and a short path for river access is on the far side of the bridge. This area is good for colorful leaves in the fall.

Just past the bridge, reach a junction with Colonel Devin Trail 290 and go left (north), leaving the Highline Trail. Join the other end of the equestrian bypass at 0.1 mile, and reach another sign that lists mileages to the railroad tunnel and Forest Service Road 300.

The trail climbs gently through the ponderosa pines. If you live at a low elevation, you may feel a little short of breath due to reduced oxygen. Get a view of the East Verde River in 0.2 mile; the AZT follows the waterway. The East Verde, a tributary of the Verde River, flows southwest through central Arizona, and its headwaters are nearby. The natural flow is supplemented by water piped in from the C. C. Cragin Reservoir on East Clear Creek on the Mogollon Rim.

In 0.1 mile cross the river on a log bridge and, 0.2 mile beyond that, another metal bridge. Access to the river is before you cross on your right (north). In 0.1 mile make two switchbacks, and reach a second log bridge in 0.1 mile. Just past the bridge is a pretty little cascade. You can either go 50 feet up the creek or cross above it on the AZT, at a switchback to the right (west). A small seating area on rocks is to your left (west).

The trail switchbacks and enters an open burn area in 0.2 mile. Pass the back of a trail sign that lists mileage to the Washington Park Trailhead. **This is the end of the short hike (6,836'), at 2.2 miles round-trip and 350 feet of elevation gain.**

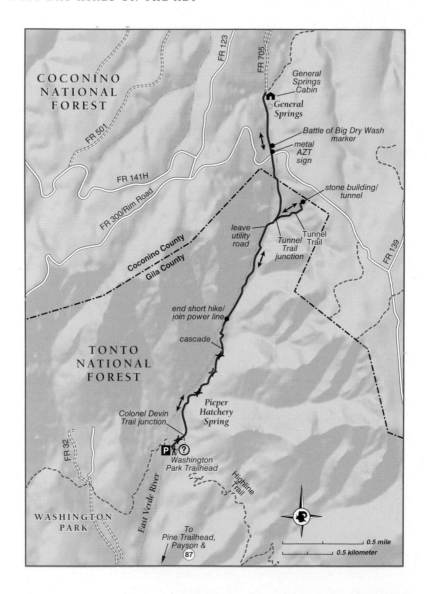

To continue on the AZT, join the power-line road to the right (northeast). In 0.2 mile the trail steepens and you join the utility road coming in from the right (south). This part of the trail does not have shade or tree cover. The trail leaves the utility corridor in 0.4 mile at a sign. Turn right (east) and cross the drainage. The trail switchbacks up 0.1 mile to a junction with the Railroad

Tunnel Trail. Don't take this turn—instead, switchback left (west) and then right (east) to reach a second junction in 0.1 mile.

The railroad tunnel was the dream of Colonel James W. Eddy and the result of the Arizona Mineral Belt Railroad wanting to move ore between Globe and Flagstaff. In 1883 work began on drilling a 3,100-foot tunnel through the Mogollon Rim—but they made it just 70 feet before the funds were exhausted and the project was abandoned.

This part of the hike is very steep; the rocks are loose and mixed with sand. Leave the AZT and take the Tunnel Trail straight (east) and steeply climb the left (north) side of the canyon. Reach the top in 0.2 mile (7,002'). Straight ahead there is a stone seating area and fire rings, and a building to the right (east); the tunnel is directly ahead to the north. The railroad tunnel is, unfortunately, filled with graffiti. You can explore the area, but be careful because it's rocky and often wet inside. Return to the AZT junction in 0.2 mile. On your hike down, don't be afraid to get low to the ground and hang on to branches or rocks, or even butt-scoot if you need to.

To reach the top of the Mogollon Rim requires an additional 0.4-mile/400-foot climb, and then it's a mostly flat 0.4-mile dirt road walk to General Springs Cabin. If you're not in the mood for more climbing, you can turn around here and go back the way you came.

To continue on the AZT, make a right (west) and climb 0.3 mile to join the utility corridor. In 0.1 mile reach FR 300, and carefully cross it. A marker commemorating the Battle of Big Dry Wash is on your right (east).

Continue north on FR 705 for 0.3 mile, passing a sign for General Springs, and arrive at the trailhead for General Springs Cabin. The cabin is 100 feet to your right (east). See the first hike in the next chapter for information on the cabin.

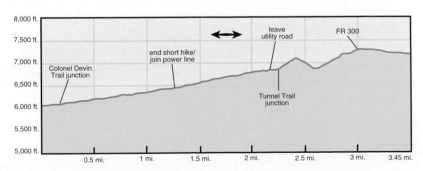

Spotlight: The Battle of Big Dry Wash

Fought on July 17, 1882, the Battle of Big Dry Wash is considered the last big combat between the Apache and the U.S. Army. In the wake of European and American colonization, the Indigenous peoples who had lived in the area for centuries fought to keep their land, and during the 1800s many Apache were forcibly relocated to reservations.

The White Mountain Apache, led by Na-ti-o-tish, had prepared an ambush for the Army in a tributary of East Clear Creek at a spot where the canyon narrows. They mistakenly thought the Army was coming from only one direction, but instead they were surrounded. Twenty-two Apache, including Na-ti-o-tish, were killed in the battle, along with one Army soldier. The area now bears the name Battleground Ridge.

The last band of Apache, led by Geronimo, surrendered to the Army in 1886. Today the San Carlos, Tonto White Mountain, and Yavapai–Apache Reservations are located in central Arizona.

On your return, make sure to leave the utility road 0.1 mile after you cross FR 300, and also make sure to leave the roadbed to the right (southwest) to follow singletrack at the point where the road descends to cross the creek. For the return trip, the trail stays on the right (west) side of the creek and does not cross. Then, in 1.1 miles, leave the utility road to the left (east).

Gateway Community: PAYSON *(see page 150)*
DISTANCE FROM TRAILHEAD: 15.0 miles **POPULATION:** 15,710 **ELEVATION:** 5,003'

Gateway Community: PINE *(see page 157)*
DISTANCE FROM TRAILHEAD: 16.0 miles **POPULATION:** 1,963 **ELEVATION:** 5,367'

Gateway Community: STRAWBERRY *(see page 157)*
DISTANCE FROM TRAILHEAD: 18.0 miles **POPULATION:** 961 **ELEVATION:** 5,889'

Getting There
WASHINGTON PARK TRAILHEAD: N34° 25.812' W111° 15.635', elevation 6,048'

ROAD CONDITIONS: *From Payson:* All vehicles; gravel for 5.0 miles. *From Pine:* All vehicles; gravel for 13.6 miles.

FACILITIES: None

DIRECTIONS *From Payson:* From the junction with AZ 260, drive 2.0 miles north on AZ 87, and turn right (east) onto Houston Mesa Road (Forest Service Road 199) across from The Home Depot; *zero your odometer here.* A sign indicates that it's 15.0 miles to Washington Park.

At mile 0.1 pass Houston Mesa Campground on the left (north), at mile 0.8 pass the Houston Mesa Trailhead, and at mile 1.7 stay right (east) at a sign for Mesa del Caballo.

The Shoofly Village Archaeological Site (see page 151) is to the right (east) at mile 2.9.

At mile 7.0 make the first crossing of the East Verde River, with restrooms and paid parking on the right (east). The Water Wheel Trailhead is to the right (east) at mile 7.5; the second crossing, at mile 8.1, has parking and restrooms on the left (west). The third crossing, with parking and picnic tables, is at mile 9, and you then pass through the community of Whispering Pines. At mile 10 Houston Mesa Road ends at the junction with Control Road 64. Turn left (west) onto this gravel road.

At mile 10.6 make a right (north) onto FR 32, and pass a sign that says WASHINGTON PARK TRAILHEAD 5 MILES. At mile 11.2 pass Shadow Rim Ranch Road, and at mile 12.5 enter private land. At mile 13.3 turn right (east), and straight ahead there is a closed gated road. Turn left (north) onto FR 32A; a sign states that the area is closed to camping by the U.S. Forest Service for the next 1.0 mile because of impact on resources. The road is a little rough, but it's still passable for passenger vehicles.

At mile 15.0 the road ends at the Washington Park Trailhead. At the time of this writing, a sign at the trailhead reads, "This area is temporarily closed to camping to allow the land to heal." The East Verde River can be heard flowing to the right (east).

From Pine Trailhead (see page 159 for GPS coordinates and driving directions): Turn left (south) onto AZ 87, drive 1.6 miles to the junction with Control Road 64, and turn left (east). Reach FR 32 in 9.3 miles; then turn left (north) and pick up the directions at the beginning of the previous paragraph. The total distance is 15.4 miles.

North (Hikes 20–30)

Gateway Communities are highlighted in yellow.

NORTH

General Springs Cabin (see Hike 20, next page) is part of a network of historic fire-lookout structures on the Mogollon Rim.

20

General Springs Canyon
Streamside amble with a historic cabin

SCENERY: ★★★★
TRAIL CONDITION: ★★★★
CHILDREN: ★★★★★
DIFFICULTY: ★★
SOLITUDE: ★★

Sunrise in General Springs Canyon

DISTANCE & CONFIGURATION: 6.0-mile out-and-back

HIKING TIME: 3–4 hours

ACCUMULATED ELEVATION GAIN: 530'

SHORT HIKE OPTION: It's up to you—amble out as far as you'd like, enjoy the views, and return the way you came. Not all hikes have to have an end objective.

OUTSTANDING FEATURES: Historic cabin, water in General Springs Canyon, ponderosa pine forest

LAND-MANAGEMENT AGENCY: Coconino National Forest, Flagstaff Ranger District, 928-526-0866, fs.usda.gov/coconino

MAPS: USGS 7.5' *Kehl Ridge and Dane Canyon, AZ*

AZT PASSAGE: 27/Blue Ridge, aztrail.org/explore/passages/passage-27-blue-ridge

ANCESTRAL LANDS: Apache, Hopi

SEASON: Spring, summer, fall

ACCESS: No fees or permits; open 24-7, year-round, but be aware of seasonal road closures (see Travel Note, page 175)

Overview

This hike on the Arizona National Scenic Trail (AZT) begins with a visit to a picturesque fire-lookout cabin. It's a pleasant walk through the ponderosa pines past a flowing creek, without a lot of elevation gain or loss. In summer, ferns cover the ground and you may find wildflowers blooming.

On the Trail

From the trailhead (7,198'), walk 100 feet east to visit General Springs Cabin, one of a series of cabins that have been used as fire-guard stations over the years. Signs at the cabin list both 1918 and 1914–15 as dates for the cabin's construction by Louis Fisher.

After visiting the cabin, head back east and turn right (northeast) to follow Forest Service Road 705. In 0.1 mile reach a sign for Fred Haught Trail 141 and a trail register. In this area, the AZT is also signed as the Cabin Loop Trail, and it becomes singletrack after the register. The fencing to your right (east) ends after 0.2 mile, and the trail crosses the canyon. In 0.2 mile the trail turns right (east) and climbs, switchbacking on sand and striated stone steps. Follow brown carsonite posts and cairns, slowly gaining elevation and then descending to cross the creek again in 0.3 mile. A seasonal waterfall may be flowing downstream from this crossing. Just before you cross the creek, go left (west) and follow the creek 100 feet to the overlook.

Climb out the other side of the creek and follow the rim of the canyon for a short distance; then switchback down, crossing the canyon again in 0.2 mile. I was delighted to find ripe blackberries during August when I was doing my research for this book.

The trail stays close to the bottom of the canyon and crosses it twice in the next 0.3 mile. The AZT makes a brief climb and flattens, traveling next to the creek and then above it. In 0.6 mile reach a small meadow; then, in 0.2 mile, you cross a small ravine and the trail nestles close to the creek again.

Ponderosa pine trees are said to smell like butterscotch or vanilla; take a sniff of one of the larger ones on this hike to see if you can smell it. For more information about ponderosa pines, see page 209.

This section of the AZT is a favorite of northbound thru-hikers: it's the first passage on top of the Mogollon Rim, which marks a significant geographic change in the terrain. The big ups and downs of southern Arizona are behind

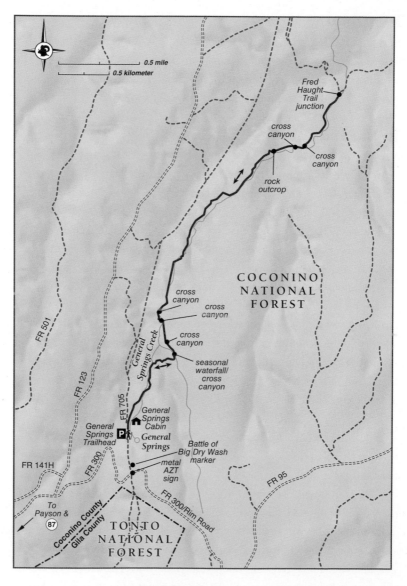

them, and as long as it isn't muddy season, it's smooth sailing—there's very little elevation gain through the world's largest ponderosa pine forest until you hit Flagstaff and the San Francisco Peaks.

In 0.5 mile cross another small ravine, and there are rocks ahead to sit on at an outcrop of sandstone on the left (north). The trail surface is sparkly due to the mica in the soil. Cross the creek two more times over the next 0.25 mile, and descend on stone steps 0.1 mile farther. Pass a campsite and then hike a beautiful stretch of trail next to the creek.

You reach the low point and end of the hike in 0.3 mile (3.0 total miles), at the junction with the Fred Haught Trail (6,932'). Return the way you came.

Gateway Community: PINE *(see page 157)*

DISTANCE FROM TRAILHEAD: 26.0 miles **POPULATION:** 1,963 **ELEVATION:** 5,367'

Gateway Community: STRAWBERRY *(see page 157)*

DISTANCE FROM TRAILHEAD: 4.0 miles **POPULATION:** 961 **ELEVATION:** 5,889'

Getting There

GENERAL SPRINGS TRAILHEAD: N34° 27.513' W111° 15.087', elevation 7,198'

ROAD CONDITIONS: No low-clearance vehicles; gravel for 12.0 miles

FACILITIES: None

TRAVEL NOTE: Forest Service Road 300—known locally as the **Rim Road**—is closed in winter, generally whenever there's snow and ice on the ground. To check whether this and other roads in Coconino National Forest's Mogollon Rim District are open, call 928-474-7900 or check tinyurl.com/rimroadupdates. The website also links to free digital maps of the area; the PDF maps are suitable for printing from a computer; the mobile files are suitable for use on smartphones and some Garmin GPS units.

DIRECTIONS *From Flagstaff (I-17/I-40 interchange):* Drive south on Lake Mary Road for 52.3 miles, and turn right (southwest) onto AZ 87 South. In 9.2 miles, turn left (south) onto the Rim Road (FR 300). *Zero your odometer here.*

At mile 0.1 take a left (east) to stay on FR 300. **Note:** Some of this road has steep drop-offs and no railings on the rim side. There is plenty of developed as

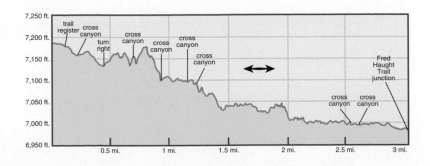

well as dispersed (primitive) camping along the Rim Road. At mile 1.4 you reach a sign about the General Crook Trail, a historical wagon road, to your left (west). At mile 3.6 reach a junction with FR 147 and FR 218—stay straight to continue on FR 300. At 5.6 miles pass a junction with FR 308 on the left (northeast); continue going straight.

There is an expansive view of the Mazatzal Mountains (MAH-zat-zal or Madda-ZELL) in the distance. At mile 6.8 Kehl Spring Forest Camp is on your left (north), and at mile 7.3 you pass a junction for FR 141. Cross the General Crook Trail again at mile 8.6, then again at the junction for FR 123 at mile 11.2.

Reach a metal AZT sign at mile 12 where the trail crosses FR 300, and turn left (north). Immediately to your right is a marker commemorating the Battle of Big Dry Wash (see page 168 for more information). Go 0.5 mile, passing a small sign for General Springs on the way to the parking area. The General Springs Trailhead is a dirt parking lot—*please leave the turnaround clear for people pulling trailers.*

From Payson: From the junction of AZ 87 and AZ 260, take the second exit off each of two successive roundabouts to stay on AZ 87 North. Drive about 28 miles through the Gateway Communities of Pine and Strawberry; then turn right (south) onto the Rim Road (FR 300), zero your odometer, and pick up the directions above. Total distance is 40.5 miles.

From Phoenix Sky Harbor Airport: Take AZ 143 North to Exit 3A for AZ 202 Loop East toward Mesa. In 7.0 miles take Exit 13 to AZ 87 North, and turn left (north). In 84.0 miles reach the Gateway Community of Payson and continue northbound on AZ 87. Past the junction with AZ 260 on your right (east), take the second exit off each of two successive roundabouts to stay on AZ 87 North. Drive about 28 miles through the Gateway Communities of Pine and Strawberry; then turn right (south) onto the Rim Road (FR 300), zero your odometer, and pick up the directions above.

21

Mormon Lake

Historical railway in the ponderosa pines

Mormon Lake is Arizona's largest natural lake, but it is often dry. In September, it fills with yellow wildflowers.

DISTANCE & CONFIGURATION: 6.2-mile point-to-point, 12.4-mile out-and-back

HIKING TIME: 3–4 hours point-to-point, double for out-and-back

ACCUMULATED ELEVATION GAIN: 600' point-to-point/1,000' out-and-back

SHORT HIKE OPTION: 3.2-mile out-and-back to railroad sign/350' elevation gain

OUTSTANDING FEATURES: Ponderosa pines, summer vacation getaway, wildflowers in September

LAND-MANAGEMENT AGENCY: Coconino National Forest, Flagstaff Ranger District, 928-526-0866, fs.usda.gov/coconino

MAPS: USGS 7.5' *Mormon Lake, AZ*

AZT PASSAGE: 29/Mormon Lake, aztrail.org/explore/passages/passage-29-mormon-lake

ANCESTRAL LANDS: Hopi, Yavapai–Apache, Western Apache

SEASON: Spring (watch for mud), summer, fall

ACCESS: No fees or permits; open 24-7, year-round

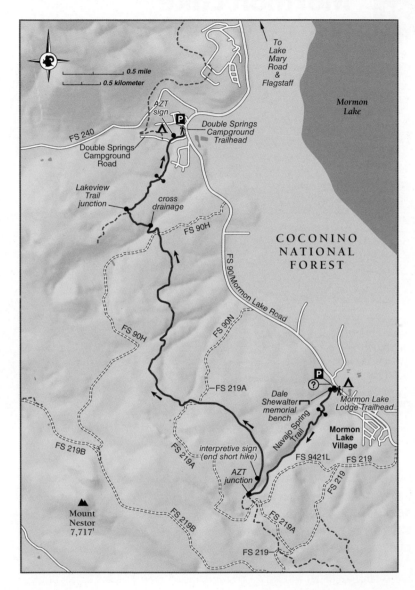

Overview

This hike on the Arizona National Scenic Trail (AZT) traverses through ponderosa pine and Gambel oak on slopes above Mormon Lake, Arizona's largest natural lake. But this being arid Arizona, the lake is often dry. It's a great getaway from the summer heat in southern Arizona—on the August day that I did the research for this hike, it was 115°F in Phoenix, yet it was only in the 80s at Mormon Lake. You may find the lake filled with yellow wildflowers in early September.

On the Trail

The start of the trail is right across from mile marker 2, through the wooden arch past the pizzeria. Go south through the courtyard and reach a memorial bench for Dale Shewalter, "Father of the Arizona Trail" (see page 1). Turn right (west) at the bench toward an information kiosk and mileage sign in 50 feet; then turn left (southwest) to follow the Navajo Spring Trail to the AZT. Join an old roadbed and, at 0.1 mile, take the right (southwest) fork marked for Navajo Spring Trail.

The tread is rocky, and you'll be sharing portions of this trail with equestrians taking advantage of the horseback rides offered at Mormon Lake. Whenever you see a horse, step to the side of the trail and greet the rider so that the horse knows you're not a threat. In 0.2 mile join a road, and look to your left (south) for trail signs and a pedestrian gate. The trail gradually gains elevation heading for the AZT. You might be feeling a little out of breath—that's because the air is thinner here, at more than 7,000 feet.

The trail passes through Gambel oak and ponderosa pine, curving left and reaching a fenced area in 0.7 mile. The fence protects young aspens from being eaten by elk, deer, and livestock until they are of an age to withstand it without dying. In 0.2 mile the trail is fenced on both sides as you reach Navajo Spring; a sign points right (west) to the AZT. The trail continues past concrete catchments and curves southwest for the final stretch to meet the AZT in 0.2 mile.

Go right (northwest) toward Double Springs Campground. Pass signs reading CLOSED TO ALL MOTOR VEHICLES, and the trail curves right (north). In 0.2 mile pass an interpretive panel—part of a series of signs about the old

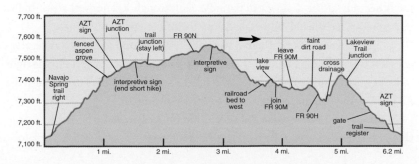

logging railroad—that talks about what loggers in the late 19th and early 20th centuries had to eat to fuel their work. **This sign marks the turnaround for the short hike, at 3.2 miles round-trip and 350 feet of elevation gain.**

Another sign (not on this hike) provides a brief account of the railroad's history as both an industrial route and a passenger route for visitors to the resort at Mormon Lake: "The Flagstaff Lumber Company extended their logging railroad from Lake Mary toward Mormon Lake and Mormon Mountain beginning in 1923. The railroad was constructed primarily to haul logs cuts from the forest to sawmills in Flagstaff, Williams, and other areas. On weekends the railroad would carry as many as 300 passengers to the Mormon Lake area."

You might notice some cross-country-skiing signs high up in the trees—this area can get a tremendous amount of snow some years. Also beware of mud season, usually in early spring, which can turn a pleasant walk into a messy ordeal. In 0.2 mile reach a trail junction, stay left (northwest) to continue on the AZT, and enjoy a pleasant walk through the trees. The tread is dirt with rocky footing in spots. You might hear the squawk of scrub jays, blue birds with black heads, in the same family as ravens.

Mormon Lake is Arizona's largest natural lake, but it is often filled with grasses and wildflowers rather than water. It used to be as deep as 16–26 feet in the early 1900s, but since the mid-1900s the lake has reached maximum annual depths of only about 10 feet, and even less in some years.

In 0.8 mile reach Forest Service Road 90N and cross it to the west, looking for a brown carsonite sign across the road for the continuation of the trail. Another interpretive sign, in 0.3 mile near the high point of the hike (7,542'), discusses railroad construction and logging practices; here you can also see old railroad ties and spikes, plus a remnant of a wall.

The trail curves right (northeast) in 0.3 mile and descends to continue on the other side of the drainage in 0.4 mile. Go through a canopy of trees. In 0.2 mile you can see the old railroad bed atop the hill to your left (west).

The trail ascends gently to a view out to Mormon Lake in 0.2 mile, then goes left (west) to join FR 90M. The AZT follows the road as it curves to the right to head north and then east, then ascends to a junction in 0.3 mile where the AZT leaves the road onto singletrack to the right (north).

Heads-Up: Do not make the very common AZT mistake of getting lost in thought and missing your turn off the dirt road onto the singletrack. Look for a carsonite sign and a big cairn where the trail descends from the junction. Cross a faint dirt road in 0.4 mile, and then cross FR 90H in 0.1 mile.

The trail goes between a pair of boulders; one of them has a message from Bambi about keeping the forest clean. The trail descends and switchbacks left (west) to cross a drainage in 0.1 mile. More switchbacks climb out the other side, and the trail winds its way uphill (northwest) for 0.2 mile to the top of the climb. Reach a junction with the Lakeview Trail in 0.1 mile—the AZT goes right (north) toward Double Springs Campground. Descend on rocky tread to the northeast, and pass through a gate in 0.4 mile. In 0.3 mile there is a trail register to sign.

Cross the meadow toward a small green building. The creek is just beyond the building; the trail curves right (northeast) and crosses a small wooden bridge, then left across the creek on a wooden bridge in 0.1 mile. Just beyond the bridge, reach the campground road and a metal AZT sign. Restrooms are across the road.

If you didn't stage a car, turn around here and go back the way you came. To return to your shuttle car for the point-to-point hike, continue right (east) and walk down the road 0.2 mile to reach the trailhead parking area.

Gateway Community: MORMON LAKE VILLAGE

DISTANCE FROM TRAILHEAD: NA **POPULATION:** 50–5,000 **ELEVATION:** 7,100'
A sign as you enter Mormon Lake Village lists the population as 50–5,000. Folks flock here to recreate among the pines and escape the long, hot summers of southern Arizona, but in winter things are pretty quiet due to the cold and snow at 7,000 feet. The cabins and campsites at **Mormon Lake Lodge** can be booked year-round, but amenities are seasonal and operating hours depend on yearly snowfall levels. Before you go, it's a good idea to contact the lodge to confirm what's open, especially during the shoulder seasons of May and October.

The lodge has a general store, a saloon with live music on the weekends, a restaurant, and a pizzeria. Horseback riding is offered in cooperation with **High Mountain Trail Rides;** packages are available that combine a trail ride with a meal and lodging.

In addition to cabins, the lodge has an RV park and campground with tent sites, full hookups, and coin-operated showers and laundry facilities. **Double Springs** and **Dairy Springs Campgrounds** are located northwest of the resort on Mormon Lake Road. Dispersed (primitive) camping can be found along the many dirt roads in Coconino National Forest surrounding Mormon Lake.

Mormon Lake is often dry, but **Upper Lake Mary,** about 15 miles north, has water in it and is stocked with fish. Nearby **Lakeview Campground** has 30 sites with tables, fire rings, and cooking grills; RVs under 28 feet are welcome, but no hookups are available.

MORMON LAKE LODGE: 1991 South Mormon Lake Road, 928-354-2227 or 877-386-4383, mormonlakelodge.com. Cabins and campsites are open year-round; amenities are open seasonally (generally mid-spring–mid-October), so call ahead to confirm hours.

Steakhouse and Saloon Across the street from the trailhead for this hike

Pizzeria Across the street from the campground and next to the trailhead

High Mountain Trail Rides 928-354-2359 (reservations); stables open 8 a.m. daily in season

Country Store Open 8 a.m. daily; closing times vary depending on season

MORMON LAKE CAMPGROUND Has 74 tent/RV sites, some with hookups. Nightly rates: $20 tent sites, $22 RV sites, $46 full-hookup sites.

DOUBLE SPRINGS CAMPGROUND: About 2.7 miles northwest of Mormon Lake Lodge on Mormon Lake Road (Forest Service Road 90), 928-526-0866, tinyurl.com/doublesprings campground. Has 15 single sites for tents and RVs (up to 35') with water, vault toilets, and picnic tables. Nightly rate: $19; open spring–mid-October. Availability is first come, first served.

DAIRY SPRINGS CAMPGROUND: About 4 miles north of Mormon Lake Lodge on Mormon Lake Road (FR 90), 928-526-0866, tinyurl.com/dairyspringscampground. Has 30 single sites with picnic tables and grills, plus 2 group sites; water and vault toilets on-site. Nightly rate: $22 single sites, $120 group sites; open spring–mid-October. Availability is first come, first served and by reservation (877-444-6777, recreation.gov/camping/camp grounds/232144).

UPPER LAKE MARY: About 14 miles southeast of Flagstaff/14 miles north of Mormon Lake Lodge on Lake Mary Road, 928-526-0866, tinyurl.com/upperlakemary. Day-use fee: $9. Open mid-May–mid-October. Two boat ramps; paved parking; picnic area with picnic tables, ramadas, and barbecue grills; vault toilets.

LAKEVIEW CAMPGROUND: About 12 miles southeast of Flagstaff/15 miles north of Mormon Lake Lodge on Lake Mary Road, 928-526-0866, tinyurl.com/lakemarycampground. Nightly rate: $24; open spring–mid-October. Availability is first come, first served.

Getting There

MORMON LAKE LODGE TRAILHEAD (HIKE START):
N34° 54.706' W111° 28.096', elevation 7,125'

ROAD CONDITIONS: All vehicles; paved

FACILITIES: Restrooms located across the street at the campground. See Gateway Community information (page 181) for the full list of amenities at Mormon Lake Lodge.

DIRECTIONS *From Flagstaff (I-17/I-40 interchange):* Take Lake Mary Road about 19 miles south toward Payson; then, just past a sign for Mormon Lake Village, turn right (west) onto Mormon Lake Road (FR 90), and follow it west and south for 7.7 miles along the west side of Mormon Lake. The trailhead will be on your right (west), and the campground and RV park will be on your left (east).

From Phoenix Sky Harbor Airport: Take AZ 143 North to Exit 3A for AZ 202 Loop East toward Mesa. In 7.0 miles take Exit 13 to AZ 87 North, and turn left (north). In 84.0 miles reach the Gateway Community of Payson, and take the second exit off each of two successive roundabouts to stay on AZ 87 North. In 35.0 miles turn left (north) onto Lake Mary Road. In 27.0 miles turn left (west) onto Mormon Lake Road (FR 90), and in about 1.6 miles the Mormon Lake Lodge Trailhead will be on your left (west).

> **DOUBLE SPRINGS CAMPGROUND TRAILHEAD (HIKE END):**
> N34° 56.558' W111° 29.481', elevation 7,140'
>
> **ROAD CONDITIONS:** All vehicles; paved
>
> **FACILITIES:** Restrooms 0.2 mile west on the campground road

DIRECTIONS *From the north:* The trailhead parking is about 5 miles south of the turn west onto Mormon Lake Road (FR 90) from Lake Mary Road—see directions from Flagstaff above. From Mormon Lake Road, turn right (west) at the signed turnoff for the campground, and leave a shuttle vehicle in the dirt lot to your left (south); then retrace your route to Mormon Lake Road, turn right (southeast), and continue about 2.7 miles farther to the Mormon Lake Lodge Trailhead, on your right (west).

From Mormon Lake Lodge Trailhead: Continue left (northwest) on Mormon Lake Road and, after about 2.7 miles, turn left (west) at the signed turnoff for Double Springs Campground. Leave a shuttle vehicle in the dirt lot to your left (south); then retrace your route to Mormon Lake Road, turn right (southeast), and drive about 2.7 miles back to the Mormon Lake Lodge Trailhead, now on your right (west).

22

Sandy's Canyon to Fisher Point

A cave and colorful sandstone

SCENERY: ★ ★ ★ ★ ★
TRAIL CONDITION: ★ ★ ★ ★
CHILDREN: ★ ★ ★ ★
DIFFICULTY: ★ ★
SOLITUDE: ★ ★

Coconino sandstone cliffs in Walnut Canyon

DISTANCE & CONFIGURATION: 4.2-mile out-and-back

HIKING TIME: 2–3 hours

ACCUMULATED ELEVATION GAIN: 265'

SHORT HIKE OPTION: 1.8-mile out-and-back to sandstone cliffs/220' elevation gain

OUTSTANDING FEATURES: Colorful sandstone cliffs and a cave; wildflowers in the summer

LAND-MANAGEMENT AGENCY: Coconino National Forest, Flagstaff Ranger District, 928-526-0866, fs.usda.gov/coconino

MAPS: USGS 7.5' *Flagstaff West, AZ*

AZT PASSAGE: 31/Walnut Canyon, aztrail.org/explore/passages/passage-31-walnut-canyon

ANCESTRAL LANDS: Hopi, Yavapai–Apache, Western Apache

SEASON: Spring, summer (be careful of monsoons; see page 35), fall

ACCESS: No fees or permits; open 24-7, year-round

Overview

This hike on the Arizona National Scenic Trail (AZT) descends into Walnut Canyon and visits colorful sandstone cliffs on the way to a cave beneath Fisher Point. This hike is a great option for children, beginners, and anyone in search of a hike that doesn't take a lot of time. The scenery payoff for the short distance is spectacular!

On the Trail

From the trailhead (6,832'), take the trail signed SANDY'S CANYON AND AZT ACCESS EAST. In 400 feet, reach the junction with Sandy's Canyon Trail. The sign says Arizona Trail 0.9 mile. Take the left (east) trail heading down into the canyon. The descent is rocky, and the steepest part is at the beginning of the downhill. If you are doing this hike in winter, there could be snow and ice and you may want to wear traction devices to avoid slipping. There may be poison ivy growing near this part of the trail, so take precautions when you pull off to the side to take a break or let people pass. The plant has three leaves and has a glossy shine to it and is only found in the first part of the hike.

At 0.25 mile the trail curves to head north and sandstone cliffs come into view. The trail is briefly flat, then descends to cross a drainage in 0.1 mile. Keep an eye out for purple (Rocky Mountain) iris blooming in the springtime. There are many varieties of wildflowers that bloom through the summer months. The trail climbs out the other side and becomes a wide, flat roadbed. In 0.2 mile the trail gradually goes downhill and the trail tread gets rockier.

Reach a junction in 0.4 mile, and make a right (east) onto the AZT: we'll be visiting some beautiful sandstone cliffs before going to Fisher Point. The trail dips down to cross Walnut Canyon. Reach the viewpoint in 0.1 mile.

The first time I hiked this section of the AZT in 2008, this was one of those unexpected places that made me drop my pack and stay awhile. It's a place I've visited time and time again, and I enjoy bringing people here because it's a beautiful destination for a short hike. These cliffs are Coconino sandstone, which is composed of sand from 275-million-year-old fossilized dunes. The striations in the cliffs are called crossbedding, which happened when the wind shifted directions.

This is also the turnaround for the short hike option, at 1.8 miles round-trip and 220 feet of elevation gain. After you've enjoyed the view, turn back north the way you came and curve to cross the canyon again. This is the low point of the hike, at 6,620 feet. Back at the junction (mile 1.0), turn right (north) to continue

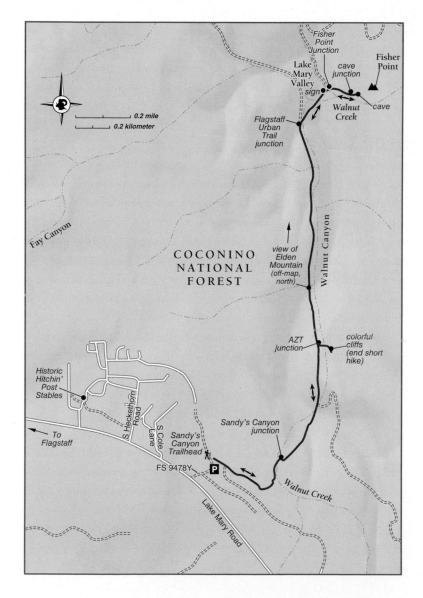

hiking. Continuing on, the trail parallels Walnut Canyon heading north; Walnut Canyon National Monument is about 9 miles north and east of this junction.

In 0.2 mile crest a small rise and get a view of Elden Mountain. Hike 24, Buffalo Park (page 196), is at the base of that mountain. The trail is sometimes singletrack, sometimes double- or tripletrack, and it makes for very pleasant,

Spotlight: Sinagua Culture

These trails were used by people long before the state of Arizona was founded. Evidence of occupation and travel through Walnut Canyon can be found as far back as Archaic times. The Sinagua Culture was an Indigenous civilization who lived in central and northern Arizona from about 600 to 1450 CE; *Sinagua* is derived from *Sierra Sin Agua* ("Mountains Without Water"), the Spanish name for the area.

The Sinagua foraged and farmed the area, growing corn, beans, and squash using irrigation techniques to water their fields. Sinaguan artists adorned the area with petroglyphs (pecked into the rock; see Hike 23, page 190) and pictographs (painted onto rock), made pottery with elaborate painted designs, and created jewelry from shell and stone. They had an extensive trade network with nearby tribes such as the Ancestral Puebloan and Hohokam.

The Hopi Tribe consider the Sinagua *Hisatsinom,* or ancestors. Their cliff dwellings and villages can be seen at Montezuma Castle and Tutzigoot National Monuments in the Verde Valley and Walnut Canyon, Wupatki, and Sunset Crater Volcano National Monuments near Flagstaff. Walnut Canyon National Monument has a museum and cliff dwellings accessed by two different trails.

nearly flat walking. In 0.5 mile the canyon opens, and the wall of the canyon comes into view straight ahead (north).

In 0.1 mile reach the junction with the AZT's Flagstaff Urban Route, which heads left (west) and then generally north through the middle of town. A sign at the junction lists mileages to Flagstaff, Marshall Lake, and the Fisher Point vista. For this hike, take the right (east) fork onto the AZT Equestrian Bypass and through the meadow to visit a small cave.

In 0.2 mile reach another junction where a sign again lists mileages to Marshall Lake—leave the AZT and turn right (east). You'll see the cave at the base of the sandstone cliff ahead. After passing another sign with mileages

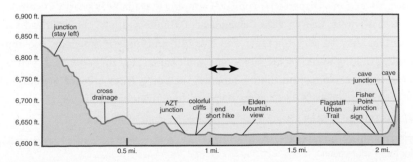

to Marshall Lake, you reach the cave—and the end of the hike—in 0.1 mile. Return the way you came.

Gateway Community: FLAGSTAFF

DISTANCE FROM TRAILHEAD: 5.0 miles **POPULATION:** 71,975 **ELEVATION:** 6,909'

Flagstaff is a fantastic town for outdoors enthusiasts. There are year-round activities, a vibrant downtown, and a great food and craft-beer scene. It's even got a trail of a different kind: the **Flagstaff Ale Trail**. The **First Friday ArtWalk**, held downtown on the first Friday of each month from 6 to 9 p.m., showcases art exhibitions, live music, performances, and more. There's often live music in **Heritage Square** during the summer.

A TALE OF TWO AZTs Because the AZT is open to hikers, bikers, and equestrians, two different routes were developed to accommodate the needs of the different trail users in the Flagstaff area. The Equestrian Bypass skirts the east side of town, avoiding city streets, while the Urban Route is the quickest way to food, resupply, and lodging for thru-hikers. Hike 23, Picture Canyon Loop (see the next hike), is on the Equestrian Bypass, while Hike 24, Buffalo Park (page 196), is on the Urban Route. The two routes rejoin south of the Schultz Pass Trailhead.

Stop in at **MartAnne's Breakfast Palace** for Chilaquiles Christmas-Style: fried corn tortillas layered with scrambled eggs, cheese, onions, and both red and green salsas. Or visit one of the many Thai restaurants in town—**Pato Thai Cuisine** is my favorite, and their curries are big enough for several meals. Learn more about the cultural and natural history of the Colorado Plateau at the **Museum of Northern Arizona**. Or visit nearby **Walnut Canyon National Monument**, which has been inhabited for thousands of years and preserves a group of Sinagua cliff dwellings (see previous page for more information).

Lodging is plentiful, ranging from hostels to hotels to Airbnbs. The historical **Hotel Monte Vista** is centrally located within walking distance to downtown attractions. Dispersed (primitive) camping is available in nearby Coconino National Forest; **Canyon Vista Campground,** 0.8 mile south of the trailhead for this hike, has 14 sites for tents and RVs (40' and under); fire rings, cooking grills, drinking water, picnic tables, and vault toilets, but no hookups. If you're looking for camping and hiking supplies, including rentals, **Peace Surplus** on Route 66 and **Babbitt's Backcountry Outfitters** downtown have you covered.

FLAGSTAFF ALE TRAIL: See flagstaffaletrail.com for more information.

FIRST FRIDAY ARTWALK: Various downtown locations; see flagartscouncil.org/artwalk for more information.

HERITAGE SQUARE: Aspen Avenue between San Francisco and Leroux Streets

MARTANNE'S BREAKFAST PALACE: 112 E. US 66, 928-773-4701, martannes.com. Open Monday–Saturday, 7:30 a.m.–9 p.m.; Sunday, 7:30 a.m.–3:30 p.m.

PATO THAI CUISINE: 20 E. US 66, 928-213-1825, patothai.com. Open Monday–Friday, 11 a.m.–3 p.m. (lunch specials) and 5–9 p.m. (dinner); Saturday, noon–9 p.m.; Sunday, noon–8 p.m.

MUSEUM OF NORTHERN ARIZONA: 3101 N. Fort Valley Rd., 928-774-5213, musnaz .org. Admission: $12 adults (ages 18–64); $10 seniors (ages 65 and older); $8 youth (ages 10–17) and Indigenous persons with tribal ID; free for kids (age 9 and younger) and Northern Arizona University students with ID. Open Monday–Saturday, 10 a.m.–5 p.m.; Sunday, noon–5 p.m.; closed Thanksgiving and December 25.

WALNUT CANYON NATIONAL MONUMENT: 3 Walnut Canyon Rd., 928-526-3367, nps .gov/waca. Admission: $15 for a 7-day pass. Open daily, 9 a.m.–5 p.m.; closed December 25 and January 1.

GRAND CANYON HOSTEL: 19 S. San Francisco St., 928-779-9421, grandcanyonhostel.com

HOTEL MONTE VISTA: 100 N. San Francisco St., 928-779-6971, hotelmontevista.com

CANYON VISTA CAMPGROUND: About 5.5 miles southeast of Flagstaff on Lake Mary Road, 928-526-0866, tinyurl.com/canyonvistacampground. Nightly rate: $22; open spring–mid-October. Availability is first-come, first served.

PEACE SURPLUS: 14 W. Historic Route 66, 928-779-4521, peacesurplus.com. Open Monday–Friday 8 a.m.–9 p.m.; Saturday 8 a.m.–8 p.m.; Sunday, 8 a.m.–6 p.m.

BABBITT'S BACKCOUNTRY OUTFITTERS 12 E. Aspen Ave., 928-774 4775, babbitts backcountry.com. Open Monday–Saturday, 8 a.m.–8 p.m., and Sunday, 9 a.m.–6 p.m.

Getting There

SANDY'S CANYON TRAILHEAD: N35° 07.878' W111° 36.340', elevation 6,832'

ROAD CONDITIONS: All vehicles; dirt for 0.2 mile

FACILITIES: None

DIRECTIONS *From Flagstaff (I-17/Lake Mary Road interchange):* Take Lake Mary Road southeast for 4.7 miles to Forest Service Road 9478Y, and go left (east) at a sign reading SANDY'S CANYON ACCESS—if you pass the turnoff for Canyon Vista Campground, you've missed the turn. In 150 feet reach a sign that reads SANDY'S CANYON TRAILHEAD, 0.25 mile to right; stay left (east) for 0.1 mile to reach the trailhead parking for the AZT.

23 Picture Canyon Loop

Ancient petroglyphs and a restored river environment

SCENERY: ★★★★
TRAIL CONDITION: ★★★★
CHILDREN: ★★★★
DIFFICULTY: ★
SOLITUDE: ★★

Picture Canyon petroglyphs were made by the Sinagua people between 700 and 1300 CE.

DISTANCE & CONFIGURATION: 3.5-mile loop

HIKING TIME: 1–2 hours

ACCUMULATED ELEVATION GAIN: 260'

SHORT HIKE OPTION: 2.6-mile out-and-back (40' elevation gain) to petroglyphs

OUTSTANDING FEATURES: Picture Canyon petroglyphs, waterfall, wildlife

LAND-MANAGEMENT AGENCY: City of Flagstaff, 928-213-2000, flagstaff.az.gov /1786/arizona-trail

MAPS: USGS 7.5' *Flagstaff West, AZ*

AZT PASSAGE: 32/Elden Mountain, aztrail.org/explore/passages/passage -32-elden-mountain

ANCESTRAL LANDS: Hopi, Navajo, Yavapai–Apache, Yavapai–Prescott, Pueblo of Zuni, Havasupai, and Hualapai

SEASON: Spring, summer (be careful of monsoons; see page 35), fall

ACCESS: No fees or permits; open daily, sunrise–sunset; pets must be leashed

Overview

Readily accessible from Flagstaff, this day hike on the Arizona National Scenic Trail (AZT) highlights the rich Indigenous culture of the area and petroglyphs of the Sinagua people.

Picture Canyon Natural and Cultural Preserve was acquired as open-space parkland by the City of Flagstaff in 2012. One mile of the Rio de Flag and 480 acres of surrounding forest, meadow, and stream habitat have been restored, making it an excellent spot for bird- and wildlife-watching.

On the Trail

From the trailhead, pass a sign that reads TOM MOODY TRAIL/PICTURE CANYON OUTER RECREATION LOOP, ARIZONA TRAIL/1.25 MILES VIA TOM MOODY TRAIL. Visitor brochures are available at the trailhead. Take the wide path east to an intersection in less than 0.1 mile and curve left (northeast) toward a sign reading TOM MOODY LOOP, OUTDOOR CLASSROOM, WATCHABLE WILDLIFE. Pass a marker noting that Picture Canyon was added to the National Register of Historic Places on January 10, 2008.

Just past this sign you'll see a trail register and a small stone amphitheater with interpretive signs about volcanoes, geology, archaeology, the Rio de Flag, wildlife and birds, and restoration efforts. Dale Shewalter, "Father of the Arizona Trail" (see page 1), was also involved in preserving Picture Canyon.

On your right (south), after the outdoor classroom, is a sign for Watchable Wildlife Site 11, a trail that leads to a pond—our loop continues straight (east). (More than 150 species of birds have been recorded at Picture Canyon.) In 0.2 mile reach the junction with the Tom Moody Loop—turn right (east) onto the wide path leading to the base of the hill. Cross under power lines and arrive at the Deepwater Pond, which is a good place to look for wildlife.

Signs talk about work done to rehabilitate the Rio de Flag stream channel and the value of volunteers. Cross the Rio de Flag and go left (north). Note that the water in the Rio de Flag—reclaimed from the Wildcat Hill treatment plant—is not potable.

Cross back under power lines at 0.1 mile, and stay straight at a junction going up the hill on your right (east). The Tom Moody Loop is marked by orange diamonds on the trees. In 0.2 mile the trail climbs a small hill to an interpretive sign about the historic remnants of a railroad trestle.

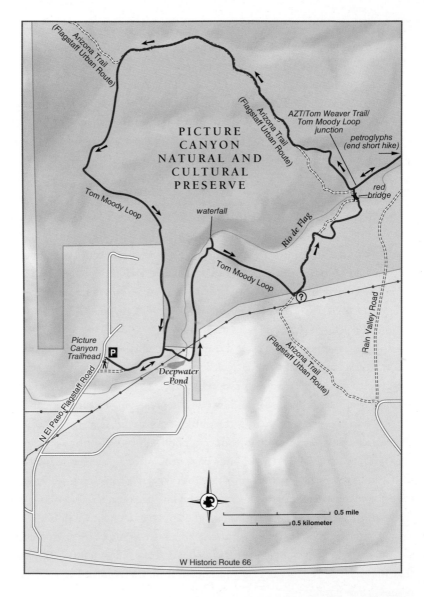

You can walk down and see the wood remnants of the trestle, then return to the trail and take a left (north) back toward the stream for 0.1 mile to view the waterfall. Return to the trail and turn left (east). Continue the loop and contour around the base of the hill as Picture Canyon deepens to your left (north).

Reach a kiosk, a power-line road crossing, and a trail junction in 0.2 mile. Take a left (northeast) onto the trail marked TOM MOODY LOOP/ARIZONA TRAIL. The trail meanders through ponderosa pine and Gambel oak. In 0.2 mile it makes a hard right to head east; then, 0.1 mile later, it makes a hard left heading north.

The trail travels northeast, then curves left (north), arriving at a little red bridge over the Rio de Flag in 0.2 mile. After crossing the bridge, come to a sign that indicates the AZT/Flagstaff Loop Trail straight ahead, the Tom Moody Loop to the right, and the Don Weaver Trail to the left.

For this hike turn right (northeast) onto the Tom Moody Loop to see the Waterbird Petroglyph Site and then return to the AZT. In 0.1 mile pass a sign that talks about making the most of a valuable resource and the ecological benefits of a meandering stream channel. Soon afterward, reach a turnoff for the Waterbird Petroglyph Site, with interpretive signs to your left (north).

The rock outcrop has Northern Sinagua petroglyphs that date from 700–1300 CE and two interpretive signs at 1.5 miles into the hike. The Sinagua ("without water" in Spanish) are the same tribe who built the cliff dwellings at nearby Walnut Canyon National Monument (see page 187). The Hopi call these ancient peoples the *Hisatsinom,* or "The People of Long Ago." These petroglyphs are just some of the 126 rock-art panels, containing 736 elements, found in the area—the largest concentration of their type.

> **PETROGLYPH ETIQUETTE** Please take care when visiting cultural sites. Petroglyphs, which are pecked into the rock, as well as pictographs, which are painted on, are very fragile and should never be touched, as your skin's natural oils can damage them. Treat the area with respect, view the petroglyphs from the designated area, do not climb around on the rocks, and do not disturb or remove any artifacts.

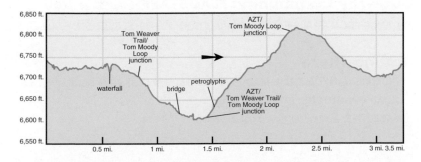

The sign at the petroglyph site reads, "The Waterbird site is sacred to seven different tribal groups, who continue to visit this area to connect with their culture and ancestors." These seven groups are the Hopi, Navajo, Yavapai–Apache, Yavapai–Prescott, Pueblo of Zuni, Havasupai, and Hualapai.

Take your time to enjoy the beauty of the petroglyphs, and think about the people who created them and the local tribes to whom they still have meaning. **This is the end of the short hike, at 1.3 miles and 40 feet of elevation gain.** Go back the way you came toward the AZT junction. To continue the loop, take a right (northwest), making sure you're on the AZT and not the Don Weaver Trail, which continues straight.

The AZT, on singletrack heading northwest, comes to a junction with a trail on the left (west). The trail ascends, curves right (northeast), crosses a road, and reaches a junction in 0.2 mile, with the Don Weaver Trail going left (southeast) and the AZT/Flagstaff Loop Trail going straight (west). Stay on the AZT as it curves north and then northwest again, crossing a couple of doubletrack roads. Follow the trail as it curves to the north and northwest, then heads west. The trail gradually ascends through a forest of oaks and pines to a junction in 0.6 mile.

Leave the AZT and turn left (south), rejoining the Tom Moody Loop on a wide trail. In 0.4 mile and again less than 0.1 mile later, cross closed doubletrack roads. The trail curves to the east and then the southeast. At mile 3.0, reach a junction and take a left (south). In 0.1 mile come to a junction with the Don Weaver Trail to the left (east)—go straight (south) on the Tom Moody Loop.

Pass the water-treatment facility and reach the junction to close the loop on the Tom Moody Trail, near the outdoor classroom in 0.2 mile. Turn right (west) to return to the trailhead; then turn right again (northwest) in 0.1 mile to reach the parking lot, and the end of the hike, at mile 3.5.

Gateway Community: FLAGSTAFF *(see page 188)*

DISTANCE FROM TRAILHEAD: NA **POPULATION:** 71,975 **ELEVATION:** 6,909'

Getting There

PICTURE CANYON TRAILHEAD: N35° 13.616' W111° 33.427', elevation 6,739'
ROAD CONDITIONS: All vehicles; paved
FACILITIES: Restrooms but no potable water

DIRECTIONS *From Flagstaff:* From the junction of US 180 and Historic Route 66, travel east on Route 66 for 4.0 miles. Turn right (east) at the AUTO PARK sign to remain on Route 66, and in 1.8 miles turn left (north) onto El Paso Flagstaff Road. In 0.6 mile the trailhead will be on your right (east), past the Wildcat Hill Wastewater Plant.

From Phoenix: Take I-17 North about 140 miles to Flagstaff, and use the right two lanes to take Exit 340A onto I-40 East toward Albuquerque. In 5.6 miles take Exit 201 left (north) onto Country Club Drive (US 180 West). In 0.5 mile turn left (southwest) onto AZ 89 South/US 180 West; then, in another 0.3 mile, turn left again (east) onto Historic Route 66. Drive 1.8 miles; then turn left (north) onto El Paso Flagstaff Road. In 0.6 mile the trailhead will be on your right (east), past the Wildcat Hill Wastewater Plant.

The bridge over the Rio de Flag

24

Buffalo Park

Scenic city getaway for all ages

Sunflowers and other wildflowers bloom in Buffalo Park in September.

> SCENERY: ★ ★ ★ ★
> TRAIL CONDITION: ★ ★ ★ ★ ★
> CHILDREN: ★ ★ ★ ★ ★
> DIFFICULTY: ★
> SOLITUDE: ★

DISTANCE & CONFIGURATION: 1.9-mile loop

HIKING TIME: 1–2 hours

ACCUMULATED ELEVATION GAIN: 100'

SHORT HIKE OPTION: None. This hike is short and doable for hikers of all ages.

OUTSTANDING FEATURES: Dale Shewalter Memorial, views of the San Francisco Peaks, sunflowers in late summer

LAND-MANAGEMENT AGENCY: City of Flagstaff, 928-213-2000, flagstaff.az.gov /1786/arizona-trail

MAPS: USGS 7.5' *Flagstaff West, AZ*

AZT PASSAGE: 33/Flagstaff, aztrail.org/explore/passages/passage-33-flagstaff

ANCESTRAL LANDS: Hopi, Navajo, Yavapai–Apache, Yavapai–Prescott, Pueblo of Zuni, Havasupai, and Hualapai

SEASON: Year-round, but be careful of monsoons July–September (see page 35). In winter trails may be snowy or require traction for hiking on ice.

ACCESS: No fees or permits; open daily, sunrise–sunset; pets must be leashed

Overview

This hike on the Arizona National Scenic Trail (AZT) is readily accessible from Flagstaff and provides a good loop for families and beginners, though hikers of all fitness levels will enjoy the expansive views and the tribute to Dale Shewalter, "Father of the Arizona Trail." The AZT splits into two routes south of Flagstaff: the Flagstaff Urban Route, which goes right through town and serves as a resupply route for thru-hikers, and the Equestrian Bypass, which lets horseback riders skirt Flagstaff to the east. Hike 23, Picture Canyon Loop (see previous hike), uses part of the Equestrian Bypass, while this one uses the Flagstaff Urban Route.

On the Trail

The start of this hike is located on the east side of the parking lot, to the south of the green water tank. You'll go through the main gate upon your return, but for now look for a silver pole with yellow-and-white stripes and an AZT sticker on it. Past this, take the Switzer Canyon Trail for 100 feet, turn left (northeast) on the marked AZT, and follow it as it curves to the north.

Walk past the water tank and pass a fence in 0.1 mile. The trail curves northwest and reaches the Dale Shewalter Memorial. A Flagstaff math teacher and hiking enthusiast who longed to tackle the Appalachian Trail but never found the time, Dale got the idea for a long-distance trail spanning Arizona from Mexico to Utah and first hiked it in 1985 (see page 1 for more on him). The Arizona Trail Association was established in 1994, and the construction of the trail was the largest volunteer project in the state's history. In 2011 the final section of the AZT was completed near the Gila River, thus making all 800 miles of trail completely contiguous; you can visit that spot on Hike 12, Gila River Canyons, on page 116.

Take time to read the memorial plaque and thank Dale for his wonderful idea; then visit the memorial bench beneath a ponderosa pine and a juniper. The bench, which commemorates Dale and his parents, was commissioned by Laurie Martin, Dale's sister. Other memorial benches are located along the AZT and in the Gateway Communities. The other ones in this book are on Hike 21 near the Mormon Lake Trailhead and Hike 26 in the Gateway Community of Tusayan.

In 0.2 mile reach the Nate Avery Trail/AZT, and turn right (north). Immediately afterward, the Nate Avery Trail splits off to the east—take the left (north) fork to stay on the AZT. To the east is the lava dome of Elden Mountain, the Dry Lake Hills are to the north, and behind them are the San Francisco Peaks,

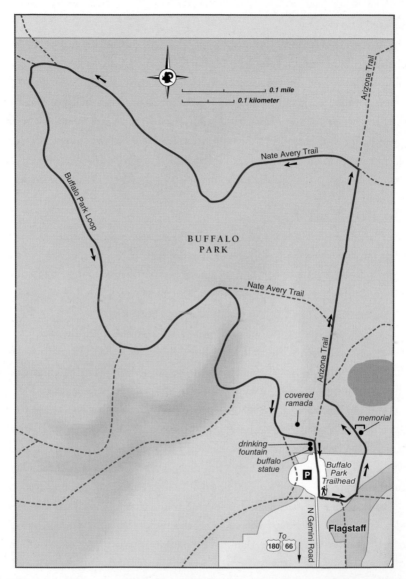

which once made up a stratovolcano called San Francisco Mountain that reached some 16,000 feet tall. The highest visible mountain in this area is Agassiz Peak (12,360'). Humphreys Peak—Arizona's highest mountain (12,667')—can't be seen from this part of town. The San Francisco Peaks are of cultural and ceremonial significance to 13 different tribes in the Four Corners area. It is one of the four sacred mountains of the Navajo, who call it *Dook'o'oosłííd*, or "Abalone Shell

Mountain." The Hopi consider the San Francisco Peaks—which they call *Nuva'tuk-ya'ovi,* or "Place of Snow on the Very Top"—the home of the *Katsinam,* or the spirit messengers of the universe. (The next hike, Aspen Loop to Bismarck Lake, affords views of Humphreys Peak.)

The trail passes exercise stations and reaches a junction with the Nate Avery Trail in 0.3 mile—turn left (west) and leave the AZT. This is the end of the wheelchair-accessible portion of this hike. Past a sign that says 1 MILE, the trail curves briefly to the southwest. The Nate Avery Trail is the wide gravel path that you want to stay on—ignore dirt trails leading off to the left and right. At 1.0 mile into the hike, reach the northwest corner of the loop, and follow the trail as it curves left (south).

In 0.5 mile another wide gravel path comes in from the right (east), at the balance beams—take a right to head south. Staying straight on the path will also take you back to the AZT, but that way is shorter. Our trail descends and curves to the left (east); then, after 0.2 mile, the trail continues turning left and begins a climb to the east. At the top of the climb, a trail to your right (south) will take you directly to the parking lot—to conclude this hike, reach the AZT in 0.1 mile and turn right (south) to go through the awning and snap a picture with the buffalo statue on the way back to your car. (Buffalo Park is also the location of Arizona Trail Day, held on the second Saturday in September.)

Gateway Community: FLAGSTAFF *(see page 188)*

DISTANCE FROM TRAILHEAD: NA **POPULATION:** 71,975 **ELEVATION:** 6,909'

Getting There

BUFFALO PARK TRAILHEAD: N35° 13.033' W111° 37.952', elevation 7,085'
ROAD CONDITIONS: All vehicles; paved
FACILITIES: Restrooms and water

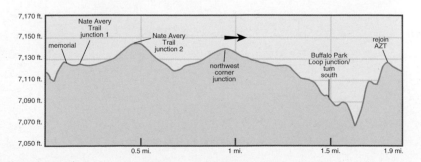

DIRECTIONS *From downtown Flagstaff:* From Historic Route 66, go north on Humphreys Street (US 180) for 0.6 mile; then turn left (west, then north) onto Fort Valley Road for 0.3 mile and go right (east) onto Forest Avenue, and follow it as it curves north. In 1.2 miles turn left (west) onto Gemini Drive, and go 0.3 mile farther to reach the Buffalo Park Trailhead. The AZT takes off to the right (east).

From Phoenix: Take I-17 North about 141 miles to Flagstaff, and then take Exit 341 to continue north on South Milton Road. Drive 1.5 miles, passing numerous hotels, restaurants, and gas stations along the way; then, just past the Northern Arizona University campus, curve right (east) onto Historic Route 66 in downtown Flagstaff. In 0.1 mile turn left (north) onto Humphreys Street (US 180) for 0.6 mile; then turn left (west, then north) onto Fort Valley Road for 0.3 mile and go right (east) onto Forest Avenue, and follow it as it curves north. In 1.2 miles turn left (west) onto Gemini Drive, and go 0.3 mile farther to reach the Buffalo Park Trailhead.

The San Francisco Peaks, Dry Lake Hills, and Elden Mountain as seen from the Dale Shewalter Memorial

25

Aspen Nature Loop to Bismarck Lake

Peak views and awesome aspen groves

SCENERY: ★★★★★
TRAIL CONDITION: ★★★★
CHILDREN: ★★★★
(short hike)
DIFFICULTY: ★★★
SOLITUDE: ★★

The San Francisco Peaks are sacred to 13 different Indigenous tribes.

DISTANCE & CONFIGURATION: 8.3 mile round-trip with out-and-back and loop sections.

HIKING TIME: 3–5 hours

ACCUMULATED ELEVATION GAIN: 900'

SHORT HIKE OPTION: Aspen Nature Loop plus viewpoint, 2.7 miles/350' elevation gain

OUTSTANDING FEATURES: Spectacular views of Humphreys Peak, aspen groves, Hart Prairie Meadow, fall color

LAND-MANAGEMENT AGENCIES: Coconino National Forest, Flagstaff Ranger District, 928-526-0866, fs.usda.gov/coconino; Arizona Snowbowl Ski Resort, 928-779-1951, snowbowl.ski

MAPS: USGS 7.5' *Humphreys Peak, AZ*

AZT PASSAGE: 34/San Francisco Peaks, aztrail.org/explore/passages/passage-34-san -francisco-peaks

ANCESTRAL LANDS: The San Francisco Peaks have cultural and ceremonial significance to 13 Indigenous groups in the area: the Hopi, Navajo, Hualapai, Havasupai, Yavapai, Zuni, Southern Paiute, and Acoma, plus five Apache tribes (San Carlos, Northern and Southern Tonto, White Mountain, and Yavapai–Apache).

SEASON: Spring, summer (be aware of monsoons July–September; see page 35), fall

ACCESS: No fees or permits to hike. The trail is open 24-7 year-round, but be aware of seasonal road closures.

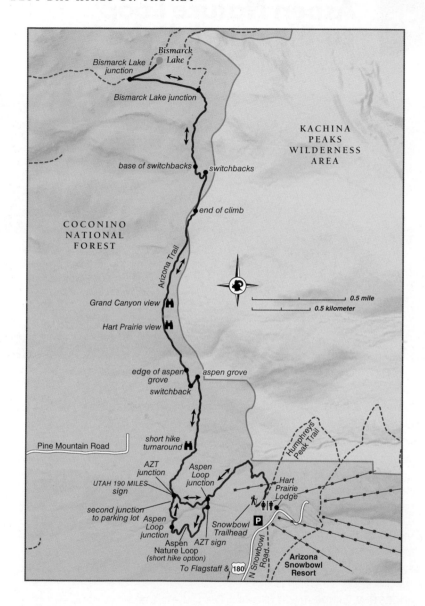

Overview

This hike on the Arizona National Scenic Trail (AZT) travels the slopes of Arizona's highest peak. The trail goes through groves of quaking aspen that are beautiful in the summer and spectacular in fall color season, turning the mountain yellow. Enjoy views of Hart Prairie Meadow and tiny Bismarck Lake on the full version of the hike.

Note: Arizona Snowbowl Ski Resort, where the trailhead for this hike is located, reopened in June 2020 for the summer season under strict social-distancing restrictions due to the coronavirus. Face coverings are required, and only a limited number of guests are allowed through the gates at a time (this does not affect trailhead parking). Guests are urged to maintain a 6-foot distance from one another. If you wish to ride the ski lift or partake of other resort activities, you must buy tickets online. For full details, see snowbowl.ski /the-mountain-summer/safety-guidelines.

On the Trail

The hike begins at the north end of the Humphreys Trail parking lot at Arizona Snowbowl Ski Resort. Go up the stairs and take Humphreys Trail 151, which goes to Humphreys Peak, the highest mountain in Arizona (12,667'). You can see quite a few mountains to the east: from south to north, the major peaks are Bill Williams Mountain (9,256'); Sitgreaves Mountain (9,390'); and Kendrick Peak (10,425'), the large mountain to the right (north). In 500 feet, the Aspen Nature Loop leaves the Humphreys Trail to the left (north). The trail curves left (southwest) and enters a grove of trees in 0.2 mile and curves right (north) for 0.1 mile then left (southwest) for 0.4 mile to reach the Aspen Nature Loop junction.

Turn right (west), and the trail breaks out into the open and switchbacks down the hill. Look back and you can see Humphreys Peak. In 0.4 mile reach a junction for the AZT. **Here, you have a decision: you can do just the Aspen Nature Loop (see page 205), or you can do the full version of the hike that takes you to Bismarck Lake.** Whichever you choose, turn right (north) to check out a beautiful

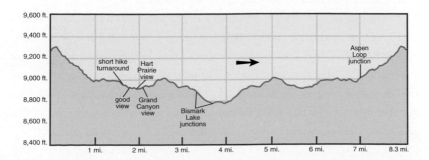

viewpoint. Reach a sign that says ARIZONA TRAIL, UTAH 190 MILES, and go north. In 0.3 mile reach the picturesque meadow, 1.3 miles into the hike.

The trail opens up to a meadow ringed with quaking aspen that is particularly pretty in the fall color season. (See page 97 for more information about these trees.)

To do the shorter loop hike, go back the way you came to the previous junction, and follow the directions on the next page for the Aspen Nature Loop/ AZT. To continue on the main hike, keep north on the AZT. The trail goes back into the trees, and this part of the hike is shady and cool no matter what the season. The forest here is primarily pine and fir. In 0.3 mile go through a beautiful stand of aspen, and the trail switchbacks down the hill. The trail exits the aspen stand in 0.2 mile, and Humphreys Peak appears again above the meadow.

Pass an informational sign about the Hart Prairie Meadow restoration in 0.2 mile; just beyond the sign are expansive views of the meadow and Fern Mountain below. In 0.3 mile get a glimpse of the Grand Canyon's North Rim if it's a clear day. There is seating uphill to the east, past the large boulder, for lunch or a break. The North Rim, at 8,000 feet of elevation, is 1,000 feet higher than the South Rim, adding to its visibility. Continuing to Bismarck Lake, the trail ascends briefly and then levels back out.

In 0.2 mile the trail goes back into the trees and climbs for 0.3 mile (9,010'). The trail passes through another grove of aspens and then descends through several switchbacks for another 0.3 mile. In the meadows you might see purple lupine, red Indian paintbrush, white yarrow, and other wildflowers, as well as various kinds of mushrooms.

In 0.5 mile reach a junction with the Bismarck Lake Trail and a metal AZT sign that says UTAH 189, MEXICO 611. Go left (west) toward Bismarck Lake. The trail descends and then passes through a large meadow.

The trail turns sharply right (northeast) in 0.4 mile at a sign that indicates Bismarck Lake to the left and the AZT to the right. This is the low point of the hike, at 8,764 feet. In 0.1 mile reach Bismarck Lake—which may or may not have water in it. If you don't see anything in the first pool, keep walking along the path; the lake may be as small as a kiddie pool. (You may laugh at what passes for a lake, but in arid Arizona we take what we can get.) The rock that makes up most of this area is very porous, so there is very little standing or flowing water available.

Water levels aside, you have commanding views of the San Francisco Peaks and Agassiz Peak. Humphreys Peak is of cultural and ceremonial significance to 13 different tribes in the Four Corners area. It is one of the four sacred mountains of the Navajo, who call it *Dook'o'oosłííd,* or "Abalone Shell Mountain." The Hopi consider the San Francisco Peaks—which they call *Nuva'tukya'ovi,* or "Place of Snow on the Very Top"—the home of the *Katsinam,* or the spirit messengers of the universe.

Return the way you came and go right (south) at the Bismarck Lake/AZT junction. In 3.1 miles reach the Aspen Nature Loop junction again. You can go back the way you came for 1.0 mile to the trailhead, for a total mileage of 8.0, or you can take the Aspen Nature Loop described below, for a total of 8.3 miles.

Short Hike Option: Aspen Nature Loop/AZT

From the northern junction of the AZT and the Aspen Nature Loop, go straight (south) on the trail for 0.25 mile. At a junction with the southern end of the loop, turn left (east) to leave the AZT and close the loop. Turn right (southeast) in 0.5 mile, and follow the trail an additional 0.7 mile back to the trailhead.

Gateway Community: FLAGSTAFF *(see page 188)*

DISTANCE FROM TRAILHEAD: 14.0 miles **POPULATION:** 71,975 **ELEVATION:** 6,909'

Getting There

SNOWBOWL TRAILHEAD: N35° 19.869' W111° 42.698', elevation 9,297'

ROAD CONDITIONS: All vehicles; paved

FACILITIES: Restrooms, no water

DIRECTIONS Drive north on I-17 until it ends at Exit 341, at the south end of Flagstaff, and becomes South Milton Road, about 0.5 mile north of the I-17/I-40 interchange. Drive north for 1.5 miles, passing numerous hotels, restaurants, and gas stations along the way; then, just past the Northern Arizona University campus, curve right (east) onto Historic Route 66 in downtown Flagstaff. In 0.1 mile turn left (north) onto Humphreys Street (US 180); then, in another 0.6 mile, turn left (west, then north) onto Fort Valley Road (US 180). In 6.6 miles turn right (north) onto Snowbowl Road (Forest Service Road 516), and drive another 6.6 miles, following the signs for the Humphreys Trail parking lot.

26 Grandview

Fire lookout in the ponderosa pine forest

SCENERY: ★★★★
TRAIL CONDITION: ★★★★★
CHILDREN: ★★★★★
DIFFICULTY: ★
SOLITUDE: ★★★

Grand Canyon vista from the 80-foot Grandview Lookout Tower

DISTANCE & CONFIGURATION: 4.0-mile out-and-back

HIKING TIME: 1.5–2 hours

ACCUMULATED ELEVATION GAIN: 50'

SHORT HIKE OPTION: 2.0-mile out-and-back/30' elevation gain

OUTSTANDING FEATURES: Grandview Lookout Tower, Mistletoe Interpretive Loop, ponderosa pine forest

LAND-MANAGEMENT AGENCY: Kaibab National Forest, Tusayan District, 928-638-2443, fs.usda.gov/kaibab

MAPS: USGS 7.5' *Grandview Point, AZ*

AZT PASSAGE: 36/Coconino Rim, aztrail.org/explore/passages/passage-36-coconino-rim

ANCESTRAL LANDS: The Grand Canyon region has 11 traditionally associated tribes: the Havasupai Tribe, Hopi Tribe, Hualapai Tribe, Kaibab Band of Paiute Indians, San Juan Southern Paiute Tribe, Las Vegas Band of Paiute Indians, Moapa Band of Paiute Indians, Paiute Indian Tribe of Utah, Navajo Nation, Pueblo of Zuni, and Yavapai–Apache Nation.

SEASON: Spring, summer (be careful of monsoons; see page 35), fall (road may be closed after snowfall)

ACCESS: Though the hike lies within Kaibab National Forest, just outside the boundaries of Grand Canyon National Park, you must pay the entrance fee ($35/car, good for a week) to drive to the trailhead on eastbound or westbound AZ 64 (aka East Rim Drive and Desert View Drive). See "Getting There," page 211, for an alternative route that bypasses the park. The South Rim of Grand Canyon and the trailhead are open 24-7, year-round; again, though, be aware of seasonal road closures.

206

Overview

This hike on the Arizona National Scenic Trail (AZT) visits a beautiful ponderosa pine forest and has a series of interpretive signs that discuss the effects of dwarf mistletoe, a parasitic plant, on the ecosystem. This part of the AZT is almost completely flat and is great for beginners. The glimpse of Grand Canyon from the 80-foot Grandview Lookout Tower is well worth the vertigo-inducing climb up the ladders.

On the Trail

At the trailhead find a series of interpretive signs at a kiosk. The 80-foot Grandview Lookout Tower and two-room cabin was built by the Civilian Conservation Corps (CCC) in 1936. You can climb the tower to the base of the cabin to get a glimpse into Grand Canyon, but it is staffed only during fire season.

Go through the AZT entrance and immediately turn right (east) at the junction marked VISHNU TRAIL AND ARIZONA TRAIL. (The Vishnu Trail, a 1.1-mile round-trip hike to a viewpoint overlooking Grand Canyon, is not part of the AZT.)

This is a dwarf mistletoe interpretive area with signs explaining the plant's life cycle. The signs describe this parasitic plant's effects on ponderosa pine trees, as well as measures for controlling its spread. (For more information about ponderosa pines, see page 209.) Pass a sign that reads ARIZONA TRAIL COCONINO RIM SECTION, RUSSELL TANK TH 12 MILES, FOREST BOUNDARY 24.2 MILES. The trail makes a wide switchback before sweeping east. At 0.1 mile a cross-country ski trail comes in from the left (north)—stay on the white-gravel path to the east.

Reach the sign for the interpretive loop on your right (south) in 0.1 mile—turn right to hike the loop, which returns to the AZT in 0.1 mile. Turn right to continue south on the AZT. After the loop, the trail changes from gravel to dirt singletrack and winds in a southern direction through the ponderosa pine forest.

Forest Service Road 302 appears in 0.1 mile—look across the road and to your left (south) for the continuation of the trail. The AZT takes a left (southeast) onto the road, goes through a cattle guard (road grate), and continues on the right (south) side of the road on singletrack. Pass a sign that says ARIZONA TRAIL FS 310-9.5, RUSSELL TANK-11, MEXICO-676, and take a moment to think about what it would feel like to walk all the way to Mexico.

The trail goes east, resumes its path heading south, and passes another interpretive sign. The AZT goes southwest and rounds a couple of curves

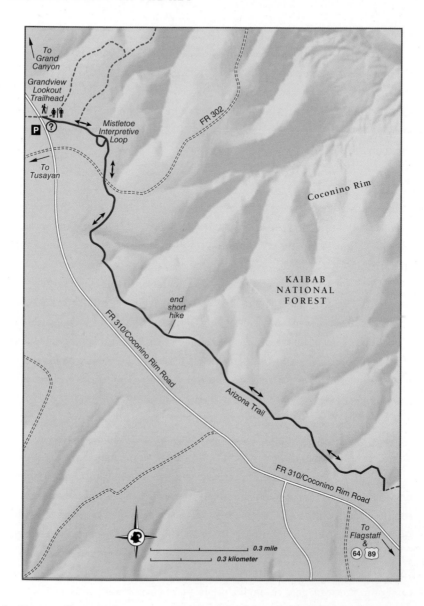

before trending southeast. At 1.0 mile you reach a clearing with some stumps and logs to sit on; this would make a nice spot for a break. If you're in search of shade, you'll find some just down the hill at the bottom of a small draw. **The clearing is the turnaround for the short hike option, at 2.0 miles round-trip and a mere 30 feet of elevation gain.**

A sign facing away from you says GRANDVIEW TRAILHEAD 1 MILE, but we're actually 1.1 miles away because we took the interpretive loop. You may see flight traffic, both helicopter and small planes, because one of the corridors for scenic flights over Grand Canyon is in this area.

Reach a giant ponderosa pine in a clearing in 0.4 mile as the trail continues to the southeast. The trunks of large ponderosa pines sometimes smell like butterscotch or vanilla; your best bet is to go to the side that's in the sun and get up close for a deep sniff. Ponderosa pines have evolved to adapt to fire and need it as a natural part of their forest ecosystem; they shed their lower branches and have thick bark, so that fires that burn low to the ground leave the tree uninjured. Unfortunately, fire-suppression techniques of the last 100 years have largely eliminated frequent low-intensity burns. The understory has become more vegetated, and today's forest fires burn much hotter and higher. Forest-thinning initiatives and controlled burns are helping to restore the ponderosa pine habitat to its natural state, however.

Go through a large clearing with many downed trees in 0.2 mile, and pass another interpretive sign about dwarf mistletoe. Continue on the AZT, noting how very different this forest looks from the others we've hiked through: the forester removed mistletoe-infested trees in this area and planted new ones.

At 2.0 miles the trail reaches the end of the restored area and this hike and heads back into the thick forest. Return the way you came, but feel free to skip the interpretive loop if you want.

Gateway Community: TUSAYAN

DISTANCE FROM TRAILHEAD: 18.0 miles **POPULATION:** 558 **ELEVATION:** 6,612'

Tusayan is both a Gateway Community for the AZT and the gateway to Grand Canyon National Park. Dining options include everything from fast food to a

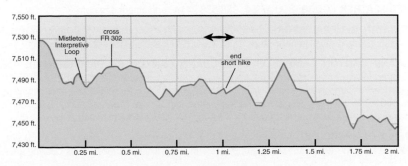

BEST DAY HIKES ON THE AZT

fancy dinner at **Big E Steakhouse & Saloon. We Cook Pizza and Pasta** serves Italian fare, plus beer and wine, while **Plaza Bonita,** next to **Red Feather Lodge,** has Mexican food and a full bar. Delaware North runs **Tusayan Village General Store,** which sells groceries, sundries, and souvenirs.

A memorial bench for Dale Shewalter, "Father of the Arizona Trail," is located outside of the **Grand Canyon Visitor Center** next to the shuttle stop. The Visitor Center has an IMAX theater, a Pizza Hut, and a gift shop; it also houses **Pink Jeep Tours.**

Tusayan has many hotels, ranging from basic to luxurious. Because of the traffic from Grand Canyon, reservations are strongly recommended if you want to stay overnight. **7 Mile Lodge** usually has the best rates but does same-day phone bookings only—no reservations. The private **Grand Canyon Camper Village** has tent and RV sites, and the public **Ten-X Campground** is just south of town on AZ 64. If you're into dispersed (primitive) camping, Tusayan is bordered on three sides by Kaibab National Forest, where camping is permitted except where NO TRESPASS-ING signs are posted. There are spots near the trailhead as well as along several graded-dirt U.S. Forest Service roads leading out of Tusayan.

GRAND CANYON VISITOR CENTER/IMAX THEATER/PIZZA HUT: 450 AZ 64, 928-638-2468, explorethecanyon.com. *March 1–October 31:* Open daily, 8 a.m.–10 p.m. *November 1–February 28:* Open daily, 9 a.m.–8 p.m.

PINK JEEP TOURS: Grand Canyon Visitor Center, 800-873-3662, pinkadventuretours.com

7 MILE LODGE: 208 AZ 64, 928-638-2291, 7milelodge.com

BIG E STEAKHOUSE & SALOON: 395 AZ 64, 928-638-0333, bigesteakhouse.com. Open daily, noon–9 p.m.

WE COOK PIZZA AND PASTA: 605 AZ 64, 928-638-2278, wecookpizzaandpasta.com. Open daily, 11 a.m.–9 p.m.

PLAZA BONITA: 352 AZ 64, 928-638-8900, myplazabonitatusayan.com. Open daily, 7 a.m.–10 p.m. Call ahead to confirm evening hours, as the restaurant sometimes closes early.

RED FEATHER LODGE: 300 AZ 64, 928-638-2414 redfeatherlodge.com

TUSAYAN GENERAL STORE: 577 AZ 64, 928-638-2854, visitgrandcanyon.com/dining -and-shopping/tusayan-general-store. Open daily; check website for seasonal hours.

GRAND CANYON CAMPER VILLAGE/GRAND CANYON RV CAMPGROUND: 549 Camper Village Ln., across AZ 64 from the Grand Canyon Visitor Center; 928-638-2887, grandcanyoncampervillage.com. Nightly rates range from $25 for tent sites without hookups to $66 for RV sites with full 50-amp hookups. Amenities include showers, picnic tables, and a camp store. Tent sites are first come, first served; RV sites can be reserved at the website.

TEN-X CAMPGROUND: Two miles south of Tusayan on the east side of AZ 64. Has 70 sites for tents and RVs (up to 35') and 2 group sites. Amenities include potable water, cooking grills, and restrooms but no showers or RV hookups. Nightly rate: $20 single sites, $175 group sites; open mid-May–early October. Availability is first come, first served and by reservation (877-444-6777, recreation.gov/camping/campgrounds/234488). *Note:* In 2020 work began to expand the campground from 70 sites to 300; see tinyurl.com/ten-x-campground for additional information.

Getting There

GRANDVIEW LOOKOUT TRAILHEAD: N35° 57.448' W111° 57.313', elevation 7,524'

ROAD CONDITIONS: All vehicles; graded dirt for 1.3 miles

FACILITIES: Restrooms, no water

DIRECTIONS *From Grand Canyon National Park:* From the first roundabout in Tusayan, drive north for 2.2 miles on AZ 64 to the park entrance; the admission fee ($35/car) is valid for one week. In 4.0 miles turn right (east) onto East Rim Drive (AZ 64) toward Desert View. FR 310 is 11.0 miles from the previous turn; after you pass a brown sign on your right for Grandview Point, look on the right (south) side of the road for the junction in 2.0 miles (you'll also pass a yellow sign indicating a T-intersection just before the turn). Turn right (south) onto FR 310, a gravel road accessible to passenger vehicles, and cross a cattle guard (road grate). Pass a sign that says ARIZONA TRAIL 1.3 MILES 2.1 KM. No camping is allowed until you reach the Kaibab National Forest boundary in 0.5 mile. Then pass a sign that says GRANDVIEW 1.0 MILE–FOREST SERVICE ROAD 310. An AZT sign points to the trailhead, on the left (east) side of the road (7,524').

From Tusayan: If you prefer to avoid driving through Grand Canyon National Park and don't mind driving 15.9 miles of dirt road, turn right (east) onto graded dirt FR 302 just north of the roundabout, with the Best Western on your left; then drive 15.8 miles on FR 302, and turn left (north) onto gravel FR 310. The lookout tower will be on your right (east) in 0.1 mile. Both Forest Service roads are suitable for passenger vehicles.

From Flagstaff and Cameron: Drive north on US 89 for 51.0 miles, and take the eastbound exit for Grand Canyon National Park/AZ 64 at the roundabout. The left (south) turn onto FR 310 is 42.0 miles down AZ 64 from the junction with US 89 and 11.0 miles west of the East Entrance Station for Grand Canyon National Park. Pick up the directions above to reach the trailhead.

27 Grand Canyon:
SOUTH KAIBAB TRAIL
Step back through time

SCENERY: ★★★★★
TRAIL CONDITION: ★★★
CHILDREN: ★★★ *(Ooh Aah Point)*
DIFFICULTY: ★★★ *(Ooh Aah Point)*,
★★★★ *(Cedar Ridge)*,
★★★★★ *(Skeleton Point)*
SOLITUDE: ★

Dramatic Grand Canyon views from Ooh Aah Point

DISTANCE & CONFIGURATION: Ooh Aah Point, 2.0-mile out-and-back; Cedar Ridge, 3.2-mile out-and-back; Skeleton Point, 6.4-mile out-and-back

HIKING TIME: Ooh Aah Point, 1–2 hours; Cedar Ridge, 2–3 hours; Skeleton Point: 4–6 hours

ACCUMULATED ELEVATION GAIN: Ooh Aah Point, 680'; Cedar Ridge, 1,140'; Skeleton Point, 2,050'

SHORT HIKE OPTION: Ooh Aah Point (see above)

OUTSTANDING FEATURES: Fascinating geology, expansive views across Grand Canyon, view of the Colorado River from Skeleton Point

LAND-MANAGEMENT AGENCY: Grand Canyon National Park, 928-638-7888, nps.gov/grca

MAPS: USGS 7.5' *Phantom Ranch, AZ*

AZT PASSAGE: 38/Grand Canyon–Inner Gorge, aztrail.org/explore/passages /passage-38-grand-canyon-inner-gorge

ANCESTRAL LANDS: The Grand Canyon region has 11 traditionally associated tribes: the Havasupai Tribe, Hopi Tribe, Hualapai Tribe, Kaibab Band of Paiute Indians, San Juan Southern Paiute Tribe, Las Vegas Band of Paiute Indians, Moapa Band of Paiute Indians, Paiute Indian Tribe of Utah, Navajo Nation, Pueblo of Zuni, and Yavapai–Apache Nation.

SEASON: Year-round, but in winter you may need traction for hiking on ice and snow. I recommend turning around at Cedar Ridge during the summer.

ACCESS: There is no personal vehicle access for the South Kaibab Trailhead, and it can only be reached via the Orange/Kaibab route shuttle bus. See Getting There, page 221, for details. The entrance fee for Grand Canyon National Park is $35/vehicle and is valid for 7 days; no permits are required for day hikes, but dogs are not allowed on trails. The South Rim of Grand Canyon is open 24-7, year-round, but be aware of seasonal road closures and weather extremes.

Overview

The AZT is the only National Scenic Trail that passes through one of the Seven Natural Wonders of the World: Grand Canyon. The South Kaibab Trail is on a ridgeline with expansive views of the canyon's multicolored geologic layers. See page 214 for an overview of Grand Canyon geology.

This hike is divided into three segments of varying lengths; choose the one that best fits your hiking ability. Remember, however, that when it comes to Grand Canyon, what goes down must come up—and hiking uphill at 7,000 feet will take your breath away in more ways than one. In general, it takes twice as long to ascend as it does to descend, so make sure to factor in that extra time.

In general, it's a good idea to check trail conditions before you go (see nps.gov/grca and explorethecanyon.com). The terrain on this hike is extremely challenging, even for the shortest option, with lots of irregular steps and a steep grade. The amount of erosion on the trail can change from year to year, and gravel on parts of the trail can be slippery. Kids may need help getting up and down some of the larger steps.

During winter you may need to bring traction devices such as microspikes and crampons. Hiking poles come in handy during any season—if you don't own a pair, you can rent some at **Grand Canyon Outfitters** (inside Canyon Village Market; call 928-638-2262 to reserve).

WEATHER AND WATER Temperatures increase the farther you descend into the canyon, and the high elevation is dehydrating. I don't recommend hiking past Cedar Ridge during the summer. Also: **There is no water on the South Kaibab Trail.** See page 29 for a discussion of water requirements, but a couple of good rules of thumb are to bring along 0.5 liter (16 ounces) of water per hour for every hour you plan to spend on the trail, or 1 liter (32 ounces) per hour during hot weather.

MULE MANNERS The South Kaibab Trail has mule rides that go down to Phantom Ranch. Mules always have the right-of-way: when you encounter a mule train, step to the inside of the trail, and follow the directions of the mule wrangler to let them pass.

CRAFTY CRITTERS The ravens and squirrels at Grand Canyon are used to humans and won't think twice about stealing your snacks when your back is turned. **Don't feed the animals,** and make sure that your food is always secured or where you can see it.

On the Trail

Take the paved path from where the South Rim shuttle bus drops you off, past the water filling station to the north. The path curves right (northeast) and reaches an information kiosk in 200 feet. The first view of the canyon is on your left at the

Spotlight: Grand Canyon Geology

Grand Canyon is considered one of the Seven Natural Wonders of the World, not only for its beautiful scenery but also the fascinating geology contained within. The designation was awarded by Seven Natural Wonders (sevennaturalwonders.org), a conservation organization dedicated to protecting these marvels of nature. The other six, in case you're curious, are the Aurora Borealis (Northern Lights); Australia's Great Barrier Reef; the harbor of Rio de Janeiro, Brazil; Mount Everest; Paricutín, a cinder cone in Michoacán, Mexico; and Zambia's Victoria Falls, the largest waterfall in the world in terms of combined width and height.

Grand Canyon is part of the Grand Staircase, a vast series of sedimentary rock layers extending like stairsteps from Zion National Park and Bryce Canyon in Utah south to Grand Canyon. The diagram opposite shows a cross-section of Grand Canyon's geologic layers.

The different layers of rocks are individually millions of years old, each layer incrementally older than the one above it. The oldest rocks in Grand Canyon are up to 1.84 billion years old! The Great Unconformity notes a period where there is a time gap in the series of rocks, up to 500 million years' worth. The layers fall into three main groups, from youngest to oldest: **Layered Paleozoic Rocks** (270–525 million years old), **Grand Canyon Supergroup Rocks** (700 million–1.2 billion years old), and **Vishnu Basement Rocks** (1.68–1.86 billion years old).

Here's a list of the layers that are visited on the hikes in this book, all from the Layered Paleozoic Rocks group:

KAIBAB FORMATION (270 million years old) This is the limestone that forms the rims of Grand Canyon and the Kaibab Plateau. It was created in shallow sea environments that contain many fossils.

TOROWEAP FORMATION (273 million years old) Like the Kaibab Formation, this is limestone that was created in a shallow sea environment. The Toroweap forms a slope, while the layers on either side form cliffs.

COCONINO SANDSTONE (Ooh Aah Point and Coconino Overlook, 275 million years old) These cliff-forming, fossilized sand dunes, up to 300 feet thick, contain fossilized footprints.

HERMIT SANDSTONE (280 million years old) This layer was created in shallow seas and made from slope-forming siltstone and mudstone. High iron content gives this layer its red color; Hermit Sandstone is nicknamed "Desert Painter" because water percolating down through it stains the rocks below.

SUPAI GROUP (Cedar Ridge, 285–315 million years old) This layer is composed of sandstone and siltstone created by seas that got deeper and shallower over time. Four sublayers within the Supai Group indicate progression and regression of the ancient seas.

REDWALL LIMESTONE (Skeleton Point, 340 million years old) This cliff-forming limestone is one of the biggest barriers to travel in Grand Canyon, as the cliffs can be up to 500 feet thick. *Redwall* refers to the rock being stained red by the rock layers above; you can see the limestone's natural gray color at Skeleton Point.

The Trail of Time interpretive walk on Grand Canyon's South Rim is an excellent way to learn about geology as well as see and touch rocks from each layer. See page 218 for more information.

Grand Canyon's Three Sets of Rocks

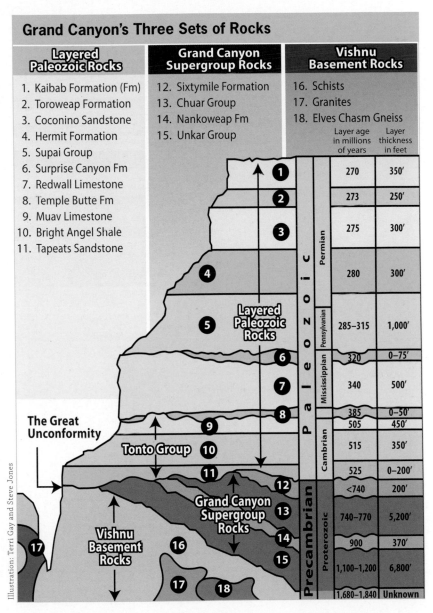

Layered Paleozoic Rocks	Grand Canyon Supergroup Rocks	Vishnu Basement Rocks
1. Kaibab Formation (Fm)	12. Sixtymile Formation	16. Schists
2. Toroweap Formation	13. Chuar Group	17. Granites
3. Coconino Sandstone	14. Nankoweap Fm	18. Elves Chasm Gneiss
4. Hermit Formation	15. Unkar Group	
5. Supai Group		
6. Surprise Canyon Fm		
7. Redwall Limestone		
8. Temple Butte Fm		
9. Muav Limestone		
10. Bright Angel Shale		
11. Tapeats Sandstone		

Illustration: Terri Gay and Steve Jones

The Great Unconformity

Tonto Group

			Layer age in millions of years	Layer thickness in feet
1		Permian	270	350'
2			273	250'
3			275	300'
4	Paleozoic		280	300'
5		Pennsylvanian	285–315	1,000'
6		Mississippian	320	0–75'
7			340	500'
8			385	0–50'
9			505	450'
10		Cambrian	515	350'
11			525	0–200'
12	Precambrian	Proterozoic	<740	200'
13			740–770	5,200'
14			900	370'
15			1,100–1,200	6,800'
			1,680–1,840	Unknown

beginning of the descent. The trail immediately does a series of switchbacks in the Kaibab Formation (see opposite page for more on the ancient rock layers in Grand Canyon). This part of the trail, known as The Chimney, holds ice longer than the rest of the trail, which is on a ridgeline. Pass signs indicating that dogs are not

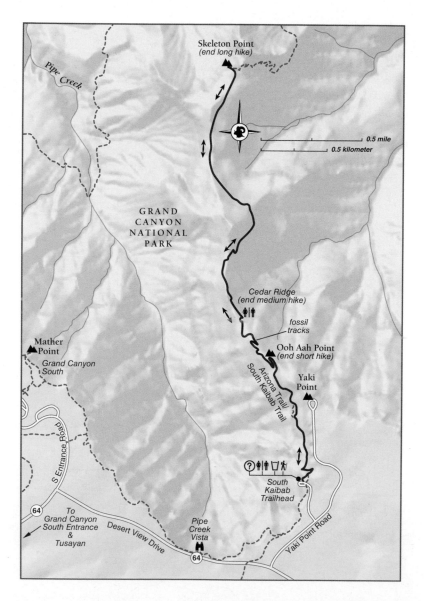

allowed on the trails, that there is no trash service in the canyon, and that guests may not cut switchbacks or throw or roll rocks, for the safety of hikers below.

In 0.3 mile reach the last switchback in The Chimney and start a traverse in the Toroweap Formation. In 0.1 mile the trail flattens, and you pass a sign that warns people not to try to hike to the Colorado River and back in a day. To

216

drive the point home, the sign has an illustration of a man doubled over and throwing up.

Descend through pinyon pine and alligator juniper along the side of the canyon, trending north. In 0.3 mile the trail levels briefly, then passes between two rocks in 0.1 mile. Look to your left (northwest) to see Ooh Aah Point, and reach the sign at 1.0 mile (6,580'). At the bend in the switchback are some slanted Coconino Sandstone slabs to take photos on, complemented by a beautiful canyon backdrop—be careful here, as the drop is steep on the far side of the slabs. From this point you can see O'Neill Butte and the trail zigzagging down the red Supai Group sandstone. **This is the turnaround for the shortest hike option, a round-trip of 2.0 miles and 680 feet of elevation gain.** The trail makes a hard left (southeast) to continue descending to Cedar Ridge. The striated Coconino Sandstone is made from fossilized sand dunes.

In 0.2 mile the trail curves right (northeast), then turns left (west) to go down Windy Ridge for 0.1 mile—be mindful of the steep drop-offs on both sides. The trail turns right (southeast) and, in 250 feet, switchbacks left (northwest). Keep your eyes open for a slanted slab of rock on your left (west) in 50 feet.

Small indentations on the face of the slab are fossilized footprints made by a mammal-like reptile walking up a sand dune. The tracks are estimated to be 275 million years old, based on the Coconino Sandstone rock layer that they are in. *Do not touch the tracks.* The red slope just before Cedar Ridge is part of the Hermit Sandstone rock layer, also known as the "Desert Painter" because water percolating through it stains the layers below with iron oxide.

Reach a sign for Cedar Ridge in 0.3 mile (6,120'). **This is the turnaround for the second leg of the hike, a round-trip of 3.2 miles and 1,140 feet of elevation gain.** The three composting toilets to the right (east) are the only restrooms on the hike; there is no water here, however.

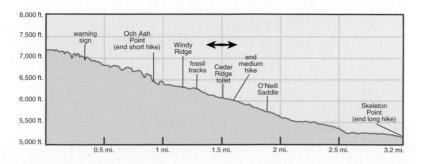

The trees are junipers, not cedars (as the name of the ridge would seem to indicate), and have rocks around them for sitting and taking a break. You're now in the red Supai Group sandstone layer. From the sign at Cedar Ridge, you can take a use trail to your left (northwest) to a viewpoint in less than 0.2 mile. There are two hitching posts for mules: one to the north and one to the east by the restrooms.

Make sure to check the amount of water you have—as well as the amount of time and energy you have—before proceeding to Skeleton Point. Hiking past Cedar Ridge is not recommended in the summertime.

To find the continuation of the trail, go toward the hitching post behind the sign, and look right (east) for a trail that continues descending from Cedar Ridge.

The trail immediately switchbacks to the left (west) and continues its descent toward O'Neil Butte saddle. In 0.2 mile you reach two tight switchbacks, and the trail reaches the saddle in 0.2 mile. The trail continues to the right (east) of O'Neill Butte and does three switchbacks in 0.1 mile, then continues traversing and descending north. The trail curves left (northwest) around the butte, and Skeleton Point comes into view in 0.2 mile.

In 0.3 mile the trail stops its relentless descent and traverses beneath the ridge. To your left (west) you can see the Bright Angel Trail and green cottonwoods as well as the trail going out to Plateau Point. To your right (northeast) are Brahma Temple and the triangular white top of Zoroaster Temple.

In 0.3 mile you pass the end of the ridge, and the rock-lined trail descends, reaching a sign for Skeleton Point in 0.1 mile. From the sign, go past the hitching post to the left (northwest) 0.1 mile for a view of the river and the end of the hike, at 3.2 miles (5,181'). This is the top of the Redwall Limestone, and there are ledges that make for a scenic spot to take in views of the Colorado River, the cottonwood trees of Bright Angel Canyon, and Phantom Ranch (see next page). The Redwall is its natural gray color here—in most of Grand Canyon, it has been stained red by the layers above it.

Go back the way you came, making sure to take frequent breaks and pace yourself. The return trip has 2,050 feet of elevation gain, and the air has less and less oxygen as you ascend to the trailhead, so you might find the going harder than you thought, especially if you live at a low elevation. Think of it as the prettiest Stairmaster you've ever seen.

Gateway Community: TUSAYAN *(see page 209)*

DISTANCE FROM TRAILHEAD: 8.0 miles **POPULATION:** 558 **ELEVATION:** 6,612'

Gateway Community: GRAND CANYON VILLAGE

DISTANCE FROM TRAILHEAD: 2.5 miles **POPULATION:** 2,004 **ELEVATION:** 6,804'

Open year-round, Grand Canyon Village serves the millions of visitors who come to Grand Canyon National Park each year. Reservations are strongly recommended for lodging and developed camping in both Grand Canyon Village and the Gateway Community of Tusayan, 2.0 miles south of the park's South Entrance (see page 209 for details). **Bright Angel, Kachina, Maswik,** and **Thunderbird Lodges,** along with the historic **El Tovar Hotel,** are managed by Xanterra. Delaware North runs **Yavapai Lodge & Trailer Village RV Park.** The National Park Service operates **Mather Campground,** next door to Yavapai Lodge. Dispersed (primitive) camping is allowed in Kaibab National Forest, which borders the park, and in Tusayan. At the bottom of Grand Canyon next to Bright Angel Creek, **Phantom Ranch** (Xanterra) caters to hikers, rafters, and mule riders with rustic cabins and bunkhouse-style accommodations that are the only permanent lodging in the park below the canyon rim. These reservations are offered via a lottery process, 15 months in advance. An advance permit is required to camp overnight in Grand Canyon, as is a trip with 4,000 feet of elevation gain and loss. **Note:** Through 2021, Phantom Ranch will be open with limited services while undergoing repairs. Visit grandcanyonlodges.com/lodging/phantom-ranch for details.

Dining options include the cafeteria and pizza pub at **Maswik Food Court;** the **Arizona Steakhouse** for steaks, chicken, ribs, and fish; and **Fred Harvey Burger.** Fine dining is available by reservation at the **El Tovar Dining Room.**

Just south of the Grand Canyon Visitor Center on South Entrance Road, **Bright Angel Bicycles and Café** has grab-and-go breakfasts and lunches and a coffee shop in addition to providing bike rentals and tours of the canyon rim.

Located next to Yavapai Lodge, **Market Plaza** consists of a grocery store, a delicatessen, a store that sells and rents camping and hiking gear, a gift shop, and the only bank and post office inside the park. The parking lot has four universal chargers for electric cars.

There's plenty to do once you're done with your hike. One of my favorite activities is the interpretive walk called **The Trail of Time,** a 2.83-mile, ADA-accessible geologic timeline where each meter you walk equals one million years of Grand Canyon's history. The main part of the trail is 1.3 miles, and along the way, you'll be able to see and touch samples from each of the rock layers found in the canyon. You can start at Verkamp's Visitor Center and walk The Trail of Time from oldest rocks to youngest (west–east), or you can start at the Yavapai Geology Museum and walk the trail from youngest rocks to oldest (east–west). The park shuttle will return you to your starting point if you don't want to walk back.

A brochure called **"Grand Canyon: Access Your Park,"** available online as a printable PDF, provides details on facilities, services, and activities that are ADA-accessible for people with mobility, sight, or hearing concerns.

Ranger talks and **guided walks and hikes** address a variety of subjects. East Rim Drive takes you to different viewpoints along the canyon rim on a 25.0-mile journey to the 70-foot-tall **Desert View Watchtower,** just northeast of the park's East Entrance. The **Tusayan Ruin and Museum,** located along the route, has an Ancestral Puebloan dwelling with an interpretive trail and exhibits that explain the history of the area. The **Grand Canyon Conservancy Store** sells books, maps, gifts, and more.

Formerly an observation tower and gift shop, the Desert View Watchtower has been repurposed as a cultural center that tells the stories and shares the work of artisans from the 11 traditionally associated tribes of Grand Canyon (see page 242). Demonstrations of pottery, carving, weaving, and jewelry making by Indigenous artisans take place daily. To the south of the tower are a gas station and general store, a gift shop, a picnic area, and an ice-cream stand. Just to the east of these is **Desert View Campground,** which has tent and RV sites (no hookups).

Cap your day by finding an overlook to watch the sunset. *Pro tip:* The sunset colors often develop and last long after the sun has dipped beneath the horizon—so stay and watch!

GRAND CANYON NATIONAL PARK LODGES (BRIGHT ANGEL, KACHINA, MASWIK, AND THUNDERBIRD LODGES; EL TOVAR HOTEL; PHANTOM RANCH): For reservations, call 888-297-2757 or book online at grandcanyonlodges.com. *Note:* Reservations for Phantom Ranch are hard to get and available via an online lottery system; see grandcanyon lodges.com/lodging/phantom-ranch for details.

NORTH YAVAPAI LODGE & TRAILER VILLAGE RV PARK: For reservations call 877-404-4611 (801-449-4139), or book online at visitgrandcanyon.com. Pet-friendly (Yapavai Lodge charges a $25 pet fee). *Yavapai Lodge:* 11 Yavapai Lodge Road; *Trailer Village RV Park:* 100 Trailer Village Road.

MATHER CAMPGROUND: Grand Canyon Village south of North Yavapai Lodge & Trailer Village RV Park, 928-638-8888, nps.gov/grca/planyourvisit/cg-sr.htm. Has 327 sites for tents and RVs (up to 30'), each with a fire ring/cooking grate, picnic table, parking space, and room for up to 3 tents. Nightly rate: $18; reservations: 877-444-6777, recreation.gov.

MASWIK FOOD COURT: Maswik Lodge, 202 S. Village Loop Dr., 928-638-2631, grand canyonlodges.com. Open daily, 6 a.m.–8 p.m.; pizza pub open noon–8 p.m.

ARIZONA STEAKHOUSE: Bright Angel Lodge, 202 S. Village Loop Dr., 928-638-2631, grandcanyonlodges.com. Open daily, 11:30 a.m.–3 p.m. (lunch); 4:30–9:30 p.m. (dinner and lounge).

FRED HARVEY BURGER: Bright Angel Lodge, 202 S. Village Loop Dr., 928-638-2631, grandcanyonlodges.com. Open daily, 7–10:30 a.m. (breakfast); 11:30 a.m.–3:30 p.m. (lunch); and 4:30–9 p.m. (dinner). Lounge open daily, 11:30 a.m.–10 p.m.

EL TOVAR DINING ROOM: El Tovar Lodge, 928-638-2631, grandcanyonlodges.com. Open daily, 6:30–10:30 a.m. (breakfast); 11:15 a.m.–2 p.m. (lunch); and 4:30–9:30 p.m. (dinner). Lounge open daily, 11:30 a.m.–11 p.m. Guests not staying at El Tovar can make reservations up to 30 days in advance by phone (928-638-2631, ext. 6432) or email (csrdining@xanterra.com).

BRIGHT ANGEL BICYCLES AND CAFÉ: 10 South Entrance Rd., 928-679-0992, bikegrand canyon.com. Hours vary by season, usually 7 a.m.–6 p.m.

MARKET PLAZA: 1 Market Plaza Rd., 928-638-2262, visitgrandcanyon.com/dining-and -shopping/canyon-village-market-deli. Open daily, 6:30 a.m.–9 p.m.

TRAIL OF TIME: Located between Verkamp's Visitor Center and the Yavapai Geology Museum, tot.unm.edu. This wheelchair-accessible interpretive hike is 1.3 miles from either end; from the museum to Verkamp's (east–west) is the downhill direction.

"GRAND CANYON: ACCESS YOUR PARK" (ADA ACCESSIBILITY GUIDE): Download at nps.gov/grca/planyourvisit/upload/grca-accessibility-guide-2018.pdf.

RANGER TALKS, GUIDED WALKS AND HIKES: For more information, check at the Grand Canyon Visitor Center on South Entrance Road, or see nps.gov/grca/planyourvisit/ranger -program.htm.

DESERT VIEW WATCHTOWER: Located 25.0 miles east of Grand Canyon Village on East Rim Drive/Desert View Drive (AZ 64), at the park's East Entrance; nps.gov/grca/plan yourvisit/desert-view.htm

TUSAYAN RUIN AND MUSEUM: Located 3.0 miles west of Desert View Watchtower on East Rim Drive/Desert View Drive (AZ 64). Open daily, 9 a.m.–5 p.m. See tinyurl.com/tusayan ruin for a printable brochure.

GRAND CANYON CONSERVANCY STORE: 6 South Entrance Rd., 928-638-2481, shop .grandcanyon.org. Open daily, 8 a.m.–7 p.m.

DESERT VIEW CAMPGROUND: Next to the Desert View Watchtower at the park's East Entrance; 928-638-8888, nps.gov/grca/planyourvisit/cg-sr.htm. Has 50 sites for tents and RVs (up to 30'); fire rings/cooking grates, picnic tables, drinking water, and restrooms, but no hookups or showers. Nightly rate: $12; availability is first come, first served.

Getting There

SOUTH KAIBAB TRAILHEAD: N36° 03.177' W112° 05.037', elevation 7,260'

ROAD CONDITIONS: South Kaibab Trailhead: **Shuttle only; no vehicle access.** Grand Canyon Visitor Center access: All vehicles; paved.

FACILITIES: Restroom, 2 picnic tables, drinking water (check before getting in the shuttle to make sure it's working, as there are often pipeline breaks).

DIRECTIONS *From Phoenix Sky Harbor Airport:* Take I-10 West 5.8 miles; take Exit 143 to merge onto I-17 North. In 139.0 miles take Exit 340B to merge onto I-40 West toward Williams. In 30.0 miles take Exit 165 onto AZ 64 North, and in 28.0 miles turn right (north) onto US 180. Drive 22.0 miles to Tusayan; just past Papillon Grand Canyon Helicopter Tours on your left, take the second exit off the roundabout to stay on AZ 64 North. Continue 0.7 mile to a second roundabout just past Grand Canyon Camper Village, and take the second exit again. Proceed 1.5 miles north to the South Entrance Station, and pay the fee. In 5.0 miles turn right (east) into the parking lots for the Grand Canyon Visitor Center.

From Flagstaff/US 180: Drive north on I-17 until it ends at Exit 341, at the south end of Flagstaff, and becomes South Milton Road about 0.5 mile north of the I-17/I-40 interchange. Drive north for 1.5 miles, passing numerous hotels, restaurants, and gas stations along the way; then, just past the Northern Arizona University campus, curve right (east) onto Historic Route 66 in downtown Flagstaff. In 0.1 mile turn left (north) onto Humphreys Street (US 180); then, in another 0.6 mile, turn left (west, then north) onto Fort Valley Road (US 180). Drive 49.2 miles to the junction with AZ 64; then turn right (north), drive 22.0 miles to Tusayan, and pick up the directions above.

From East Rim Drive/Desert View Drive via Cameron*: From I-17 North in Flagstaff, take Exit 340A onto I-40 East toward Albuquerque. In 5.6 miles take Exit 201 left (north) onto Country Club Drive (US 180 West). In 0.5 mile turn right (northeast) onto US 89 North, and drive 46.7 miles to Cameron. Take the third exit at the roundabout to continue west on East Rim Drive/Desert View Drive (AZ 64), and reach Grand Canyon National Park's East Entrance in 30.7 miles. In 22.0 miles turn right (north) onto South Entrance Road and, in 0.5 mile, reach the parking lots for the Grand Canyon Visitor Center.

From the north: Take US 89 South to Cameron, cross the bridge over the Little Colorado River, and in 1.8 miles take the first exit onto AZ 64 at the roundabout; then pick up the directions above.

South Rim Shuttle Bus At the Grand Canyon Visitor Center, take the Orange/Kaibab route eastbound past Pipe Creek Vista to the second stop at the South Kaibab Trailhead. The shuttle is free; hours and frequency vary by season, but the last shuttle always runs 30 minutes after sunset.

28 Grand Canyon:
NORTH KAIBAB TRAIL
TO COCONINO OVERLOOK
Wonder of the world

SCENERY: ★★★★★
TRAIL CONDITION: ★★★★
CHILDREN: ★★★★
DIFFICULTY: ★★★
SOLITUDE: ★

Roaring Springs Canyon from the Coconino Overlook

DISTANCE & CONFIGURATION: 1.5-mile out-and-back

HIKING TIME: 1–2 hours

ACCUMULATED ELEVATION GAIN: 520'

SHORT HIKE OPTION: None due to length

OUTSTANDING FEATURES: Grand Canyon views, aspen and maple groves for fall color, fascinating geology

LAND-MANAGEMENT AGENCY: Grand Canyon National Park, 928-638-7888, nps.gov/grca

MAPS: USGS 7.5' *Bright Angel Point, AZ*

AZT PASSAGE: 38/Grand Canyon–Inner Gorge, aztrail.org/explore/passages/passage-38-grand-canyon-inner-gorge

ANCESTRAL LANDS: The Grand Canyon region has 11 traditionally associated tribes: the Havasupai Tribe, Hopi Tribe, Hualapai Tribe, Kaibab Band of Paiute Indians, San Juan Southern Paiute Tribe, Las Vegas Band of Paiute Indians, Moapa Band of Paiute Indians, Paiute Indian Tribe of Utah, Navajo Nation, Pueblo of Zuni, and Yavapai–Apache Nation.

SEASON: May 15–October 15; be aware of monsoons July–September (see page 35)

ACCESS: The entrance fee for Grand Canyon National Park is $35/vehicle and is valid for 7 days; no permits are required for day hikes, but dogs are not allowed on trails.

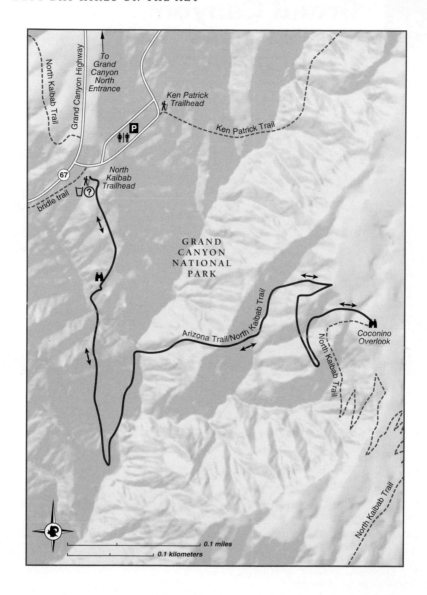

Overview

The Arizona National Scenic Trail (AZT) goes rim-to-rim through Grand Canyon, the crown jewel of the system. But you don't have to do the whole 21 miles to experience the grandeur of this Natural Wonder of the World. The North Rim receives just a tenth of the visitors of the South Rim, making it a much more intimate setting.

MULE MANNERS The North Kaibab Trail is used for mule rides that go down as far as the Supai Tunnel. Trail etiquette dictates that mules always have the right-of-way: when you encounter a mule train, step to the inside of the trail, and follow the directions of the mule wrangler to let the train pass.

On the Trail

From the trailhead (8,241'), the AZT descends on the North Kaibab Trail immediately into the forest. The view opens up a bit in 0.1 mile. At mile 0.2, reach a switchback, turn left (east), and continue to descend. You'll pass Gambel oaks, ponderosa pines, quaking aspens, and even some bigtooth maples that change color in late September to early October. In 0.1 mile switchback to your right (west) and then, in another 0.1 mile, your left (north).

Reach the Coconino Overlook at 0.7 mile. There's plenty of room to sit, take in the view, and take photos with a fantastic backdrop (7,715'). You can see the trail snaking through Roaring Springs Canyon, and the Redwall Bridge is visible below. After the bridge, you can see the trail is blasted out of the right side of the canyon. Beyond that, Roaring Springs Canyon meets Bright Angel Canyon, and the North Kaibab Trail makes a right to continue down Bright Angel Canyon to Cottonwood Camp and Phantom Ranch before reaching the Colorado River. It's a total of 14.2 miles and 5,850 feet of elevation change.

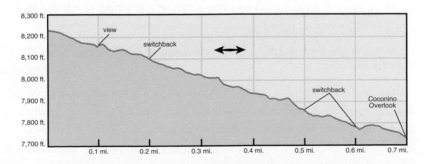

The rock that the overlook is named after is Coconino Sandstone—you're standing on 275-million-year-old fossilized sand dunes. The dark striations on the sheer rock faces above are formed by desert varnish, a thin coating made of silica, iron, and manganese. For more information about Grand Canyon's rock layers, see "Spotlight: Grand Canyon Geology," page 214.

Across the canyon on a clear day, you can see Humphreys Peak, Arizona's highest mountain (12,667'), which is of cultural and ceremonial significance to 13 different tribes in the Four Corners area. It is one of the San Francisco Peaks and one of the four sacred mountains of the Navajo, who call it *Dook'o'oosłííd,* or "Abalone Shell Mountain." The Hopi consider the San Francisco Peaks—which they call *Nuva'tukya'ovi,* or "Place of Snow on the Very Top"—the home of the *Katsinam,* or the spirit messengers of the universe.

It's tantalizing to go farther down into the canyon, but the difficulty of the trail increases considerably, and it becomes much hotter and more exposed below the Coconino Overlook. I recommend turning around at the overlook and pairing your hike with a visit to North Rim Lodge and hike to Bright Angel Point (not on the AZT; see Gateway Community section following for details).

When you're ready to return to the trailhead, take the right fork uphill from the overlook, and retrace your steps to the top. During my research for this book, I turned a corner to come face-to-face with a young deer.

A good rule of thumb for Grand Canyon hiking is that it takes twice as long to go uphill as it does to go downhill, especially at high elevations—the lower the elevation at which you live, the more the thin air at 8,000 feet will affect you. So walk at a pace where it's comfortable to hold a conversation, and take as many breaks as you need.

Gateway Community: GRAND CANYON NORTH RIM
(open May 15–October 15)

DISTANCE FROM TRAILHEAD: 2.1 miles **POPULATION:** No census data
ELEVATION: 8,200'

Unlike the South Rim, the North Rim is open just six months a year versus year-round. On the upside, it's far more compact than the sprawling South Rim, consisting of **North Rim Lodge** and nearby campground facilities. If you want to stay overnight, advance reservations are **strongly** recommended. The lodge has a fantastic sunroom with giant windows and couches, plus two verandas with Adirondack chairs—perfect for lounging with your favorite beverage while the sun sets. The veranda serves a variety of snacks and hot sandwiches. The current lodge dates to 1936. Accessed from the east corner of the lodge's back porch, the Bright Angel Point Trail (not part of the AZT) is a 0.5-mile round-trip hike. This paved path goes out to a viewpoint between Roaring Springs Canyon and Transept Canyon; hikers get spectacular views of the South Rim, with Humphreys Peak beyond it, along with Deva, Brahma, and Zoroaster Temples to the southeast. Yaqui Point and the ridge of the South Kaibab Trail/AZT are visible across the canyon.

If you really want to treat yourself, make a reservation for a meal at the lodge's main dining room—if you're lucky, you might get one of the coveted tables right next to the window. Other options for food and drink include **Bright Angel Buffet; Deli in the Pines;** and the **Coffee Shop,** which does double duty as the **Roughrider Saloon.**

Two **scenic drives** originate at the North Rim. The **Point Imperial Road,** going to the highest point on the North Rim (8,803'), has views of Mount Hayden, the Painted Desert, and Eastern Grand Canyon. It's 11.0 miles from the visitor center and takes about 20 minutes one-way to drive. The **Cape Royal Road** goes to several overlooks and ends at a 0.3-mile paved walk to Cape Royal, which juts out on a sweeping turn of the canyon with views east, south, and west. It's 23.0 miles from the visitor center and about 45 minutes one-way. No camping is allowed on these roads—dispersed (primitive) camping is available in Kaibab National Forest north of the park. Camping on the North Rim is $18–$25 per site per night. A maximum of two vehicles, six people, and three tents are allowed per site. Book at recreation.gov/camping/campgrounds/232489. A permit is required to stay overnight below the rim in Grand Canyon (nps.gov/grca/planyourvisit/back country-permit.htm).

NORTH RIM LODGE: For reservations, call 877-386-4383 or book online at grandcanyon forever.com/lodging. Open May 15–October 15. For information about the lodge, things to do at the North Rim, and dining options, see nps.gov/grca/planyourvisit/north-rim.htm.

NORTH RIM CAMPGROUND: 928-638-2611, nps.gov/grca/planyourvisit/cg-nr.htm. Three group sites plus 88 tent/RV sites (no hookups). Nightly rate: $18–$25. Reserve your site up to 6 months in advance: 877-444-6777, recreation.gov.

NORTH RIM GENERAL STORE: North Rim Campground, 928-638-2611. Open daily, 7 a.m.–8 p.m. Groceries, camping gear, gift shop, and the best Wi-Fi signal in the park.

NORTH RIM LODGE DINING:
   Main Dining Room For reservations call 928-638-8560 Monday–Friday, 9 a.m.–4 p.m., or email gnrfbmngr@gcnr.com. Open daily, 6:30–10 a.m. (breakfast); 11:30 a.m.–2:30 p.m. (lunch); and 4:30–9 p.m. (dinner).

Bright Angel Buffet Open nightly, 4:30–6:30 p.m.

Deli in the Pines Premade salads and sandwiches available daily, 10:30 a.m.–9 p.m.

Coffee Shop/Roughrider Saloon Breakfast served daily, 5:30–10:30 a.m.; full bar and beers on tap daily, 11:30 a.m.–10:30 p.m.

NORTH RIM SCENIC DRIVES: See the *North Rim Pocket Map and Services Guide* for more information; download it at nps.gov/grca/planyourvisit.

Getting There

NORTH KAIBAB TRAILHEAD: N36° 13.014' W112° 03.400', elevation 8,241'

ROAD CONDITIONS: All vehicles; paved

FACILITIES: Restrooms, seasonal water faucet. Check nps.gov/grca for water availability, as there are occasional pipe breaks that require shutting off the water.

TRAVEL NOTE: AZ 67 is open only seasonally. It opens on May 15 and closes after the first big snow, generally in November. The North Rim Lodge and other facilities are closed from October 15–May 15. Check nps.gov/grca to confirm if the road is open before you go. Finally, note that cell reception is spotty after you leave Flagstaff.

DIRECTIONS *From Flagstaff:* From Exit 201 off I-40 East, take US 89 North for 109.0 miles to Bitter Springs, crossing into the Navajo Nation at Gray Mountain. Then turn left (north) onto US 89A, and in about 14 miles drive over the Navajo Bridge, which spans the Colorado River in Grand Canyon. There is a Navajo arts market on the east side of the bridge and a visitor center and restrooms on the west side (open daily, April–October, 9 a.m.– 5 p.m.; 928-355-2319). It's a great spot to take a break and stretch your legs with a walk across and back on the pedestrian bridge. You might even see a California condor or a river trip floating 500 feet below!

Go past the Vermilion Cliffs, and after House Rock Valley the road climbs onto the Kaibab Plateau. AZT Passage 41, Kaibab Plateau: Central (not covered in this book), crosses US 89A 2.5 miles east of Jacob Lake. Then, 56.0 miles from the Bitter Springs junction, reach Jacob Lake, turn left (south) onto AZ 67, and take it 30.0 miles to the park's North Entrance Station. The North Kaibab Trailhead is 11.0 miles past the entrance on the left (east), at a small parking area.

From Kanab, Utah: Drive east on US 89A toward Jacob Lake 37.0 miles; turn right onto AZ 67, and pick up the directions above from Jacob Lake.

29 East Rim Viewpoint to Tater Canyon

Aspen-ringed meadows on the Kaibab Plateau

SCENERY: ★★★★★
TRAIL CONDITION: ★★★★
CHILDREN: ★★★★
DIFFICULTY: ★★
SOLITUDE: ★★★★

Quaking aspens on the Kaibab Plateau show off their fall colors in Upper Tater Canyon.

DISTANCE & CONFIGURATION: 9.0-mile out-and-back
HIKING TIME: 4–6 hours
ACCUMULATED ELEVATION GAIN: 715'
SHORT HIKE OPTION: 4.0-mile out-and-back to meadow/250' elevation gain
OUTSTANDING FEATURES: View of Marble Canyon, Tater Canyon meadow, fall colors
LAND-MANAGEMENT AGENCY: Kaibab National Forest, North Kaibab District, 928-643-7395, fs.usda.gov/kaibab
MAPS: USGS 7.5' *Telephone Hill, AZ*
AZT PASSAGE: 40/Kaibab Plateau South, aztrail.org/explore/passages/passage-40-kaibab-plateau-south
ANCESTRAL LANDS: Southern Paiute, Ute
SEASON: May 15–October 15; be aware of monsoons July–September (see page 35)
ACCESS: No fees or permits; open 24-7, year-round, but be aware of seasonal road closures

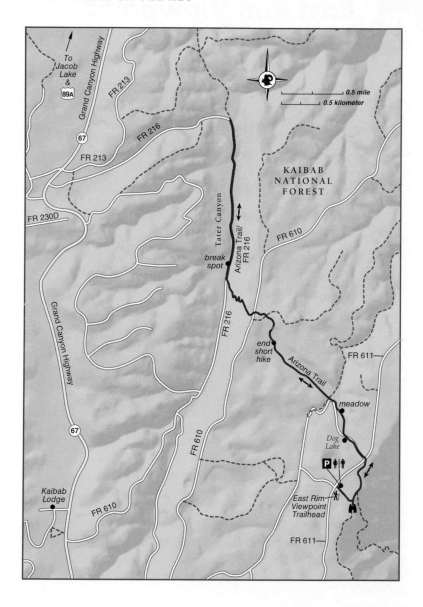

Overview

A hike on the Arizona National Scenic Trail (AZT) from the East Rim Viewpoint Trailhead is a great way to experience the unique environment of the Kaibab Plateau, its meadows ringed with fir, aspen, and spruce, and enjoy great views

230

into Marble Canyon. You might even see one of the white-tailed squirrels found only on the Kaibab Plateau and nowhere else in the world.

On the Trail

From the East Rim Viewpoint Trailhead, hike in on an ADA-accessible paved trail 0.2 mile to reach the AZT. A metal AZT sign welcomes you and lets you know it's 59.0 miles north to Utah and 743.0 miles south to Mexico. This is the high point of the hike (8,852'), and the end of the ADA-accessible trail. Turn right (south) and go to the base of a big ponderosa pine with a picnic table and spectacular views.

The East Rim Viewpoint affords a sweeping panorama of the Saddle Mountain Wilderness and beyond. You can see Marble Canyon, which makes up the first 60.0 miles of Grand Canyon, cutting through House Rock Valley below. Directly east are South Canyon and Bedrock Canyon. The domed mountain in the distance is Navajo Mountain, important in Hopi, Paiute, and Navajo traditions. The Echo and Vermilion Cliffs are also visible. Saddle Mountain is the peak to the left with the long, sloping ridge.

After you've enjoyed the view, return north the way you came toward Utah on Trail 101. Pass a sign for the Saddle Mountain Wilderness and Saddle Mountain Trail 7, which descends from the rim. Join a road in 0.4 mile at a camping area.

Heads-up: Immediately look to your left for a brown carsonite sign for a singletrack trail leaving the road. The white-tailed Kaibab squirrel is featured on the signage, and the forested parts of the trail are the best place to see these animals. Kaibab squirrels live in an area of only about 638 square miles. Due to the extreme isolation of the Kaibab Plateau, they evolved a different coloring than the gray Abert's squirrels found across the Grand Canyon on the South Rim. Cross Forest Service Road 611 and reach a sign that says KAIBAB PLATEAU

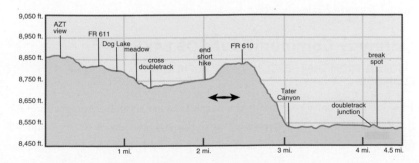

TRAIL #101–E. RIM VIEW 0.5 MILE, GRAND CANYON BOUNDARY 8 MILES.
The trail continues between the fence posts and the tree.

Follow a closed roadbed for 0.2 mile to tiny Dog Lake, which has a gated entrance at the north end. Continue on the trail until it reaches a beautiful grassy meadow in 0.3 mile. The trail skirts the meadow's left (southwest) side. **The end of the meadow marks the turnaround point for the short hike option, at 4.0 miles round-trip and 250 feet of elevation gain.**

After the trail goes back into the trees, it crosses FR 610 in 0.5 mile. The trail descends for 0.5 mile and then opens onto a larger meadow. In 0.1 mile reach a mileage sign and doubletrack dirt road; then turn right (north) to continue down gorgeous Upper Tater Canyon.

One of my favorite spots on the whole AZT, Tater Canyon is ringed with quaking aspens that yield spectacular fall color in late September and early October (check fs.usda.gov/kaibab for updates). However, the canyon is lovely any season it's accessible. For more information about quaking aspens, see page 97.

Keep your eyes peeled for fossils in the limestone of the Kaibab Formation, which was created in a marine environment 270 million years ago in the Permian Age. Brachiopods, corals, mollusks, and other vertebrates and invertebrates can be found in this layer, which forms the surface of the Kaibab Plateau as well as both rims of Grand Canyon.

In 1.0 mile reach a junction with a faint doubletrack that climbs the hill to the left (west) and stay to the right (north). In 0.2 mile there is an outcropping of white Kaibab Limestone on the left (west) that makes a perfect spot for a snack break or picnic lunch. Continue north to a junction with a Forest Service road coming in from the left at mile 4.5, where the singletrack AZT goes right (north).

Return the way you came, keeping in mind that the air is quite thin at more than 8,000 feet of elevation. You'll probably be huffing and puffing on the climb back out of Tater Canyon.

Gateway Community: JACOB LAKE

DISTANCE FROM TRAILHEAD: 31.0 miles **POPULATION:** No census data
ELEVATION: 7,925′

This tiny community consists of the **Jacob Lake Inn**; a public campground; and the **Kaibab Plateau Visitor Center,** all near the intersection of US 89A and AZ 67. Jacob Lake Inn has rooms and cabins, a country store and gift shop, a gas station, and a restaurant. Their famous cookies are in a display case just as you walk in—try one of their classics such as lemon raspberry or a cookie in a cloud.

South of Jacob Lake, **Kaibab Lodge, DeMotte Campground,** and **North Rim Country Store** are all just north of the intersection of Forest Service Road 611 and AZ 67. Dispersed (primitive) camping is available in Kaibab National Forest.

JACOB LAKE INN: AZ 67 at US 89A, 928-643-7232 or jacoblake.com.

JACOB LAKE RECREATION AREA CAMPGROUND: North of Jacob Lake Inn on Forest Service Road 567, just west of US 89A; 928-643-7395, tinyurl.com/jacoblakecampground. Has 51 tent/RV sites (no hookups) and 4 group sites; fire rings/cooking grills, picnic tables, vault toilets, and drinking water. Nightly rate: $5 single sites, $105 group sites; open year-round. Available by reservation mid-May–September (877-444-6777, recreation.gov/camping /campgrounds/234529); first come, first served the rest of the year.

KAIBAB PLATEAU VISITOR CENTER: AZ 67 at US 89A, 928-643-7298, tinyurl.com /kaibabplateauvisitorcenter. Open mid-May–mid-October daily, 8 a.m.–5 p.m.

KAIBAB CAMPER VILLAGE: Forest Service Road 461, about 1.25 miles south and west of the Kaibab Plateau Visitor Center; 928-635-5251 (October 16–May 13), 928-643-7804 (May 14–October 15), kaibabcampervillage.com. Open May 14–October 15.

KAIBAB LODGE: AZ 67 at milepost 605.0, 26.0 miles south of Jacob Lake; 928-638-2389, kaibablodge.com. Cabins and a lodge with a cozy fireplace. At the time of this writing, dining service was limited to takeout and room delivery; contact the lodge for the latest information.

DEMOTTE CAMPGROUND: AZ 67 at milepost 605.0, 26.0 miles south of Jacob Lake; 928-643-7395, tinyurl.com/demottecampgroundaz. Has 38 tent/RV sites (no hookups) with fire rings/cooking grills, picnic tables, vault toilets, and drinking water. Nightly rate: $22; open May 15–October 14. Availability is first come, first served and by reservation (877-444-6777, recreation.gov/camping/campgrounds/234722).

NORTH RIM COUNTRY STORE: Across AZ 67 from Kaibab Lodge and DeMotte Campground at milepost 605.0, 26.0 miles south of Jacob Lake; 928-638-2383, northrimcountry store.com. Open daily year-round, 8 a.m.–6 p.m. The owner, Betsy, is a volunteer Trail Steward for the AZT and very hiker-friendly.

Getting There

EAST RIM VIEWPOINT TRAILHEAD: N36° 25.013' W112° 05.489', elevation 8,826'

ROAD CONDITIONS: All vehicles; graded dirt for 4.0 miles

FACILITIES: Restrooms but no water, ADA-accessible trail

TRAVEL NOTE: AZ 67 is closed seasonally October 15–May 15. Winter often covers the Kaibab Plateau with many feet of snow. (I once got snowed on June 4 while on this hike.) Also, note that phones sometimes pick up cell towers in the Utah or Navajo Nation, which will register daylight saving time (which Arizona does not observe).

DIRECTIONS *From Flagstaff:* From Exit 201 off I-40 East, take US 89 North for 109.0 miles to Bitter Springs, crossing into the Navajo Nation at Gray Mountain. Then turn left (north) onto US 89A, and in about 14 miles drive over the Navajo Bridge, which spans the Colorado River in Grand Canyon. There is a Navajo arts market on the east side of the bridge and a visitor center and restrooms on the west side (open daily, April–October, 9 a.m.–5 p.m.; 928-355-2319). It's a great spot to take a break and stretch your legs with a walk across and back on the pedestrian bridge. You might even see a California condor or a river trip floating 500 feet below!

Go past the Vermilion Cliffs, and after House Rock Valley the road climbs onto the Kaibab Plateau. AZT Passage 41 (not in this book) crosses US 89A 2.5 miles east of Jacob Lake. Then, 56.0 miles from the Bitter Springs junction, you reach Jacob Lake and turn left (south) onto AZ 67. Pass the North Rim Country Store and the turnoffs for Kaibab Lodge and DeMotte Campground. Note that all facilities south of Jacob Lake are open only seasonally.

At 27.0 miles south of Jacob Lake, take a left (southeast) onto Forest Service Road 611, signed EAST RIM VIEW 4 MILES, ARIZONA TRAIL 4 MILES. The road is graded dirt, and in 1.3 miles you reach a junction with FR 610 to the right, signed for the AZT in both directions—continue straight (south) on FR 611 toward the East Rim Viewpoint. In 2.2 miles pass a NO CAMPING sign, and in 0.5 mile reach a sign that reads EAST RIM VP TO RIGHT, ARIZONA T.H. RIGHT, NORTH CANYON T.H. Then turn right (east) to reach a parking area 4.1 miles from AZ 67.

From Kanab, Utah: Take US 89A East toward Jacob Lake for 37.0 miles to the junction with AZ 67. Turn left (south) and pick up the directions above from Jacob Lake.

30 Stateline Trailhead to Coyote Valley Overlook

Sublime sandstone at the state line

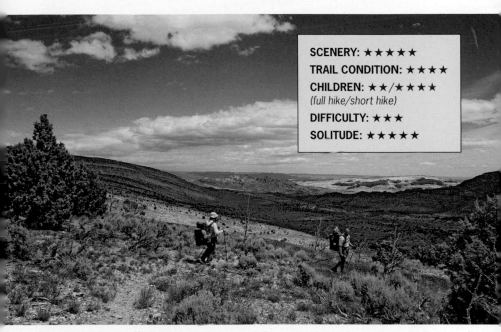

SCENERY: ★ ★ ★ ★ ★
TRAIL CONDITION: ★ ★ ★ ★
CHILDREN: ★ ★ / ★ ★ ★ ★
(full hike/short hike)
DIFFICULTY: ★ ★ ★
SOLITUDE: ★ ★ ★ ★ ★

Thru-hikers from the Warrior Expeditions program for veterans close to completing their 800-mile journey at the Utah border

DISTANCE & CONFIGURATION: 4.8-mile out-and-back

HIKING TIME: 3–4 hours

ACCUMULATED ELEVATION GAIN: 1,090'

SHORT HIKE OPTION: 2.0-mile out-and-back to hillside view/400' elevation gain

OUTSTANDING FEATURES: Spectacular views into Utah, Border Monument, northern terminus of the AZT

LAND-MANAGEMENT AGENCY: Bureau of Land Management, Arizona Strip Office, 435-688-3200, blm.gov/office/arizona-strip-district-office

MAPS: USGS 7.5' *Coyote Buttes, AZ*

AZT PASSAGE: 43/Buckskin Mountain, aztrail.org/explore/passages/passage-43-buckskin-mountain

ANCESTRAL LANDS: Southern Paiute, Ute

SEASON: Spring, fall, winter (see Travel Note, page 239)

ACCESS: Open daily, 24-7, year-round

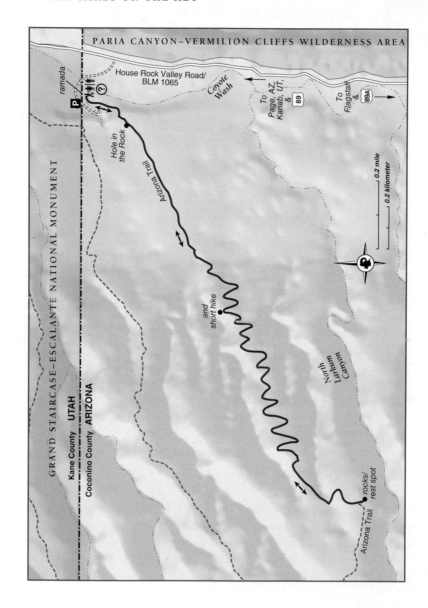

Overview

This hike on the Arizona National Scenic Trail (AZT) at the Utah border has unique scenery, with views into the colorful sandstone of Utah and the edge of the Kaibab Plateau. A beautiful stone obelisk marks the northern terminus of the trail. It's a long way from anywhere, but it's well worth the trip. You might even see thru-hikers starting or finishing their journey.

On the Trail

Pass the border obelisk that marks the Utah terminus of the AZT, and take time to read the poem "The Arizona Trail" by Dale Shewalter, who got the idea for a trail running from the Mexico border to Utah and first hiked it in 1985 (see page 37). A shade structure with interpretive signs and local information is just ahead. The trail begins to climb, with accessible pullouts for wheelchairs. A sign at mile 0.1 points left (east) to the Ridge Path. The AZT reaches a bench and interpretive sign about the geology of Coyote Valley and the end of the wheelchair-accessible portion of the trail in 100 feet.

Follow the sign that says WINTER ROAD 11, FOREST BOUNDARY 12.3 MILES. The trail switchbacks to the top of the small ridge and back down. In 0.1 mile look off to your left (south), and you'll see a rock with a window in it that's perfect for taking photos. The trail travels across the open sagebrush flat for 0.4 mile and then crosses a wash.

The trail curves left (northeast) and climbs through junipers and sagebrush. A total of 22 switchbacks ascend the slope. Views of the Coyote Valley and the edge of the Kaibab Plateau open as the trail climbs at a steady grade. In 0.4 mile, at the third switchback, views get even better as you ascend out of the junipers onto an exposed hillside. **This is the turnaround point for the short hike option, at 2.0 miles round-trip and 400 feet of elevation gain.**

The climb is sure to get your heart pumping—the good news is that there are views in every direction, so take a breather and enjoy. To the east and northeast is Utah, revealing its multiple layers of multicolored rock. The closer rock

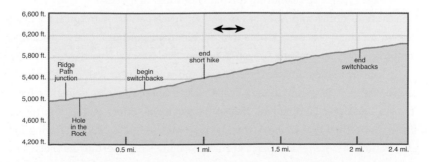

formations are the Coyote Buttes, and in the distance are the cliffs of the Grand Staircase, which encompasses rock layers up to the Pink Cliffs of Bryce Canyon. The layers of white rock on the Kaibab Plateau curve down into the Coyote Valley. This is the edge of the Kaibab Monocline, a 150-mile fold in the earth that aided in the creation of Grand Canyon.

Junipers reappear in 0.5 mile, and the trail continues to switchback up the hill. Reach the last of the 22 switchbacks in 0.6 mile. The trail becomes less steep but continues to climb. Pass some small rock ledges in 0.2 mile; some good rocks for resting and eating lie just ahead in 0.1 mile. Turn left (east) 70 feet toward a juniper with more rocks for sitting and enjoying the view you've worked so hard to attain. This is the high point of the hike, at 6,041 feet and 2.4 miles. Return the way you came.

Other Hikes Nearby

BUCKSKIN GULCH The Wire Pass Trailhead is 1.5 miles north on House Rock Valley Road. Buckskin Gulch, at 16.0 miles, is one of the longest slot canyons in the world. You can get a taste of it by day-hiking; the canyon narrows about 3.5 miles in. Self-serve permits are available at the trailhead. The Wave, a unique, photo-op-worthy rock formation, is also accessed through this trailhead, but mandatory permits are in high demand and must be obtained in a lottery. Information at recreation.gov.

Gateway Community: PAGE

DISTANCE FROM TRAILHEAD: 45.0 miles **POPULATION:** 7,247 **ELEVATION:** 4,117'

At 45.0 miles from the Stateline Trailhead, the town of Page seems an unlikely Gateway Community until you look at a map and realize how remote the northern terminus is. The only other community nearby with services is Kanab, Utah—49 miles away.

Page is a hub for exploring the many outdoor activities in the area. There are plenty of hotels and Airbnbs, as well as developed campgrounds, on Lake Powell (including **Wahweap Marina RV Park and Campground**). At-large primitive camping is available in **Paria Canyon–Vermilion Cliffs National Monument.**

Lake Powell dominates the scenery, and you can rent watercraft no matter what your style—from the smallest kayak to a houseboat big enough to have its own helicopter landing pad. **Hidden Canyon Kayak** offers rentals and tours, some where they tow you and your boat to an interesting spot, allowing for exploration of more remote parts of the lake along with side-canyon hikes.

Page is also home to two iconic points of interest: **Horseshoe Bend** and **Antelope Canyon**. Horseshoe Bend is an overlook on a sweeping curve of the Colorado River, reached by a 1.5-mile ADA-accessible hike. Navajo guides are required to tour Antelope Canyon, a sinuous, orange-hued slot canyon. Tours are easily arranged at several places in town. The **Powell Museum** explores the history of boating on the Colorado River in Grand Canyon. Local dining favorites are **Big John's Texas BBQ, State 48 Tavern,** and **Fiesta Mexicana.**

PARIA CANYON–VERMILION CLIFFS NATIONAL MONUMENT: 435-688-3200, blm .gov/visit/paria-canyon-vermilion-cliffs-wilderness. Comprises 112,500 acres of public land at the Arizona–Utah border.

WAHWEAP MARINA RV PARK AND CAMPGROUND: 100 Lake Shore Dr., 888-896-3829, lakepowell.com/rv-camping/wahweap-rv-campground. Has 36 tent-only sites, 112 tent/RV sites, and 139 full-hookup RV sites; all have restrooms, picnic tables, fire rings, and/or cooking grills. Check the website for current nightly rates when you reserve your site.

HIDDEN CANYON KAYAK: 908 N. Navajo Dr., 928-660-1836, lakepowellhiddencanyon kayak.com. Day, overnight, and multiday tours and rentals on Lake Powell. Operates February–November; call or email info@hiddencanyonkayak.com for details.

HORSESHOE BEND: Located 3.0 miles south of Page on AZ 89 between mileposts 544.0 and 545.0, on the west side of the road; cityofpage.org/hsb. Admission: $10/vehicle. Open daily, sunrise–sunset.

ANTELOPE CANYON: Requires a Navajo guide; visit navajonationparks.org for a list of companies based in Page.

POWELL MUSEUM: 6 N. Lake Powell Blvd., 928-645-9496, powellmuseum.org. Free admission. Open Monday–Saturday, 9 a.m.–5 p.m.

BIG JOHN'S TEXAS BBQ: 153 S. Lake Powell Blvd., 928-645-3300, bigjohnstexasbbq.com. Open Wednesday–Sunday, 11 a.m.–9 p.m.

STATE 48 TAVERN: 614 N. Navajo Dr., 928-645-1912, state48tavern.com. Open for dinner Wednesday–Monday, 5–10 p.m., and for brunch Saturday and Sunday, 10 a.m.–5 p.m.

FIESTA MEXICANA: 125 S. Lake Powell Blvd., 928-645-4082, fiestamexrest.com/mexican -restaurants/page-az. Open Sunday–Thursday, 11 a.m.–10 p.m.; Saturday and Sunday, 11 a.m.–11 p.m.

Getting There

STATELINE TRAILHEAD: N37° 00.072' W112° 02.092', elevation 4,994'

ROAD CONDITIONS: All vehicles; graded dirt for 9.0 or 19.0 miles (see Travel Note below)

TRAVEL NOTE: The northern terminus of the AZT at the Utah border is in the middle of nowhere, accessed by a bumpy dirt road on the Arizona Strip. There is both a north and a south route to get there. Do *not* attempt to drive to the Stateline Trailhead when roads are wet and it becomes, as they say in these parts, "slick as snot." It's always a good idea to check the weather to make sure a big storm isn't coming in during your visit. The road is appropriate for passenger cars, but make sure to allow for slower travel. At the time of this writing, cell reception is spotty to nonexistent on the road to the trailhead. Phones sometimes pick up cell towers in the Utah or Navajo Nation, which will register Daylight Saving Time (which Arizona does not observe).

FACILITIES: Stateline Campground (blm.gov/visit/search-details/261735/1) has free camping and about seven spots with shade ramadas, fire pits, and restrooms, but no water or garbage service.

DIRECTIONS *From Page, Arizona:* Take US 89 into Utah, and pass the Paria River in 31.0 miles. In 3.0 miles the highway cuts through a rock formation called The Cockscomb; the turnoff for House Rock Valley Road (Bureau of Land Management Road 1065) is just after the cut to the left (south). Take this road 9.0 miles to the Stateline Trailhead, which will be on your right (west). Park in the spots designated for the AZT.

From Kanab, Utah: Take US 89 North for 38.0 miles east toward Page, Arizona. Turn right (south) onto House Rock Valley Road (BLM 1065), and pick up the directions above.

From Flagstaff: From Exit 201 off I-40 East, take US 89 North for 109.0 miles to Bitter Springs, crossing into the Navajo Nation at Gray Mountain. Then turn left (north) onto US 89A, and in about 14 miles drive over the Navajo Bridge, which spans the Colorado River in Grand Canyon. There is a Navajo arts market on the east side of the bridge and a visitor center and restrooms on the west side (open daily, April–October, 9 a.m.– 5 p.m.; 928-355-2319). It's a great spot to take a break and stretch your legs with a walk across and back on the pedestrian bridge. You might even see a California condor or a river trip floating 500 feet below!

At 28.0 miles west of the Navajo Bridge, look for a signed turn for House Rock Valley Road (BLM 1065). If the road gets curvy and you start ascending onto the Kaibab Plateau, you've missed the turn. Go right (north) and follow this wide dirt road for 19.0 miles to the left (west) turn into Utah for the Stateline Trailhead. Road conditions get rougher after you pass a sign for Winter Road indicating that the AZT is 4.0 miles ahead. Park in the spots designated for the AZT.

Appendix 1:
INDIGENOUS TRIBES

EACH HIKE IN THIS BOOK lists the Indigenous peoples who inhabited a particular adjacent area before Europeans and Americans colonized the United States. (Also see "Ancient Trails Through Ancestral Lands," page 17.) Though the Arizona National Scenic Trail (AZT) does not pass directly through tribal reservations, the places that it does visit remain important to local Indigenous communities to this day. *(See the map below and the resources on the following page.)*

TRIBAL HOMELANDS IN ARIZONA

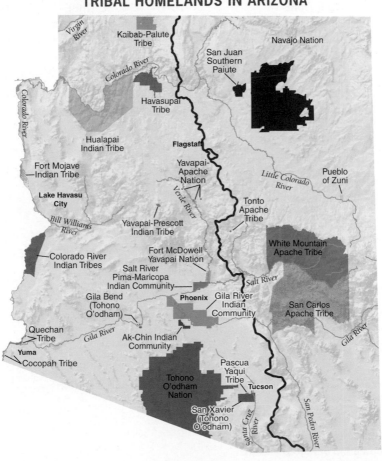

Arizona has 22 sovereign Indigenous tribes. Below is a list of these communities that are located near the AZT, from south to north, as well as an alphabetical list of 11 tribes—some of them outside of Arizona—that have historical connections to the land that makes up today's Grand Canyon National Park.

For more information, visit the website of the **Inter Tribal Council of Arizona** (itcaonline.com).

TOHONO O'ODHAM NATION
tonation-nsn.gov
PO Box 837
Sells, AZ 85634
520-383-2028

PASCUA YAQUI TRIBE
pascuayaqui-nsn.gov
7474 S. Camino de Oeste
Tucson, AZ 85757
520-883-5000

SAN CARLOS APACHE TRIBE
sancarlosapache.com
Apache Gem Road, Marker 2
San Carlos, AZ 85550
928-475-2361

TONTO APACHE TRIBE
itcaonline.com/member-tribes
 /tonto-apache-tribe
Tonto Apache Reservation Road 30
Payson, AZ 85541
928-474-5000

THE 11 TRADITIONALLY ASSOCIATED TRIBES OF THE GRAND CANYON REGION

Havasupai Tribe
theofficialhavasupaitribe.com
PO Box 10
Supai, AZ 86435
928-448-2731

Hopi Tribe
hopi-nsn.gov
PO Box 123
Kykotsmovi, AZ 86039
928-734-2441

Hualapai Tribe
hualapai-nsn.gov
PO Box 179
Peach Springs, AZ 86434
928-769-2216

Kaibab Band of Paiute Indians
kaibabpaiute-nsn.gov
HC 65, Box 2
Fredonia, AZ 86022
928-643-7245

Las Vegas Band of Paiute Indians
lvpaiutetribe.com
1 Paiute Dr.
Las Vegas, NV 89106
702-386-3926

Moapa Band of Paiute Indians
moapabandofpaiutes.com
1 Lincoln St.
Moapa, NV 89025
702-865-2787

Navajo Nation
discovernavajo.com
PO Box 663
Window Rock, AZ 86515
928-810-8501

Paiute Indian Tribe of Utah
utahpaiutes.org
440 N. Paiute Dr.
Cedar City UT 84721
435-586-1112

The Pueblo of Zuni
ashiwi.org
PO Box 339
Zuni, NM 87327
505-782-7022

San Juan Southern Paiute Tribe
sanjuanpaiute-nsn.gov
50 S. Main St., Ste. 101
Tuba City, AZ 86045
928-212-9794

Yavapai–Apache Nation
yavapai-apache.org
2400 W. Datsi St.
Camp Verde, AZ 86322
928-567-3649

Appendix 2:
LAND-MANAGEMENT AGENCIES

LISTED GENERALLY FROM SOUTH TO NORTH, these agencies administer the public lands through which the AZT passes.

CORONADO NATIONAL MEMORIAL
nps.gov/coro
4101 E. Montezuma Canyon Rd.
Hereford, AZ 85613
520-366-5515

CORONADO NATIONAL FOREST
fs.usda.gov/coronado

Sierra Vista Ranger District
5990 S. AZ 92
Hereford, AZ 85615
520-378-0311

Nogales Ranger District
303 Old Tucson Rd.
Nogales, AZ 85621
520-281-2296

Santa Catalina Ranger District
5700 N. Sabino Canyon Rd.
Tucson, AZ 85750
520-749-8700

BUREAU OF LAND MANAGEMENT
blm.gov

Tucson Field Office
blm.gov/office/tucson-field-office
3201 E. Universal Way
Tucson, AZ 85756
520-258-7200

Arizona Strip District Office
blm.gov/office/arizona-strip-district-office
345 E. Riverside Dr.
St. George, UT 84790
435-688-3200

PIMA COUNTY NATURAL RESOURCES, PARKS AND RECREATION
webcms.pima.gov/recreation
3500 W. River Rd.; Tucson, AZ 85741
520-724-5000

Colossal Cave Mountain Park
colossalcave.com
16721 E. Old Spanish Trail
Vail, AZ 85641
520-647-7275

ORACLE STATE PARK
azstateparks.com/oracle
3820 E. Wildlife Dr.
Oracle, AZ 85623
520-896-2425

TONTO NATIONAL FOREST
fs.usda.gov/tonto

Globe Ranger District
7680 S. Six Shooter Canyon Rd.
Globe, AZ 85501
928-402-6200

Mesa Ranger District
5140 E. Ingram St.
Mesa, AZ 85205
480-610-3341

Tonto Basin Ranger District
28079 N. AZ 188
Roosevelt, AZ 85545
602-225-5395

Payson Ranger District
1009 E. AZ 260
Payson, AZ 85541
928-474-7900

continued on next page

continued from previous page

COCONINO NATIONAL FOREST
fs.usda.gov/coconino

Flagstaff Ranger District
5075 N. US 89
Flagstaff, AZ 86004
928-526-0866

CITY OF FLAGSTAFF
flagstaff.az.gov/1786/arizona-trail
211 W. Aspen Ave.
Flagstaff, AZ 86001
928-213-2000

ARIZONA SNOWBOWL SKI RESORT
snowbowl.ski
9300 N. Snowbowl Rd.
Flagstaff, AZ 86001
928-779-1951

GRAND CANYON NATIONAL PARK
nps.gov/grca
PO Box 129
Grand Canyon, AZ 86023
928-638-7888

KAIBAB NATIONAL FOREST
fs.usda.gov/kaibab

Tusayan Ranger District
176 Lincoln Log Loop
Grand Canyon, AZ 86023
928-638-2443

North Kaibab Ranger District
430 S. Main St.
Fredonia, AZ 86022
928-643-7395

Appendix 3:
BOOK UPDATES

FOR POST-PUBLICATION UPDATES on the book and to buy a personalized copy from the author, visit sirenarana.com.

For updates on hike conditions, visit the Arizona Trail Association website listed in each hike's description. For reports on trail conditions, visit aztrail .org/the-trail/trail-conditions-form.

To report errors in the book, please e-mail dayhikesazt@gmail.com.

Appendix 4:
AZT RESOURCES

HERE'S A LIST OF RESOURCES, both official and unofficial, that will aid you in researching, navigating, and enjoying this spectacular National Scenic Trail.

ARIZONA TRAIL ASSOCIATION (ATA)
aztrail.org

738 N. Fifth Ave., Ste. 201
Tucson, AZ 85705
Voicemail: 602-252-4794
Contact form: **aztrail.org/contact**

Official AZT Mobile App (Atlas Guides)
Available for Android and iOS; $9.99. It works in airplane mode after initial setup, thus helping extend your phone's battery life. For more information, see atlasguides.com/arizona-trail and aztrail.org/explore/maps/mobile-app.

Arizona Trail Day Hiker's Guide
by Jake Baechle and the Arizona Trail Association ($33 or free download with ATA membership)
This guide splits the 800 miles of the AZT into 89 day hikes for people interested in section-hiking the trail. For more information and to order, see aztrail.org/product/arizona-trail-day-hikers-guide

Your Official Guide to the Arizona National Scenic Trail
By Matthew J. Nelson and the Arizona Trail Association (Wilderness Press, $25.95)
Available at aztrail.org/product-category/books, Amazon, and other retailers nationwide.

ATA Online Resources
ATA Store: aztrail.org/store
Gateway Communities: aztrail.org/explore/gateway-communities
Giving: aztrail.org/get-involved/donate
Interactive Maps: aztrail.org/explore/maps
Junior Explorer Handbook: aztrail.org/youth/junior-explorers
Passages: aztrail.org/explore/passages
Trail Finishers: aztrail.org/the-trail/trail-finishers
Trail Skills Institute: aztrail.org/get-involved/trail-skills-institute
Trail Stewards: aztrail.org/explore/trail-stewards

MEMBERS-ONLY CONTENT Join the ATA (see aztrail.org/get-involved/join) and get access to exclusive content including GPS data, trail elevation profiles, the *Arizona Trail Databook,* the *Arizona Trail Mountain Bike Databook,* maps for loop routes, topographic maps, and more.

Unofficial Resources
The Arizona Trail Driver's Guide: By Robert Garber, $5.99 (Kindle); tinyurl.com/aztdriversguide
HikeArizona AZT Forum: hikearizona.com (click "Connect," choose "HAZ Forums" from the pull-down menu, click the "Forums" tab, and then select "Arizona National Scenic Trail")

Golden quaking aspens light up in October in the San Francisco Peaks.

Index

Trails Inspire

Connecting Trails and Communities

Sirena Rana, Founder

Trails Inspire, LLC, provides consulting services dedicated to promoting the outdoors as a place of personal health, economic development, and tourism through public speaking, freelance writing, photography, and trail design and development. Trails Inspire is committed to promoting diversity and inclusion for outdoor spaces.

Services include the following:

Content Creation

- *Best Day Hikes on the Arizona National Scenic Trail,* by Wilderness Press
- Freelance writing
- Photography (outdoor, wildlife, astrophotography, light painting)

Public Speaking and Virtual Presentations

- Subjects include recreation, economic benefits of trails, backpacking and hiking for beginners, desert hiking, the Arizona National Scenic Trail, and more. Custom presentations upon request.

Trail Project Management

- Trail design, planning, and development
- Outreach, interpretation, and marketing for communities and public and private lands

Contact Us

Web / email: trailsinspire.com, sirena@trailsinspire.com

Social media: facebook.com/trailsinspire, @trailsinspire (Instagram and Twitter)

Trails Inspire Patreon

Join our Patreon community at patreon.com/desertsirena and get access to a monthly newsletter; videos; advance notice of events and projects; behind-the-scenes looks at Sirena's writing, photography, travels, and stories; and more.

About the Author

SIRENA RANA is an advocate for the outdoors and wildlife. She aims to inspire others by sharing the experiences she has while hiking, backpacking, rafting, and canyoneering. She developed her passion for the outdoors while recovering from an accident that left her with fibromyalgia, a condition that causes chronic pain.

Sirena's company, Trails Inspire, LLC, provides consulting services that promote the outdoors in the contexts of mental and physical health, economic

Photo: Mike Bieke

development, and tourism, through public speaking, freelance writing, photography, trail design, and community engagement. Trails Inspire is also committed to promoting diversity and inclusion for outdoor spaces.

Sirena has partnered with organizations such as the Arizona Office of Tourism, REI, the Partnership for the National Trails System, the Continental Divide Trail Coalition, and the Florida Trail Association. Her photography, writing, and personal story have been featured in numerous articles, TV programs, and podcasts and radio shows across the country.

Since 2007 Sirena has helped build, maintain, and promote the 800-mile AZT, and she has hiked the entire trail twice, on a section hike in 2008–09 and a thru-hike in 2014. She has an eclectic work history that includes time working in the video-game industry, as an archaeologist, as the Gateway Community Liaison for the Arizona Trail Association, and as a rafting guide on the Colorado River in Grand Canyon.

Sirena is currently section-hiking the length of Grand Canyon, and she volunteers at Wildlife Rehabilitation in Northwest Tucson, which specializes in raptor rescue. Originally from the Chicago suburbs, she is a first-generation American with parents from India and Italy. Sirena earned a bachelor's degree in anthropology and classics from the University of Arizona, which brought her to the state she now calls home.